LINGUISTIC BEHAVIOUR

Linguistic Behaviour

JONATHAN BENNETT

Professor of Philosophy at the
University of British Columbia

CAMBRIDGE UNIVERSITY PRESS

CAMBRIDGE

LONDON · NEW YORK · MELBOURNE

Published by the Syndics of the Cambridge University Press
The Pitt Building, Trumpington Street, Cambridge CB2 IRP
Bentley House, 200 Euston Road, London NWI 2DB
32 East 57th Street, New York, NY 10022, USA
296 Beaconsfield Parade, Middle Park, Melbourne 3206, Australia

© Cambridge University Press 1976

Library of Congress catalogue card number: 75–44575

ISBN 0 521 21168 9

First published 1976

Printed in Great Britain at the Alden Press, Oxford

CONTENTS

PREFACE

This book presents in some detail a view of language – that is, language
in general, not any particular tongue – as essentially a matter of systematic communicative behaviour. Those last three words point to
three major emphases in the book. A glance down the table of Contents
will show something of what I regard as the main obstacles to my way
of looking at language, and of how I try to remove them. The Select
Bibliography might also help. It lists the thirty works I have found
most helpfully relevant to what I am doing here, and so it provides a
clue to what my book is like. Items in the Bibliography are referred to,
in the text and footnotes, only by author's name and a date where
necessary; but that use of the Bibliography is strictly secondary.

   The spadework for the book was done in courses on the philosophy of
language which I have taught at various times and places since 1965. I
owe a great deal to students at the Universities of Cambridge, Michigan and British Columbia, and at Cornell and Simon Fraser Universities. My ideas were modified by stimulating discussions of talks which
I gave during one-night stands at several campuses of the University of
California and at Stanford University, and during longer visits to the
Universities of London and Wisconsin.

   The shift from lecture notes to the draft of a possible book occupied
a year when I was a Fellow at the Center for Advanced Study in the
Behavioral Sciences in Stanford. For that privilege, with all its attend-
ant benefits – especially the freedom to think slowly about problems –
I am immeasurably in the Center's debt.

   Several friends have read the entire work, in one version or another,
offering criticisms and suggestions which have led to many improve-
ments. For this remarkable generosity I thank David M. Armstrong,
Michael Beebe, Christopher Hookway, Sydney Shoemaker and, above
all, Dorothy Edgington.

   Secretarial expenses in connection with the last two versions of the
book were covered by a grant from the Canada Council, which I
gratefully acknowledge.

At a time when I planned to include an extensive treatment of animal communication, I was helped and welcomed by Peter Marler, David Premack, W. John Smith and Adrian Wenner. In the event, the help counteracted the welcome, for it showed me that I was far too ignorant to be able properly to carry out my plan; and §62 below is all that remains of it. Still, I recommend the borderlands between philosophy and ethology as fertile territory for any philosopher who thinks it important that men are animals.

Vancouver, B.C.   J.F.B.
December 1975

1

PROGRAMME FOR A SYNTHESIS

§1. Identifying language

Someone visited the planet Margo, and found that its inhabitants have a language. How could such a discovery be made? We can usually tell at a glance, or at a hearing, whether language is being used by humans; because our species has a physically recognizable sort of behaviour ('vocalizing'), in which vocal cords, tongue and lips collaborate to produce variegated sequences of sounds which we use for linguistic purposes and, as adults, for little else. That is why one can recognize something as a conversation, say, without understanding it. But this basis for recognizing a performance as linguistic is not illuminating: it infers 'They are using a language' from 'They are vocalizing' on the grounds that *most human vocalizing is linguistic*; and this must rest on some other basis for classifying performances as linguistic. What is it?

Here is one answer: 'I just directly know that my own vocal performances are linguistic – there is no basis on which I recognize them as such. Then I can classify some other people's vocalizings as linguistic because they involve my language: I know that you are using language, for instance, because I understand what you say. So I can learn that certain humans vocalize only when using language; others could similarly learn this about other groups; and by assembling all the testimonies we learn that throughout the species most vocal behaviour is linguistic.' That answer, though, teaches us nothing about language, and merely rubs our noses in it. Of course when I use a language I know that I do, but that still leaves me unclear about what this knowledge amounts to, that is, unclear about my concept of language. And of course when you speak I understand; but my proper confidence about this does not greatly help me to understand what understanding is.

Nor does any of this help to explain how we could discover that the Margolese have a language. No one is bilingual as between Margolese and any human language, and the Margolese do not communicate vocally;[1] so how could we learn that they have a language?

---

[1] See Kurt Vonnegut, Jr, *Breakfast of Champions* (New York, 1973), ch. 5.

The Margolese are just a dramatic device. The fact is that we can, in fairly agreed ways, sort out behaviour into linguistic and non-linguistic – not just actual behaviour but also many possible sorts which do not actually occur. I want to know what we go by when we divide performances into the linguistic ones and the others. 'So you plan to explore the concept of language, or the meaning of "language". There may be something to be discovered about this, but is it worth the effort?'

Yes, because we might find that the concept of language is governed by a set of rules which are orderly enough to be manageable, yet complex enough to be interesting. We do have some such rich, disciplined conceptual structures, and they are worth studying in their own right.

Yes, also, because the inquiry is directed not only at 'language' but also at *language* – not just the word but the phenomenon. One's own first language is so familiar and all-encompassing that one cannot easily command a clear view of it; it is hard to resolve the blur of detail into a sharply focussed picture which highlights just those features which mainly serve to make language important to us. One way of developing such a picture is to discover which features of our language are relevant to our agreeing that it is a language.

This, incidentally, could also motivate a careful consideration of whether to count as 'languages' any of the natural communication systems of known non-human animals, or how to classify the supposed languages which have been taught to captive chimpanzees in recent years. So far from being a merely verbal matter, something which 'depends on the definition of language rather than on the observation of what animals do' and can be contemptuously left to 'those who have a taste for such questions',[2] this may involve a serious consideration of aspects of the human condition. When we have the raw behavioural facts about a given chimpanzee, the question of whether we should credit her with having a language forces us to compare her achievements with our own, thus coming to see ourselves more clearly. The endeavour to get straight about chimpanzees, bees, dolphins and the like – which I have reluctantly decided to omit from this book – can spring from the belief that the proper study of mankind is man.

Sometimes the question whether a given behavioural system should be counted as a language is a matter for decision or stipulation rather

---

[2] Beatrice T. Gardner and R. Allen Gardner, 'Two Way Communication with an Infant Chimpanzee', in A. M. Schrier and F. Stollnitz (eds.), *Behavior of Non-Human Primates*, vol. 5 (New York and London, 1971), p. 181.

than for conceptual discovery; but even then discovery is involved, for one cannot stipulate reasonably unless one has knowledge. The question of whether to count a given system as a language ought to depend upon how it resembles paradigm languages, and that cannot be known without conceptual investigation.

§2. The emphasis on behaviour

I stress linguistic *behaviour* because when we consider extra-terrestrials or animals or one another, outward behaviour such as the making of movements or noises is what we must go by. It may some day become possible to base claims about language on facts about neural events inside its users. Such events, however, are no part of our actual basis for distinguishing the linguistic from the non-linguistic, and indeed we know little about them. They may eventually come to dominate our picture of what language is, but I want to see what picture can be drawn with the materials now available.

Although I shall ignore neural events, I shall attend to mental ones. (Or, if physicalism is true, I shall attend to neural events in their guise as – or considered in their role as – mental events.) But statements about minds are based upon facts about behaviour, and I shall never introduce any mentalistic concept without first displaying its behavioural credentials, saying what sorts of physical behaviour would entitle us to apply it. Throughout the present work, indeed, I shall be interested in mentalistic concepts primarily as aids to intellectually organizing behavioural data, treating mental items as theoretical entities which are postulated by a certain kind of theory to explain behaviour. There is more than that to mental concepts, no doubt; but the 'more', though significant in some parts of the philosophy of mind, seems to be safely negligible in philosophy of language of the kind I am doing.

I therefore give short shrift to the private or inner uses of language, for instance as an aid to ordering one's thoughts. I have to, because I do not know how to handle such phenomena except on the basis of an understanding of the outer uses of language.

Some writers deplore any such behavioural emphasis in the philosophy of language. Chomsky, notably, has attacked those students of language who attend to linguistic behaviour at the expense of what 'underlies' it, as when he writes against Wittgenstein:

If we interpret [Wittgenstein] as merely circumscribing the task of the philosopher, limiting it to a 'purely descriptive method', to descriptions which 'are not hints of

3

explanations', then . . . he is proposing . . . to concentrate on evidence, . . . putting aside the question of what the evidence is evidence for. The traditional answer to this question was that the observed phenomena constitute evidence for an under-lying mental reality; it would not have surprised any traditional theorist of language or mind that evidence falls into unilluminating networks of family resemblances. It remains to establish the fact that there is some point in restricting one's activities to arrangement of data which are no longer regarded as evidence for the construction of a theory of language or a theory of mind.[3]

There are two targets here. One is Wittgenstein's reluctance to specu-late about the mind, and the other is his refusal to look for illuminating general theories of any sort at all. I sympathize with Wittgenstein's anti-mentalism in the philosophy of language; as I have explained, I shall use mentalistic concepts only under a tight behavioural rein. But I side with Chomsky on the other matter. Wittgenstein has an anti-theoretic streak which invites Chomsky's jibe about 'restricting one's activities to arrangement of data'. The 'networks of family resemblances' into which Wittgenstein sometimes tries to arrange data can indeed be un-illuminating, as Chomsky says, and the passage where Wittgenstein deploys his opinions about them is pertinent to my main theme:

Someone might object against me: 'You take the easy way out! You talk about all sorts of [linguistic activities], but have nowhere said what the essence . . . of language is: what is common to all these activities, and what makes them into language or parts of language . . .' And this is true. – Instead of producing some-thing common to all that we call language, I am saying that these phenomena have no one thing in common which makes us use the same word for all, – but that they are *related* to one another in many different ways. And it is because of this relationship, or these relationships, that we call them all 'language'.[4]

Since Wittgenstein gives no coherent evidence that 'these phenomena have no one thing in common which makes us use the same word for all', this is just dogmatic defeatism. And when, elsewhere, he empha-sizes 'the particular case' as an antidote to 'the craving for generality',[5] he seems to be hostile to something which is of the essence of the life of reason. None of that, however, is implied by the policy of rooting one's theory of language in facts about behaviour. I shall try through my heavily behavioural theory to establish general results of a certain kind – results which will let me, one might say, 'produce something

[3] N. Chomsky, 'Some Empirical Assumptions in Modern Philosophy of Language', in S. Morgenbesser *et al.* (eds.), *Philosophy, Science, and Method: Essays in Honor of Ernest Nagel* (New York, 1969), pp. 280–1.

[4] L. Wittgenstein, *Philosophical Investigations* (Oxford, 1953), §65.

[5] L. Wittgenstein, *The Blue Book* (Oxford, 1964), p. 18.

common to all that we call language'. Chomsky does not try to do this. In one place he implies an account of what 'language' is, an account which is quite wrong if offered as analytic of the concept of language; but in a later version the account is addressed to what 'human language' is, which makes it look like empirical description rather than conceptual analysis.[6]

Chomsky has also opposed the behavioural emphasis in the philosophy of language because it focusses on how language is used rather than on how it is structured. Let us examine this antithesis between use and structure.

Any human language is certainly a complex, orderly structure. Its complexity shows in the richness of what can be expressed in it, and its orderliness in the fact that everyone can produce brand-new sentences which others immediately understand, a feat which is miraculous unless we all have at our command some general rules or principles which govern our language. Actually to state the rules is evidently a difficult task; there is no natural language for which linguists have found a complete syntactic and semantic theory embodying all the facts about the grammatical structures in the language and how they contribute to the meanings of its sentences. Indeed, the experts even disagree about what the broad shape of such a theory would be (see §76 below). That hints at the size and complexity of this intellectual area; but it does not indicate the power of the work that has been done in it, under Chomsky's acknowledged leadership, in the past twenty years.

As well as facts about how a language is structured, there are facts about how it is used – the circumstances under which various sentences may be uttered, the purposes of the utterers, the effects on the hearers, and so on – and my main subject-matter lies in this area. Chomsky disapproves. 'If one wants to find out something significant about the nature of language', he writes, 'I think it is important to look not at its uses, which may be almost any imaginable, but, rather, at its structure.' It is futile to examine the uses of language, he thinks, because these 'may be almost any imaginable'. No doubt they may; but perhaps we can bring order into the chaos by mastering some central and basic kinds of language-use, and then with their aid elucidating others. Even if many uses are never covered by the theory, the latter may still have lit up the centre of our problem-area.

For a start, I agree with those philosophers of language who give

---

[6] For those two references, and for every remaining quotation from Chomsky in this section, see Chomsky (1967), pp. 73–4, and Chomsky (1968), pp. 61–2.

prominence to the use of language in communication between an utterer and an audience – I shall often say 'speaker' and 'hearer', just for euphony and not implying a restriction to vocal behaviour or to auditory intake of it. Furthermore, it seems likely that communication is primarily a matter of a speaker's seeking either to inform a hearer of something or to enjoin some action upon him. (Strictly speaking, 'enjoining' involves *authoritatively* trying to get someone to act; but I shall always use it to cover not just commanding but also requesting, advising and the like; and analogously with 'injunction'. There seems to be no word which is just right for the job, except perhaps 'imperative' – but that lacks a corresponding verb, and also has the disadvantage that it suggests a grammatical form rather than a use of language.) I suggest that we may get a handhold on the uses of language by starting with its uses as a means for information and injunction. Chomsky disagrees:

There is little reason to believe that the primary use of language is to modify behavior or modify thought. Language can be used for all kinds of other purposes. It can be used to inform or to mislead, to clarify one's thoughts or to show how clever one is; or, in fact, it can be used for play in a very general sense ... I am not using language any less, if I do not care whether I convince anyone or change anyone's behavior or change his thoughts.

Granted that language has many uses other than to inform and enjoin, why does Chomsky deny that these uses of it are primary? He does not say, and does not even explain what he means by 'primary'.

Perhaps information and injunction are not the most frequent uses of language on our planet, but why should we care about that merely statistical matter? The following seems more important. There could be a community which used language to inform and/or enjoin but for nothing else; but it is doubtful if one could describe in detail a community which used language for 'all kinds of purposes' but never to inform or enjoin. If that is right, then those two uses of language are 'primary' in one sense which is clearly relevant to the philosophy of language; and I conjecture that no other language-use has that kind of primacy.

That informing and/or enjoining *are* indispensable to a working communal language is an unobvious claim which needs defending – perhaps by arguing that a language must be used in those ways if it is to be closely enough linked with the world for its users to be able to learn it. But I shall not pursue this, for I do not actually need to claim primacy for informing and enjoining. It is enough for my purposes if those two uses of language make a good starting point for a certain kind of philosophical inquiry. I am sure they do, and I shall try to demonstrate this by writing a book which goes well because of its well-chosen starting point.

I take my stand, then, on a prediction that a certain kind of inquiry can yield useful results. Chomsky thinks that it cannot. The remarks I have quoted are part of his attack on the view that human languages can be fruitfully compared with systems of animal communication. Directly on that topic, he says:

If we rise to the level of abstraction at which human language and animal communication systems fall together, then we find plenty of other things incorporated under the same generalizations which no one would have regarded as being continuous with language ... Consider ... the properties of purposiveness, of having syntactic organization, and of being propositional, in a sense, informative. [And in the light of these] consider the common gestures one uses in helping someone park a car. When you indicate to him by the distance between your two hands how far he is from the car behind, your actions are purposive, integrated, and propositional. But, it is unlikely that any significant purpose would be served by studying such gestures and human language within the same framework.

That is, in effect, a prediction. I hope to falsify it in this book, and to show that the questions which Chomsky here sweeps aside as unworthy of study are profitable ones.

We can treat language-use without assuming anything about grammatical structure. Indeed, much of my subsequent inquiry into language-use will concern a communication-system – perhaps it is not a 'language', properly so called – whose utterances lack grammatical structure, but whose uses are significantly like some central uses of language.

What about the converse? Chomsky pictures the investigation of linguistic structure as an independent activity, owing nothing to assumptions about the uses of language. Certainly, one can investigate grammatical structure without explicitly mentioning uses; but in §75 below I shall argue that the investigation of structure does subtly presuppose something about meanings and thus about language-use.

§3. Meaning-nominalism

A study of communication must focus upon what speakers mean by what they say, and that requires us to become clear about how 'what he meant by x' relates to 'what x means'. Consider first the ludicrous

7

suggestion that no one has ever known what any part of our language really means. Don't say that in that case there would be no such thing as English, for that evades the question: is it conceivable that you and Milton and Henry James and all the rest of us have always been slightly wrong about the meaning of 'don't' and of 'say' and of 'that' and of 'in' . . . and so on through the English lexicon, and also about the real force of every grammatical construction in English? Granted that we know *what we mean by those items*, might we not be wrong about *what those items mean*? Obviously not; and that must be because what an expression means in language *L* is logically connected with what the users of *L* generally mean by it.

But which way does the connection run? Should we take as basic the notion of 'what *x* means' and try to elucidate 'what *U* meant by *x*' in terms of it, or should we reverse that order?

Here is one possible answer:

> We should elucidate 'What he meant was . . .' in terms of 'The meaning of what he uttered was . . .'. When the two fail to coincide, that is always because of some wrong belief the speaker has about the meaning of what he uttered. For instance, when he said, 'The episode just before the cadenza is climatic' he meant that the passage provided a climax, because that is what he thought his sentence meant. So 'what an expression means' is the basic notion, and 'what a speaker means by an expression' can be derived from it with the aid of the concept of belief.

That approach has been favoured by many writers, and one can see why. What a speaker can mean by an utterance is usually restricted to what he thinks it means in the language, and one is tempted to explain that by simply identifying 'what he means by his utterance' with 'what he thinks his utterance means'. But other explanations are possible, including one highly persuasive one which takes 'what he means by *x*' as basic and yet does abundant justice to the fact that ordinarily one can mean by an expression only what one thinks it means.[7]

What can be said in positive support of the view that 'what *U* means by *x*' is more basic than 'what *x* means'? Technical, grammatical arguments have been given for this,[8] but one simpler consideration is the fact that no one has yet succeeded in elucidating 'what *x* means' without appealing to 'what *U* means by *x*'. Davidson has tried, and I shall explain in §79 below why I think he fails; but even he does not base

[7] The explanation is Keith Donnellan's, but the fullest presentation of it is in Bennett (1973), pp. 166–8.

[8] Dennis W. Stampe, 'Toward a Grammar of Meaning', *Philosophical Review*, vol. 77 (1968). Stampe's arguments are discussed in Steven Davis, 'Meaning and the Transformational Stew', *Foundations of Language*, vol. 6 (1970).

'what U means by x' upon 'what x means', for he wishes to dispense
with the former locution altogether. So the evidence is quite strong
that 'what x means' is not the more fundamental of the two.

Even if it is not, however, the other may not be fundamental either.
Perhaps each must be explained through the other, so that together they
make a tight little conceptual circle, as I shall argue that the concepts of
intention and belief do. The state of the literature used to tempt one to
draw that conclusion; but the situation changed when H. P. Grice
showed how to give a clear sense to 'By uttering x, U meant that P'
without implying anything about any language – not that x meant
that P in any language, or that U thought it did, or that U thought that
his hearers thought it did, or . . . etc.[9] Grice's theory analyses the concept of meaning which is involved in language as distinct from the one
involved in 'Those clouds mean rain', but the analysis itself presupposes
nothing about language. Indeed, it treats of what an individual means
by an utterance on a particular occasion, without reference to what
anybody did, does, will or would mean on any other occasion.

So now we can have a meaning-nominalist account of language, that
is, one which treats as basic the individual instance of meaning, by one
speaker at one time, and gives a derivative status to every kind of
general statement about meanings – what the speaker usually means by
x, what speakers generally mean by x, what x means in the language,
and so on. Grice's work is controversial, and some of its critics object
to that aspect of it which I have been praising, namely its meaning-
nominalism.[10] I find their criticisms unconvincing; but I choose to
answer them only indirectly, by trying to carry out a thorough meaning-
nominalist programme.

Some years ago I started an inquiry in the philosophy of language by
asking how a certain animal communication-system fell short of
counting as a language.[11] Although that work may still be worth
reading, I dislike its central question – What mainly marks us off from
the brutes? – and my answer to it was wrong (see §§31–3 below). My
book's gravest fault, however, was its failure to profit from Grice's
insights about meaning. I could not avail myself of Grice, I now see,
because I did not begin in a nominalist way. Instead of attending to
isolated cases of communication, I started with a communication-

---

[9] Grice (1957).
[10] See Paul Ziff, 'On H. P. Grice's Account of Meaning', *Analysis*, vol. 28 (1967–8); N. L.
Wilson, 'Grice on Meaning: the Ultimate Counter-example', *Nous*, vol. 4 (1970).
[11] Bennett (1964).

system which is defined by certain *general* behaviour-patterns of honey-bees. This time I shall do better.

Even if our Gricean foundation is secure, can we find the materials to complete the structure? We are to start with 'what U meant by x on that occasion' and to elucidate 'what x means in L' in terms of that; but how? It seems obvious that the notion of 'what x means in L' is a covertly general one: what x means in language L is connected with what L-users *generally* do or would mean by x. But we cannot simply equate 'what x means in L' with 'what L-users generally mean by x': mere generality is too weak a foundation for the concept of meaning-in-L. For one thing, it lets us say that someone is using x in an unusual way, but not that he is using it wrongly; yet we do have the notion of linguistic malpractice, and a theory of language should account for it. It might be replied that the notion of misuse of language deserves no respect – that it merely reflects our deplorable tendency to condemn unusual kinds of behaviour. I cannot disprove this; but it is *prima facie* implausible, and we ought not to accept it without looking for an account of 'what x means' which will support the notion of wrong uses of language.

There is also a tougher objection to the equation of 'what x means' with 'what people generally mean by x'. A statement of the form 'Whenever anyone in this community utters x he means by it that P', which expresses mere generality, could be true by sheer coincidence: it does not connect one speaker's meaning that P by x with any other speaker's doing so. But it seems clear that we need something non-coincidental. If x is to mean that P in L, then your using it to mean that P must somehow be connected with my doing so. And the connection cannot be merely this: we both use it to mean that P because in our language it means that P. For that reverses the desired explanatory order.

But if mere generality is not enough, what shall we add to it? Some have said that language involves not merely regularities or general practices but rules or conventions. Early in this century, I think, most philosophers of language put their money on 'convention'; but no one explained clearly what a convention is, and suspicions grew that the concept of convention, if we did once become clear about it, would prove inapt for our purposes after all.[12] At about the same time, 'rule' came much into favour, perhaps under the influence of Wittgenstein's

---

[12] See the closing paragraphs of W. V. Quine, 'Truth by Convention', reprinted in H. Feigl and W. Sellars (eds.), *Readings in Philosophical Analysis* (New York, 1949); and William P. Alston, *Philosophy of Language* (Englewood Cliffs, N.J., 1964), pp. 56–8.

comparison of languages with games.[13] But 'rule' was never made much clearer than 'convention' had been. Two recent studies subject the concept of a rule, and especially a linguistic rule, to closer and more detailed scrutiny than it had ever had before.[14] But this work is outweighed, and the whole situation transformed, by the appearance at long last of a believable theory of convention. This is due to David Lewis. According to it, a convention is a special kind of behavioural regularity; and when one sees what kind, one can see how departures from conventions may count as wrong, what connects one person's behaviour with another's when they are conforming to a convention, and how conventions can arise in various ways which include but are not exhausted by groups' convening and agreeing on behavioural policies. As originally presented, Lewis's theory dealt better with non-linguistic than with linguistic conventions; but a slight change in the theory enables it to cope with linguistic conventions as well as with any others (see §55 below).

Eventually I shall argue that although actual human languages are Gricean and are governed by conventions, in Lewis's sense, there could be languages which did not quite satisfy Lewis's theory and which were not quite Gricean either. This will be the upshot of §§50–61 below. Even if it is right, though, this whole territory has been opened up by Grice's work and Lewis's, and I would not know how to present my results except in relation to theirs.

§4. Grice on meaning

The seminal idea which I take from Grice incorporates the view that meaning is a kind of intending. This is a commonplace; Grice's achievement was to discover a defensible version of it, which I briefly introduce in this section.

We sometimes equate 'what I meant' with 'what I intended to say'. Encouraged by the thought that saying is more straightforward than meaning, we might look to that equation for help in grasping what meaning is. But really it does not help. If a speaker says something unclear and then explains 'What I intended to say was . . .', he is not reporting what he intended to utter, as though some laryngeal mishap

---

[13] For a good recent example, see Searle (1969), *passim*.
[14] Joan Safran Ganz, *Rules: a Systematic Study* (The Hague, 1971); Raymond D. Gumb, *Rule-Governed Linguistic Behavior* (The Hague, 1972). For a useful discussion of the rival merits of 'rule' and 'convention', written in knowledge of Lewis's work, see Charles Landesman, *Discourse and its Presuppositions* (New Haven, 1972), ch. 4.

had made him produce the wrong words. Rather, he means something like 'What I meant is more clearly expressed by . . .'; and the words 'meant' and 'expressed' doubly disqualify that from helping to analyse the concept of meaning.

Here is a more promising line. If I say something to you, meaning by it that P, then I am presumably trying to 'get across to you' that P; and perhaps that metaphor means that I am trying to get you to believe P.[15] That cannot be the whole story about meaning, however, for I could try to get you to believe P in ways which obviously do not involve my meaning that P. For example, I could arrange for you to find evidence that P is true.

Granted, my displaying evidence for P's truth 'means that' I want you to believe P; but that is a fact about what my behaviour means – in the way furniture's rattling means that there is an earthquake – and not about what I mean. Grice labels as 'natural meaning' the sort of meaning where something is a natural sign or symptom of, or evidence for, something else; and he uses 'non-natural meaning' for the sort which is involved when a person, rather than an event or fact or state of affairs, means that P. For an exemplary account of the surface differences between the two sorts of meaning, see the opening pages of his original paper. Throughout this book, whenever I use 'meaning' without qualification I refer to non-natural meaning.

The point, then, was that I may try to get you to believe P without my non-naturally meaning P. Still, perhaps we can explain non-natural meaning as trying to bring it about *in some special way* that someone comes to believe something. But the 'special way' must not be anything like 'bringing it about that he believes that P because the speaker tells him that P', for 'tells' embodies the concept we want to explain. Grice's contribution was to offer a tenable theory about what this 'special way' is. I shall introduce it with an example.

During an opera performance, I look across at a friend sitting a dozen seats away; our eyes meet, and she grimaces in an exaggerated manner while holding her nose. I think that readers will be familiar with this kind of occurrence, and will agree that my friend *meant that* she was hating the performance. Let us analyse this situation, relying partly on our knowledge of the kind of real-life occurrence which my sketchy description evokes.

[15] Throughout this book I use P to abbreviate things of the form 'It is raining' and of the form '*that* it is raining', and so I say both 'the belief *that* P' and 'he believes P'. My reason is stylistic: when I always wrote 'believes that P', 'means that P' and so on, the repetitions of 'that' became burdensome.

Well, for a start, my friend intended to get me to think that she hated the performance. She might have tried other means to the same end: deliberately putting on a show of aesthetic agony, intending me to take it as natural evidence that she was suffering; or, without deceit, letting me see her trembling left hand which really is evidence that she is experiencing something hateful. But each of those devices involves something which I am to take, *independently of why I think she made it available to me*, as evidence that she hates the performance. The nose-holding and exaggerated grimaces were not like that: they were not offered, deceitfully or otherwise, as independent evidence that she hated the performance.

How, then, were they intended to get me to think that she hated the performance? Well, how did they in fact succeed? My friend's gesture led me to believe that she hated the performance because *that is what I thought she was trying to get me to believe*, and I didn't think that she would be misinformed or deceitful. Furthermore, that is just what she intended to happen: she intended to get me to think that she hated the performance, intending this to be brought about through my realizing what she was up to. Her grimaces etc. were intention-dependent evidence that she was hating the performance: their status as evidence depended essentially upon why she displayed them to me.

That is the core of Grice's account of non-natural meaning. If U does x, thereby meaning that P, he does it intending

(i)   that some audience A should come to believe P,
(ii) that A should be aware of intention (i), and
(iii) that the awareness mentioned in (ii) should be part of A's reason for believing P.

Further refinements are needed, but they can wait until chapter 5.

The above conditions are offered for statements only, not injunctions. We could stretch them to cover injunctions only by giving P values like 'A is to sit down', so that condition (i) would say that U intends that A should believe that he is to sit down; and it is not clear enough what that means. A better account of injunctions can be got if, following Grice's original paper, we say that U meant that A is to do X if U acted with the intention

(i)   that A should do X,
(ii) that A should be aware of intention (i), and
(iii) that the awareness mentioned in (ii) should be part of A's reason for doing X.

13

That too needs more discussion, which it will get in §41 below. In the meantime I shall concentrate on statements and neglect injunctions.

Note that in the opera example nothing like conventional meaning is involved. Gestures like my friend's are in common use; but their success as vehicles of meaning does not depend on that, for someone might understand such a gesture perfectly on his first encounter with this sort of behaviour.

It is true that such communications succeed only because they contain an iconic element. By that I mean that the 'utterance' provides a natural pointer to the meaning; e.g. my friend performs in a manner significantly *like* an unaffected display of a certain kind of aesthetic displeasure. This contrasts strikingly with the non-iconic relationship which usually holds between linguistic utterances and their subject-matters (a shout of 'Fire!' is not even slightly like flames), and I would not minimize the difference. But we cannot get a clear view of the difference between iconic and non-iconic cases, including a just estimate of how big a difference it is, without bringing both under a unified theory of meaning. I shall return to the difference between them in §47 below.

With Grice's theory of non-natural meaning in mind, look back at what Chomsky says about the 'common' procedure whereby 'you indicate to [someone] by the distance between your two hands how far he is from the car behind' (see §2 above). Such gestures might work even if they were not 'common', but then they would have to rely on the mechanism which figures in Grice's account of non-natural meaning. My intending that the placing of my hands should convince you that there is a yard to go would be inexplicable unless I intended you to acquire that belief partly through your recognition of my purpose.

In this mode of communication, a continuous quantity in the signal (distance between hands) is correlated with a continuous quantity in what is meant by it (distance between cars). Chomsky remarks that this is a common feature of animal communication systems, and not of human languages. That is perfectly correct; and the iconic relationship between the signal and its meaning is a further difference between this case and most linguistic utterances. It is a pity, though, that Chomsky overlooks the important feature which languages share with the distance-between-the-hands signals, and perhaps not with any communicative activities of known non-human animals, namely the reliance on the Gricean mechanism in which one produces a belief in someone else partly through his recognition that that is what one intends.

§5. Strategy: a conceptual route

Grice enables us to make sense of the form 'By doing x, U meant that P'. If you wish, replace 'doing' by 'uttering', but don't assume that x must be audible. An utterer can mean something by an action of any physical sort whatsoever.

The emphasis on actions may seem peculiar. Ordinarily we say that a speaker means something by what he utters, rather than by uttering it. I cannot escape this peculiarity: Grice links 'what he means by . . .' with 'what he intends by . . .'; and, since one intends things by actions, my Gricean approach implies that one means things by actions also.

Still, once this oddity has been squarely faced, it can be swept away by a simple device. I shall assume that any action by which someone means something is either a movement, a noise-making, or the production of an object such as a written inscription or the like. In an action of any of these kinds, the agent *makes* something – a movement, a noise, or an object – and I shall describe what he makes as the 'product' of the action. Using 'product' in this convenient way, I announce that I shall move routinely from what U meant by his action to what U meant by its product. With movements, the product *is* the action; with noises, they are hardly distinct; with objects, they are quite different, but we can still harmlessly use 'By the smoke-signal he meant P' as short for 'By making the smoke-signal he meant P'. If that seems high-handed, see the third paragraph of §65 below.

So I shall slide freely between actions and products, and thus between doing and uttering; but let it be remembered that the account starts with actions.

Observe also that it starts with the idea of someone's meaning *that P* – that the speaker is ill, that there are fish in the bay, that the opera is dreadful, that the hearer is to sit down. Anything by which someone means that P, for a propositional value of P, I shall call a 'whole utterance'. The gesture at the opera was a whole utterance, and so is my holding my hands a yard apart to tell you that you have a yard to go. I prefer 'whole utterance' to 'sentence' because sentences, properly so called, are linguistic, and I want a name for anything with a 'that P' meaning, whether it belongs to a language or not.

Whole utterances are not the only items that can have meanings. I shall start with whole-utterance meaning, and then use it to introduce the notion of the meaning of an utterance-part. Here is the route I shall follow. First, with the aid of Grice I shall introduce

(1)   By doing or uttering x, U meant that P,

where x is a particular action or product. Next, with Lewis's help I shall proceed to

(2)   There is a convention whereby the members of some community, when they utter or do x, mean by it that P,

where x is now some *kind* of action or product, so that in (2) the phrase 'when they utter x' expands into 'when they utter a token or instance of x'. I do not distinguish (2) from

(3) x means that P,

where x is a kind of product. With (3) we reach the notion of the meaning that a certain expression – a certain product-kind – conventionally has; but the expression is still a whole utterance, something more like a sentence than like a word or phrase. The final big step is from that to

(4) w means . . .

where w is an utterance-part, and the completion is a word or phrase and not a 'that P' clause where 'P' stands for a sentence.

The order could have been different, for a limited notion of utterance-part meaning could be introduced without appeal to conventional meanings. By getting in conventional meanings first, I can get a richer system of meaningful utterance-parts; but the fact that the other order could be followed is important. I shall discuss it in §80 below.

What about the notion of grammatical structure? It belongs at level (4), neither earlier nor later. It is, I shall argue in §75, of the essence of grammatical structure that it mediates between the meanings of whole utterances and the meanings of their parts: the meaning of an ordinary structured sentence depends upon the meanings of its words and upon the significance of how they are assembled. If that is right, we cannot deploy a useful concept of grammatical structure before we have meaningful utterance-parts. Conversely, we shall find that meaningful utterance-parts, except ones of a very limited kind, require grammatical structure.

The term 'language', I believe, becomes fully appropriate at level (4) but not before.

The route from (1) through (4) is worth following for its own sake: one need not take a Gricean view of (1) to think that (2) must be explained in terms of (1), and (4) in terms of (2) or (3); and the problem of giving those explanations is challenging and interesting, whether or not it belongs to any larger endeavour. But the route from (1) to (4) is really important if (1) can be elucidated without the aid of 'meaning', 'language', 'message', 'signal', or any other concepts that 'swim the same orbit of conceptual space as does "meaning" itself'.[16] If (1) can be thus treated, and the route from there to (4) followed in a disciplined manner, then the whole thing will be a fairly radical analysis of the concept of language.

Two of the steps need comment right away.

Firstly, in declining to distinguish (3) what x means from (2) what people conventionally mean by x, I do not endorse an uncritical linguistic democracy. On the contrary, I freely admit that there could be sentences to which no one ever attached their correct meanings. The meaning of a sentence is determined by the meanings of its parts and the significance of how they are put together; and these matters, although they arise directly from what language-users ordinarily mean, are possible subjects of general error – through mis-assemblage of the facts, so to speak. For instance, nurses and first-aid trainees are sometimes taught 'No head injury is too trivial to be ignored', by which their teachers mean that no head injury is so trivial that it ought to be ignored. Really the sentence means something which it would be absurd to say, namely that no head injury is so trivial that it ought *not* to be ignored. It means this because of facts about the form 'too *adjective* to be *verb*ed' – 'too wicked to be forgiven', 'too fattening to be eaten' – and these in turn rest on facts about what speakers would usually mean. This example shows how there might be some sentence which everybody got wrong, even though meanings are ultimately determined by what the language-users mean. But this essentially involves mistakes about grammatical structures, and so it cannot occur until we reach level (4). Before then, when we are dealing with whole utterances whose meanings do not result from the meanings of their parts and their structures, an utterance can only mean what people generally mean by it. That is why I can conflate (2) with (3).

§6. Sentence-meaning and word-meaning

The other part of my conceptual route which should be discussed at once is the move from (3) whole utterances to (4) meaningful parts of

[16] Dennis W. Stampe, 'Toward a Grammar of Meaning', p. 168.

utterances. Strange as it may seem to someone meeting it for the first time, the view that the concept of a whole utterance (e.g. sentence) is more basic than that of a meaningful utterance-part (e.g. word) is endorsed by all linguists and by philosophers of language as diverse as Grice, Davidson, Ziff, Austin and Quine.[17] It seems to be rejected mainly by psychologists who think that the fundamental linguistic act is one of 'naming' rather than of saying something. ('The simplest and most primitive aspect of [language] is the ability to understand names.'[18]) However, the primacy of sentence-meaning has been disputed by one considerable philosopher, Michael Dummett. He writes: 'Any attempt to express clearly . . . the idea that the meaning of sentences is primary, that of words derivative, ends in implicitly denying the obvious fact – which is of the essence of language – that we can understand new sentences which we have never heard before.'[19] This does not even *prima facie* challenge one version of the thesis that sentence-meaning is primary, namely that the concept of sentence-meaning comes, in the order of explanation, before that of word-meaning. Dummett is clearly attacking the stronger view that statements about what individual sentences mean are more basic than ones about the meanings of words. That suggests not just that 'sentence-meaning' comes first, but that sentence-meanings come first; it does *prima facie* conflict with the fact that we understand many sentences by understanding their constituent words, and thus with 'the fact . . . that we can understand new sentences which we have never heard before'; and so the view in question does seem to be Dummett's target. I accept this stronger primacy thesis; and although I am not committed to it by anything I have said so far, I shall rely heavily upon it in chapter 8 below. I therefore wish to defend it against Dummett.

Just before the quoted remark, Dummett says: 'Though it is certainly true of *some* words that [i] we can learn their sense only by learning the use of representative sentences containing them, conversely [ii] there are some sentences . . . which we understand only by already knowing the meanings of the constituent words.' He apparently takes (i) to be true of some words but not of all; and so he rejects the (stronger) primacy thesis because he reasonably takes it to imply that one can learn

---

[17] For an illuminating discussion of how this view relates to what a child learns, see L. S. Vygotsky, *Thought and Language* (Cambridge, Mass., 1962), p. 126.

[18] Jane B. Lancaster, 'Primate Communication Systems and the Emergence of Human Language', in Phyllis C. Jay (ed.), *Primates* (New York, 1968), at p. 446.

[19] Michael Dummett, 'Nominalism', *Philosophical Review*, vol. 65 (1965), p. 492.

what *any* word means only by learning how it is used in sentences. The question is: why does Dummett think that (i) fails for some words?

Well, he apparently takes his claim (ii) that some sentences can be understood only through words to conflict with the thesis that the meaning of any word must be learned by learning some of its uses in sentences. But really there is no conflict at all. All that (ii) rules out is the vastly stronger thesis that the meaning of any word must be learned by learning *all* of its uses in sentences. But *that* is not true of any words, let alone of all, and nobody has ever thought that it is. The primacy thesis maintains only that to learn the meaning of any word one must learn its use in some sentences: it does not deny that there are other sentences which, as claimed by (ii), can be understood only after the word has been understood.

The overall picture of meaning-explanation for a given language could be like this: the explanatory base contains some sentences, the next layer up contains all words, and then above that is a layer containing the infinitude of remaining sentences. That is doubtless too simple; but it serves to show how Dummett's claim (ii) is consistent with the stronger primacy thesis, i.e. with (i)'s being true of all words and not just of some.

Suppose we replace Dummett's (ii) by the seemingly extravagant claim that to understand *any* sentence one must know the meanings of its constituent words. That claim is in fact defensible; for even if someone knows the overall meaning of a sentence, if he does not know how it results from the meanings of the separate words we can plausibly deny that he *fully* understands the sentence. For example, a child who says 'Helpme' when and only when he wants help, without viewing this sentence as segmented into 'help' and 'me' with their separate meanings, can reasonably be said to have some lack in his understanding of the sentence. But that still lets us maintain a version of the primacy thesis, namely that to learn the meaning of any word one must gain an incomplete understanding of sentences containing it. If one's understanding of the sentences is incomplete then so perhaps is one's understanding of the word; but that is all right. We now have a new picture in which the bottom explanatory layer contains only sentences, as before, but now only incompletely understood; the next layer has many partly understood words, making possible a fuller understanding of the bottom layer; the third layer has more sentences, generating a still fuller understanding of the first two layers; and so on upwards.

Much more recently, Dummett has turned around. He insists that 'in a certain sense ... sentences have a primacy within language over other linguistic expressions', and alludes to 'Frege's ... insight that sentences play a unique role, and that the role of almost every other linguistic expression ... consists in its part in forming sentences.'[20] But he also hints that he still sees his earlier argument as posing a *prima facie* difficulty,[21] yet he does not show how it should be overcome. He endorses the view, which he says is Frege's, that 'in the order of *explanation* the sense of a sentence is primary, but in the order of *recognition* the sense of a word is primary';[22] but this, even if it is right, does not go far towards diagnosing the mistake in the earlier argument. So I have offered my diagnosis.

The primacy thesis can also be challenged on the grounds that word-meanings need not be grasped through sentence-meanings because they can be given in definitions.

Verbal definitions, in which a word's meaning is explained by presenting some other expression which means the same, cannot conflict with any theory about what it is for an utterance-part to have a meaning. One's favoured theory, whatever it is, can be applied to both sides of the verbal definition; and so the theory I favour interprets a verbal definition as saying that the definiendum and the definiens make about the same contribution to the meanings of sentences in which they occur, which is why they are inter-substitutable. Usually the contributions would differ slightly, and so the inter-substitutability is imperfect; but then we know that verbal definitions are indeed seldom perfectly accurate.

Where two languages are concerned, inter-substitutability is not to the point. For instance, *ultio* is Latin for 'revenge'; but if in any sentence you replace one of those words by the other, the result will usually be a Latin–English mix with no clear meaning. Still, we can construe the given explanation of *ultio* as saying that *ultio* contributes to the meanings of Latin sentences what 'revenge' contributes to comparable English ones.

What about ostensive definitions? They seem to present word-meanings without implying anything about sentences: the definer utters the word 'rose', say, while indicating a rose, then utters it again while indicating a second rose, and so on through a good sample-set of roses; he seems to have shown what 'rose' means without implying anything about how it can be used in sentences.

[20] Dummett (1973), pp. 194, 196.   [21] *Ibid.*, p. 192.   [22] *Ibid.*, p. 4.

That is an illusion. Consider the ostensive definition from the pupil's point of view: what does he learn from it? If he already knows that 'rose' is a general term which applies (in sentences) to objects of some kind, but does not know what kind, then the ostensive definition simply tops up his knowledge about how to use 'rose' by giving him the vital bit of information which lets him sort true from false among an important class of sentences containing the word. So in that case the definition does tell the pupil something about how to use the definiendum in sentences. The same holds true if the pupil initially knows nothing about 'rose' and does all his learning during the ostensive procedure. So long as what he finally gets is the idea that 'rose' is a general term which can be applied (in sentences) to objects of a certain kind, and that the teacher is showing what the kind is, there is no challenge to the claim that word-meanings must be understood through sentence-meanings.[23]

Now let us consider an ostensive definition where the pupil neither imports nor acquires the hunch that he is learning how to apply, in sentences, a general term. What can he be learning? To embarrass the primacy thesis, it must be something which does not bear on the use of 'rose' in sentences, but which does pertain to its meaning as a linguistic entity. The pupil must not learn, say, that the uttering of 'rose' is an adjunct to a flower-brandishing ceremony with no linguistic import.

Does he learn that someone confronted by a rose is permitted to utter 'rose'? That is vacuous: one is permitted to utter any word in the presence of a rose, and to utter 'rose' in the presence of any object. Perhaps, then, he learns that when confronted by a rose he *should* utter 'rose'; but that would get him into all sorts of trouble.

Objection: 'You are missing the point. What he learns is just that "rose" is the name of that kind of flower.' But that lesson has no content unless the pupil contemplates using the name in sentences about the flower. To see this, try to imagine a tribe whose only linguistic apparatus is a repertoire of names for things. Since the names could do the tribe no service, there is no content to the idea that they are names or that the tribe's 'having' them constitutes a linguistic possession.[24] In psychology books one still reads sometimes that there is an operation of naming or labelling which is not a part of using sentences to say things. This may be nourished by a conflation between words and unstructured sentences, e.g. between the noun 'rain' and the exclamation

---

[23] I have been helped here by P. T. Geach, *Mental Acts* (London, 1957), §§6, 10, 11.
[24] See Dummett (1973), p. 193.

'Rain!', or between the name 'Charles' and the cry 'Charles!' (meaning 'Charles, pay attention to me!'); but that would take me too far afield.[25]

Although it is widely agreed by philosophers that some form of the primacy thesis is correct, there is no received doctrine about just how word-meanings should be explained through sentence-meanings, or the concept of word-meaning explained through that of sentence-meaning. Grice ignored word-meaning entirely in his original paper; but he took it up in a later work which I shall discuss in §83 but which I shall not follow.[26] The approach I shall adopt owes a good deal to Ziff.

§7. Strategy: merely sufficient conditions

Grice offered a biconditional of the form: 'U does x thereby meaning that P, if and only if U does x with the intention . . .', which I now abbreviate to '[meaning]$\rightleftarrows$[intending]'. It has become clear that half of this, namely the conditional [meaning]$\rightarrow$[intending], is false; and Grice and others have tried to amend the formula so as to block the counter-examples. The results, though complicated, have still left some counter-examples standing.

I shall jettison [meaning]$\rightarrow$[intending], and defend only conditionals of the form [intending]$\rightarrow$[meaning]. That is, I shall seek results of the type 'Anything like this would be a case of meaning', without trying to cover every case of meaning. That I shall pursue sufficient but not necessary conditions for meaning is the dominating strategic fact about this book.

Traditionally, a conceptual analysis is supposed to yield a biconditional, stating conditions which are jointly sufficient and severally necessary for the application of the concept. This can be hard to achieve. Sufficiency demands strength, whereas necessity (requiredness) calls for weakness, and one needs to get the mixture just right. But if we simply drop one half of the endeavour, and look only for sufficient conditions for the application of our concept, our task will be too easy to be interesting. For example, if a community's vocal behaviour was indistinguishable from that of the characters in Chekhov's *The Three Sisters*, say, that might suffice to qualify it as linguistic; but such a

---

[25] The distinction between words and unstructured sentences is helpfully discussed in Quine (1960), §12. It is related to the thought of some psychologists in Bennett (1975), §11. [26] Grice (1968).

specialized example does not illuminate the concept of meaning or of language. What we need, at a minimum, is a statement of conditions which are strong enough to be sufficient for meaning and yet *weak enough to be instructive*. Although that is vague, it restores the problem to the form: how can we get something strong enough but not too strong?

Conditions for meaning would be 'weak enough to be instructive' if they were necessary for meaning, but I have declined to aim so high. I shall try to establish sufficient conditions which are weak enough to cover a large, central, basic class of instances of meaning. By 'central' I mean important in our everyday uses of language. By 'basic' I mean adequate as a basis for explaining all other kinds of meaning.

If I can succeed in that, then I could explain every kind of meaning, using Gricean material for my basic kind and then using it to explain the others. With a certain broadly Gricean [intending]→[meaning] conditional as my spearhead, I shall thrust through to the centre of the conceptual area I want to occupy, there establishing a base from which one could easily range out and capture the rest of the territory. It would be more orthodox to advance on a broad front, invulnerable to flanking attacks and not committed to mopping-up operations after the main campaign is over; but the concept of meaning probably cannot be conquered in that way, within tolerable limits of complexity.

I shall omit the mopping up. It certainly could be done *if* my main conceptual thrust succeeds. This is a fairly small claim because that is a very large 'if'.

Of the cases of meaning which are not covered by the sufficient conditions I shall offer, most depend upon *language*, and thus upon conventional meanings and conventional ways of resolving utterances into meaningful parts. For instance, someone may mean something by an utterance which he uses merely to give vent to his feelings, with no thought of a possible audience.[27] But I doubt if that is psychologically or even conceptually possible except in a language: the speaker's solitary cry 'I wish I were dead!' expresses his despair only because of what that sentence conventionally means in a communal language.

Everything of this sort should be set aside in the initial stages of the conceptual development. It would be futile to try to allow for the solitary cry of despair, for instance, in an absolutely general account of

[27] This is used against Grice by O. H. Green, 'Intentions and Speech Acts', *Analysis*, vol. 29 (1968-9).

meaning which was to be a *basis* for an account of conventional meaning and thus of language. A more hopeful procedure is to start with a fairly general account of meaning, on that basis to build a fairly general account of conventional meaning, and then to generate a comprehensive account of language which scoops in all those language-dependent cases which were previously omitted.

Our ordinary uses of 'mean' etc. include many subtleties which reflect the fact that most actual meanings are linguistic. For example, we distinguish 'what U meant by x' from 'what U meant by uttering x', relating the latter to motives rather than to meanings; and this seems to connect with x's having a meaning in a language. That is one reason for my ignoring the difference between meaning something by an action and meaning something by a product. The other reason is that this distinction is only a nuance, and is negligible for that reason. My attitude to nuances is thus quite unlike Ziff's. When he complains that Grice's theory conflates 'mean by x' with 'mean by uttering x',[28] he is not setting a higher standard for Grice than he sets for himself in *Semantic Analysis*, where he tries 'to adhere to every distinction that speakers of my English dialect generally make in talking about or in saying something pertaining to words'.[29] In sharp contrast with this, I shall be prepared at every stage to settle for approximations which are accurate enough for the project in hand. I reject the view, which Ziff says is 'often' advanced, that 'natural languages are horribly confused and so there is no sense in paying attention to such distinctions'. My position is that I should ignore a distinction, such as that between 'talking about' and 'saying something pertaining to', if respecting it would increase my difficulties without helping my explanatory programme.

§8. Thought and language

Any analysis leaves unanalysed materials on the right-hand side. Similarly, for my programme of analysis-by-synthesis I must help myself to an initial stock of concepts, without explaining them through anything more primitive. It is always a problem to know where to start. There is a line of conceptual dependence from 'language' to 'meaning', to 'intention' and 'belief', to 'organism', to 'physical object', and philosophical problems abound all the way down. But surely we

[28] Paul Ziff, 'On H. P. Grice's Account of Meaning', *Analysis*, vol. 28 (1967–8), p. 3.
[29] Ziff, pp. viii–ix.

can explain something without explaining its entire conceptual ancestry!

However, I shall not start with 'intention' and 'belief', because I want to lay foundations for those two concepts, showing how intentions and beliefs can be attributed to creatures which lack a language. If they could not, I should be in trouble. My meaning-nominalist programme requires me to identify cases of meaning which are untouched by convention, and are thus not linguistic, so that I can move upwards from meaning to language through a stage where conventional meaning appears as the clean overlap of two species, *convention* and *meaning*. But if intentions and beliefs were prerogatives of creatures with language, then any case of meaning would involve an agent who possessed a language even if he was not using it just then; and that would spoil the bold picture which I hope to draw – though my programme does not absolutely require it – of a situation where we are fully entitled to say that U means something by x although we do not yet know whether U has a language.

So the plan is, broadly speaking, to start with thought and move from that through meaning to language. Here is a recent argument for the conclusion that the plan is a bad one:

If thought *is* a representational system analogous to public language, then it cannot be appealed to to *explain* how representational systems succeed in representing a world. Whatever the merits of agent-semantics as a component in an account of public linguistic *performances*, the analysis of *representation* must be conducted at a level undercutting the distinction between the overt and the covert, between public language and thought.[30]

This reflects the author's assumption that there is a unitary notion of representation: he wants to discover how it is possible 'for language to represent the world'.[31] It seems also to assume that the difference between thought and language is *just* that between covert and overt representation. Since I reject that second assumption, I am free to inquire into what else is involved in the difference between thought and language, undeterred by threats about 'the ultimate sterility of agent-semantics and its intentionalist under-pinnings'.[32]

The above quotation occurs in a book which acknowledges the influence of Wilfrid Sellars. Sellars's own work is also marked by a refusal simply to start with thought and move on from it to language. A typical remark is that 'an uttering of p which is a primary expression

[30] Jay Rosenberg, *Linguistic Representation* (Dordrecht, 1974), p. 28.
[31] *Ibid.*, p. 95.   [32] *Ibid.*, p. 28.

of a belief that-*p* is not merely an *expression* of a thinking that-*p*, but is itself a *thinking*, i.e., a thinking-out-loud that-*p*'.[33] Sellars also warns of dangers which he sees inherent in 'approach[ing] language in terms of the paradigm of *action*',[34] that is, in thinking of language as essentially a kind of (outer) behaviour which is in a certain way expressive of (inner) thought. I am unsure of my grasp of this, but Sellars's warnings seem to rest on the dubious assumption that his opponents will agree with him that 'thought is analogous to linguistic activity' in some strong though unexplained way.

The crucial difference between Sellars's approach and my Gricean one, however, seems to stem from the fact that his philosophy of language gives an absolutely fundamental place to the concept of a *rule*. I do not dispute that language is rule-governed (though I would rather say that it is conventional); but I think that Grice has shown us how to connect language with thought through a mediating concept – *meaning* – which does not essentially involve any such concept as that of a rule or convention; and so I am not even slightly tempted to think that the rules governing language must be intimately related to rules governing thought. This leaves me genuinely unable to bring Sellars's warnings to bear upon anything I am doing, though I realize that I have done scant justice to what is evidently a rich and subtle body of philosophical doctrine.

The position I am adopting, in opposition to the Sellarsian one, has been well expressed by Armstrong:

Once thought has been linguistically expressed the expressions can be perceived and react back upon the mind, eventually creating more complex and sophisticated thought which in turn can be given linguistic expression. And so speech gives birth to thought. It seems also to be at least a fact of nature, and may even be a logical necessity, that certain thoughts can be manifested in *linguistic* behavior only. But both these propositions are compatible with the 'distinct existence' in every case of mental states and the linguistic behavior in which they may be manifested.[35]

In conformity with this, and following Grice, I shall start with thought

---

[33] Wilfrid Sellars, 'Language as Thought and as Communication', reprinted in *Essays in Philosophy and its History* (Dordrecht, 1974), p. 107.

[34] *Ibid.*, p. 98. For more on Sellars's basic approach to these matters, see his 'Empiricism and the Philosophy of Mind' and the ensuing correspondence with Chisholm, in A. Marras (ed.), *Intentionality, Mind, and Language* (Urbana, Ill., 1972).

[35] Armstrong (1971), pp. 427–8. The 'mentalism' of my present work is compatible with that defended in Jerrold J. Katz, 'Mentalism in Linguistics', *Language*, vol. 40 (1964), although our overall theories differ in method, aim and content.

– specifically with intentions and beliefs – and shall move from there to language through the concept of meaning. In my next three chapters I shall try to show positively and in detail how non-linguistic behaviour can support the concepts of intention and belief. First, though, I want to rebut arguments for saying that this is impossible.

§9. Thought without language?

Various writers have suggested analyses of '*x* believes that *P*' in terms of '*x* has such and such an attitude to *S*' where *S* is a *sentence*. That seems to tie belief to language, but really it does not. Quine, at any rate, says that the proposed analysis 'is not, of course, intended to suggest that the subject of the [belief] speaks the language of the [sentence], or any language'.[36] Other proponents of that sort of approach, such as Carnap, appear not to have wondered what sorts of creatures can have beliefs. Rather they have considered the normal human situation where there are both beliefs and languages, and have offered theories about the relations between the two. I shall not discuss these theories.

Quine is indeed on record as thinking that there is something inescapably vague and impressionistic about any attribution of beliefs and intentions to lower animals – he says that such attributions use an 'essentially dramatic idiom', which has no firm criterial foundations and depends upon our imaginatively putting ourselves in the animal's position and then using our (actual) language to express the beliefs we imagine we would have if thus placed.[37] In so far as this merely reflects pessimism about the chances of finding solid non-linguistic behavioural foundations for the concept of belief, the right response is just to build the foundations – which is what I shall attempt in the ensuing chapters. The other source of Quine's position involves scepticism about the legitimacy of 'He believes that . . .' even where 'he' does have a language. The reasons for that will be discussed in §78 below.

Bernard Williams has argued for a close link, of a kind, between belief and language. He presents a creature – call it *C* – some of whose belief-like epistemic states are manifested in assertion-like performances, with this peculiarity that *C* cannot 'assert' that *P* unless it 'believes' that *P*. That is, *C* cannot 'lie'. On the strength of this description of *C*, Williams contends (i) that *C*'s performances are not genuine assertions,

[36] W. V. Quine, 'Quantifiers and Propositional Attitudes', in *The Ways of Paradox* (New York, 1966), p. 192.   [37] Quine (1960), p. 219.

and (ii) that the states they manifest are not genuine beliefs.[38] I deny that he is entitled to claim (ii). He infers both conclusions from a single premiss, which he describes both as stating 'an extremely important fact about assertion' and as presenting 'a feature of belief'; and he words it both as 'Assertion can be insincere' and as 'The assertion of p is neither a necessary nor . . . a sufficient condition of having the belief that p'.[39] This, when construed in a certain way, does entail that it is not the case that C's performances are assertions which manifest C's beliefs; whence it follows that either (i) or (ii) is right. It is evidently implausible to deny (i) while maintaining (ii), that is, to say that C's performances are genuine assertions but that what they manifest are not genuine beliefs. We therefore seem to be driven by Williams's premiss to agree with him in accepting (i) that C's performances are not genuine assertions. But that leaves us with no basis whatsoever for also contending (ii) that the states manifested by those performances are not genuine beliefs. The premiss relating belief to assertion is simply irrelevant to the beliefs of a creature which, like C, does not assert.

Of any such creature, Williams says without qualification that 'Its states would not be beliefs', which suggests a very strong view about belief in relation to assertion and thus to language. I gather, though, that he wanted to deny the status of belief only to those states of C which are manifested in assertion-like performances, leaving open the possibility that C may have beliefs which it manifests in other ways. In fact, Williams attributes to languageless creatures only a concept of 'something rather like belief', or of 'belief' in an 'impoverished' sense; but his reasons for these cautions have to do not with the creature C but rather with other difficulties which I shall try to grapple with in chapter 4 below.[40]

The current situation regarding intentions and language is peculiar. Many philosophers would agree with this: 'Intention appears to be something that we can express, but which brutes . . . can *have*, though lacking any distinct expression of intention.'[41] In conversation, however, one often meets the rival view that intentions need language; yet I can find almost no direct defences of this in the literature.

[38] Williams, p. 145. As well as the argument I am now criticizing, this paper contains much that is true, interesting, and relevant to the present work.
[39] Williams, p. 140.
[40] *Ibid.*, pp. 139–40. On the whole matter of the beliefs of languageless creatures I agree with the position and the argument of Armstrong (1973), ch. 3.
[41] G. E. M. Anscombe, *Intention* (Oxford, 1957), p. 5; see also p. 85.

9. THOUGHT WITHOUT LANGUAGE?

One line of argument, which I have heard but never read, exploits a fact about intention which can easily seem to require intenders to have a language. Suppose that someone acts with a certain intention, and achieves what he intended to. Suppose further that what he achieves is getting food, emptying a rabbit-burrow, and contributing to the starvation of a bystanding buzzard. Although he achieved what he intended to, and achieved those three things, he may not have intended to achieve those three things – e.g. he may have intended to get food without intending to empty the burrow or even knowing about the buzzard. This is true of intentions generally, it seems. One must always be prepared to say 'He intended to produce G but not to produce H', even when producing G inevitably would involve producing H. For instance, he intended to drink that water but not to poison himself; and yet to drink that water would inevitably be to poison himself. Now, if we express this point in the form 'One always intends to achieve something *under a certain description*', we may be tempted to infer that an intender must have a language.

But that is all wrong. The intender need not select descriptions: *we* do that when we describe his intention. Admittedly, we have to select because the intender has, as it were, selected aspects or features of the state of affairs resulting from his action; and I must explain what this feature-selection is. Of various *prima facie* workable accounts of the matter, I shall choose one using the concept of belief. We can be entitled, in speaking of a languageless creature, to distinguish 'He believes P' from 'He believes Q' even in cases where P and Q stand or fall together. So we can distinguish 'He intended to achieve G' from 'He intended to achieve H', even if achieving G must involve achieving H, thus: the agent did A intending to achieve G because his doing A is partly explained by his believing that this would lead to G; and he did not intend to achieve H because either he did not believe that doing A would lead to H or else his having this belief does not help to explain his doing A. That, of course, is a mere promissory note: the details will be given in the following chapters. For the present, what matters is just that we are not compelled to restrict intentions to creatures with language just because intentions involve feature-selection.

The only extended written defence I know for the thesis that intentions require language is by Hampshire, who writes:

It is the *possibility* of our declaring ... our intentions ... that gives sense to the notion of intention itself. Without this possibility, the notion of intention becomes empty ... It is characteristic of an intention that it may be formed long in advance of the action intended, and also that an intention may have existed without ever having been translated into action. It is senseless to speak of what a dog intended to do before it was interrupted or prevented or changed its mind, unless 'He intended to do so-and-so next' is taken to mean the same as 'He would have done so-and-so next, if he had not been prevented'. To say of a person 'He intended to do so-and-so next' is certainly not equivalent to the statement that he would have done so-and-so if he had not been prevented . . . One might believe that someone had seriously and sincerely intended to do something, and at the same time be very doubtful whether he would in fact have done it, or even have tried to do it, if and when the occasion for action occurred.[42]

Granted, the content of 'He intended to do A, but did not do it' is not equivalent to 'He would have done A if he had not been prevented'; but that simplistic equation fails for dogs as well as people, for reasons that have nothing to do with language. Hampshire simply asserts that it is 'senseless' to attribute an unfulfilled intention to a dog unless the attribution merely means a simple conditional of the form 'It would have done so-and-so if it had not been prevented'. Why should a dog's lacking a language debar it from being the subject of *complex* truths about its behavioural dispositions? And why should not these give the behavioural content of truths about the dog's unfulfilled intentions?

Hampshire's point cannot be that some attributions of (unfulfilled) intentions have no behavioural implications at all. Such an attribution, since it implies nothing about behaviour, could not be supported by any facts about behaviour; so we, in our present state of knowledge, could have no evidence for it; so it would be idle. Of course, a statement attributing to someone an intention at a certain time might be based on his earlier behaviour yet imply nothing about the future; but that goes for dogs as well as for people.

I think that Hampshire's point must be that someone who had an unfulfilled intention can *say* that he had it, whereas a dog cannot. Indeed, that means for revealing intentions is open only to creatures with languages, but what of it? Forget the fact that we do not ordinarily accept someone's reports on his unfulfilled intentions unless they have some backing in his non-linguistic behaviour; take the line between the linguistic and the non-linguistic revelation of intention to be as sharp, deep and absolute as you like; still, where does it lead? A little later Hampshire says: 'Intentions are something that may be concealed and disguised; but they can be concealed and disguised, only because they naturally express themselves immediately either in words or in

[42] Stuart Hampshire, *Thought and Action* (London, 1959), pp. 97–8. The remaining quotations in this section are all from *Ibid.*, pp. 97 and 99.

actions.' That is ambiguous, but it serves Hampshire's turn only if it implies that the concealment of intentions requires a language. Hampshire offers no defence of that, and it is certainly not self-evident. On the face of it, a language seems to offer an extra way of revealing intentions rather than indispensable means of concealing and disguising them.

Hampshire argues that intentions require language because it is of the essence of the concept of intention that 'an intention may have existed without ever having been translated into action', or that 'intentions . . . may be concealed and disguised'. The argument is not valid, I have contended; and now I question whether the premiss is even true.

The concept of intention has 'action uses', when it helps to explain behaviour in which the agent is said to act on an intention; and it has 'non-action uses', in which one attributes intentions which are concealed, disguised, thwarted or dropped. It is the non-action cases which Hampshire says require language; to which he must add the claim that the concept of intention should be applied only to agents who admit of both uses of the concept. There are two possible bases for this last claim.

(1) The action uses of the concept of intention somehow require or involve the non-action uses.

(2) The action uses can function without the others, but the word 'intention' is improper except in describing a creature whose behaviour sometimes brings the non-action uses into play.

Hampshire offers no hint of an argument for (1), and I genuinely think that his basis is the relatively superficial and verbal claim (2). One pointer to this is the following remark, about a certain interpretation of the behaviour of a languageless creature: 'Here it might seem that the intention behind the activity is being stated, because at least the point and purpose of the activity are stated. But the more intellectual word "intention", since it is associated with the possibility of a declaration of intention, is out of place in the context of animal behaviour.' If Hampshire's basis really is just (2), a view about the meaning of 'intention', then I could harmlessly concede that his premiss is true and that his conclusion follows from it. At worst, that would imply that in my programme – which needs only the action uses – I ought not to use the word 'intention'. Instead of 'intention' then, I shall use a different word spelled in the same way. If Hampshire's premiss were about conceptual structures, this feint would be unavailing. But if his point is merely about the propriety of a word, my evasion is legitimate: verbal troubles admit of verbal remedies.

In Hampshire's book there is a hint of a different argument which he has developed for me in personal correspondence. He argues that intentions must sometimes be directed towards particular times in the non-immediate future; so an intender must be able to structure his future, e.g. to distinguish tomorrow from the day after; and Hampshire contends that this requires a language. Although his case for that last bit is not watertight, the whole line of thought is an interesting one which deserves to be developed further. But I need not let it block my present programme, which has no need for those uses of the concept of intention which involve ambitions, long-term contingency-plans and the like. Hampshire agrees, in his letter, that there is a sense of 'intention' in which 'the word can be made to march with "belief", and in step', that is, a sense in which 'intentions' can be attributed to languageless creatures just so long as they have beliefs; and that somewhat attenuated sense is all I need. Hampshire would rather express it by 'purpose' than by 'intention', but I find it convenient – and, in the context of my present work, harmless – to retain my habit of using 'intention' for both sorts of case.

§10. Putnam's deceivers

I shall seek sufficient conditions in non-linguistic behaviour for the attribution of intention (or purpose) and belief. Those conditions are to be weak enough to cover all the intentions and beliefs that I shall need to support meaning, convention and language; but they need not be weak enough to be necessary for the application of 'intention' and 'belief'. My endeavour will thus be different from a reductive analysis of the concepts of intention and belief.

It differs in another way as well, because I am not looking for conditions which are *logically* sufficient for the attribution of intentions and beliefs, merely ones which are sufficient by normal, reasonable, everyday standards. The plan is to describe kinds of non-linguistic behaviour which would be best explained by supposing the agent to have certain intentions and beliefs. But that leaves one always vulnerable to the overlooked possibility, the equally good or even better explanation which does not involve intention and belief; and that is one reason why I do not claim to be adducing logically sufficient grounds. All I need to show is how those two concepts can have an active, coherent, working life in application to languageless creatures.

My programme therefore need not be embarrassed by the claim, which I indeed accept, that no statements about physical behaviour can logically entail any statements about minds. But Hilary Putnam has supported this claim with a particular argument which threatens not just that strong form of logical behaviourism but also my thesis that there is a weaker sufficiency relation – one of the form 'P is sufficient by normal standards to entitle one to say that Q' – between premises about behaviour and conclusions about minds.[43] So although I am not defending logical behaviourism, I need to examine Putnam's attack on it.

Putnam describes creatures whose behaviour blocks the inference from behavioural premises to mental conclusions because, he says, they have a 'pathological preference function'. That is, they assign a 'relatively infinite weight' to some kind of situation, which means that there is something they will do everything possible to achieve (or to avoid) in all circumstances. I would not label as 'pathological' the preference function of someone who would do anything to avoid being tortured, say; but that is a quibble. More important is the fact that someone's having a pathological preference function need not prevent his behaviour from manifesting facts about his mind. His behaviour could show us what he gave infinite weight to, and then we could work out his other preferences by observing his behaviour in circumstances where the 'pathological' preference was irrelevant. Someone who would do anything to avoid being tortured, or to become famous, may still be discovered to like vodka, swimming and Shakespeare, and to dislike cabbage, poker and Brahms.

In fact, Putnam's examples work only because his creatures assign relatively infinite weight not just to *something* but specifically to *deceiving observers about their states of mind*. He concedes that logical behaviourism 'constitutes a kind of "near miss"',[44] but the miss is much nearer than he implies. Where he concedes that behaviourism may hold for creatures which do not have a pathological preference function, his argument lets it hold for any creatures which lack the extremely special pathological preference function which I have described.

Indeed, the miss is nearer still. We could even learn about the mind of someone who attached relatively infinite weight to deceiving us, for we might be able to observe his behaviour without his suspecting that we were doing so. If Putnam is to prevent this in the case of his

---

[43] Hilary Putnam, 'The Mental Life of Machines' and 'Brains and Behaviour', both in *Mind, Language and Reality* (Cambridge, 1975).
[44] *Ibid.*, p. 422.

supposed creatures, he must somehow guarantee them against ever being sure, wrongly, that they are unobserved. So in addition to their overwhelming distaste for being understood, he must endow them with either (a) perfect counter-intelligence skills or (b) total suspiciousness.

One might think that (b) is a manageable supposal – a mere matter of endowing psychopaths with a further pathological feature. But really it is not clear that such creatures are even logically possible. What does it mean to say that someone wants warmth, say, if there are no circumstances under which he would seek warmth with the sort of persistence that would show that he wants it? 'His wanting warmth consists in the fact that he would pursue it if he ever became sure that he was unobserved.' But that presupposes that he *does* always think that he may be under observation; and it is unclear what that alleged belief amounts to, given that it does not relate in any normal way to his sensory intake. Consider an agent who loves rum but never drinks it because whenever he sees rum he mistakenly thinks it is bouillon. What does it mean to credit him with that preference and that belief, rather than another pair (e.g. that he always recognizes rum, but hates to drink it) which would yield the same behaviour? If there is to be real content in the claim that his behaviour is explained by one particular preference-belief pair, the claim must support predictions about the conditions under which the behaviour would change – such as that he would drink rum if he were given a chance to distinguish it from bouillon by its smell. But Putnam's creatures, on the version of them I am now examining, are said to have a belief which is not answerable to evidence. It is a blanket, programmatic, essentially psychotic or philosophical scepticism about chances of not being observed. There are no environmental conditions under which this 'belief' would predictably change; so there is no content to the claim that they have that belief, and thus no content, after all, to any claim about their preferences.

That argument shows my behaviourist bias, no doubt, but it also offers a legitimate challenge. It is fair to suggest that when readers think they understand Putnam's example, it is because they think of his creatures' wants as showing up in behaviour-patterns which are suspended only on rare occasions when the creatures think they are being observed. That shifts the story from (b) pathological suspicion back to (a) all-conquering ingenuity in finding out when they are being observed.

Now, Putnam's position is that from premisses about the behaviour of some creature we can never move by sheer logic to conclusions about its mind; because the creature may be of a peculiar kind for which no such move would be valid. But the kind has turned out to be more peculiar than at first appeared: for what we must allow for is just that our creature may have an all-conquering dislike of being understood, and an infallible talent for knowing when it is being observed, even if we have no evidence for either supposition about it.

Logical behaviourism's 'near miss', if that is its measure, is as good as most hits. Certainly, there is nothing here to discomfit the claim that statements about behaviour can be sufficient, by normal evidential standards, to establish statements about minds. Nor does Putnam say that there is; but what he does offer is further from refuting the claim than his own treatment of its suggests.

In a helpful personal response to an earlier version of this section, Putnam argues like this: (a) The relationship between behaviour and psychological state depends upon facts about 'the actual functional organization that the creature has' – its scale of preferences, system of beliefs, and so on. (b) These facts are *a posteriori*, and cannot be established by logic alone; and so (c) Even if we have the premiss that a given creature is not of the peculiar kind discussed above, nothing logically follows of the form 'The creature will behave thus and so if and only if it is in psychological state P'. I fully concede (a) and (b), but deny that (c) follows. For (c) might be false, not because the facts about 'actual functional organization' are *a priori* but rather because they too could be established on the basis of behaviour. That, if it could be done, would let us use a creature's behaviour to establish its 'actual functional organization', and then to use that, and further facts about the behaviour, to establish all the creature's detailed psychological states.

Putnam points out that any such programme must grapple with the fact that any given bit of behaviour can be explained in terms of various different preference-belief pairs. I shall take this up in §15 below, where I shall try to show how one can select, from the various preference-belief pairs which fit a given single item of behaviour, the one pair which best fits the creature's behaviour-patterns as a whole. Perhaps this still won't license a logical move from behavioural premisses to mentalistic conclusions; but then logical moves are not what I am after.

2

TELEOLOGY

§11. Spinoza's challenge

To speak of what someone intended by an action is to say what the action was for, what future state of affairs it was directed to; and so the concept of intention is a teleological one – that is, it involves the notion of an *end* for which something happens. But some teleological concepts do not involve intention, as when we say that the frog flicked out its tongue so as to catch the insect. In this chapter I shall lay the behavioural foundations for teleological concepts as such, with an emphasis on rather primitive cases of teleology where intentions are not involved.

It is sometimes plausibly argued that teleological explanations are bound to be faulty, and that teleological concepts should not be used. If explaining an event is saying what caused it, then a teleological explanation seems to imply that an event's cause may post-date the event itself; which is absurd. 'That is all right, because what is involved is a special sort of cause, traditionally called a "final cause".' We should sympathize with philosophers who have refused to be mollified by that move. Spinoza, for instance, roundly rejected the doctrine that there are final causes – those 'human fictions' – on the grounds that it 'completely reverses the order of nature': 'That which is in reality a cause, it considers as an effect, and vice versa.'[1] It is not 'obvious' that Spinoza is right, as he claims it is, but still he does have a point which deserves an answer. Consider 'The bear killed the seal so as to eat it'. The later eating cannot have caused the earlier killing, in any reasonable sense of 'cause'; and if an unreasonable sense be introduced, why should we allow that the original statement in any way *explains* the killing of the seal? If the 'final cause' is final it is not really a cause; and if it is not really a cause then the adducing of it is not really explanatory.

The way to meet this objection is to present a theory of what a teleological explanation is which shows how it can refer in a genuinely

[1] Spinoza, *Ethics*, Part I, Appendix, nearly half-way through.

explanatory way to a time later than that of the event to be explained, without implying that a cause can follow its effect. That is my first task in the present chapter.

The core of the theory to be presented is not mine. The first big step towards it was made by G. Sommerhoff,[2] and Ernest Nagel made significant further progress. Then a vitally important concept which seems to be absent from Sommerhoff's account, and which is somewhat buried in Nagel's, was brought properly to the surface by Charles Taylor. To complete my acknowledgment of antecedents, I should mention the work of Ann Wilbur MacKenzie, including help she has given me in the course of our correspondence about her drafts and my own.[3] She has broadened, deepened and refined Taylor's theory, and I have availed myself of many of her insights.

An important mistake about teleology, though it is not visibly made by Nagel, seems not to have been properly corrected by anyone before Taylor. It is the mistaken view that non-intentional teleology presents problems which do not arise with, or are much more easily solved for, intentional teleology. Braithwaite, for instance, sees that the problem is to show how in the explanation of event E there can be a role for any mention of a time later than that of E, and he says that where there is a conscious intention the solution is easy: a reference to the future enters the picture because E arises from a *thought about* the future.[4] But that is not very problem-solving, as Braithwaite nearly admits; and Taylor has shown that the role of the 'thought about the future' is much better understood if one first clarifies teleology generally and then moves on to the special case of conscious intention.

The mistake in question occurs even more grievously in Sommerhoff's work. He starts perfectly, by calling attention to 'the widespread and striking *appropriateness* which organic activities show in relation to the needs of the organism', and says that he will 'take the idea of *appropriate response* as a starting-point'.[5] It could be more than a starting-point; for something like it is central in the theories of Nagel and Taylor, which are directly descended from Sommerhoff's. Yet the

---

[2] G. Sommerhoff, *Analytical Biology* (Oxford, 1950).

[3] See Ann Wilbur MacKenzie, *An Analysis of Purposive Behaviour*, Ph.D. thesis, Cornell University, 1972; published on demand by University Microfilms, Ann Arbor, Michigan. Mrs MacKenzie's forthcoming book on the theory of goals is, at the time of this writing, well advanced but still untitled.

[4] R. B. Braithwaite, *Scientific Explanation* (Cambridge, 1953), pp. 324–5.

[5] Sommerhoff, *op. cit.*, pp. 38–9. The next two quotations are from *Ibid.*, pp. 45, 46. They have some deletions.

latter seems not to give a working role to the concept of appropriateness (the theory is hard to follow, so I am not sure); and this is presumably explained by Sommerhoff's apologetic attitude towards his starting-point: 'The notion of appropriateness is based on a vague consideration of . . .' etc. And, most damagingly, he says: 'When this idea of appropriateness is applied to activities which do not spring from a conscious mind, its meaning becomes metaphorical in comparison with this psychological use.' That, we shall see, is false.

§12. Teleology: the basic theory

First, I introduce the notion of an instrumental property, expressed in language by an instrumental predicate. If F and G are monadic predicates, then F/G is an instrumental predicate, defined as follows:

> F/Ga at time T if and only if at T a is so structured and situated that the truth of Fa at a later time is causally required for and causally sufficient for the truth of Ga at a still later time.

I am sorry that 'instrumental predicate' reminds one that Fa is sufficient for Ga but not that it is required for it; but I cannot find an acceptable label that expresses both halves of the concept, and what is not expressed by mine is the half which will be dropped from the concept late in §20 below.

The F and G in an instrumental predicate can be any monadic predicates whatsoever, but in my examples F will usually concern something a does and G some state that a comes or continues to be in – e.g. 'a is kills/satiated', meaning that if and only if a kills soon a will be satiated shortly thereafter. I shall often use 'a does F' or 'a becomes [continues to be] G' as shorthand for, respectively, 'a does something which makes it the case that Fa' and 'It comes [continues] to be the case that Ga'.

I could have given instrumental predicates the more general form F/P, where Fa/P means that a's doing F is required for and sufficient for P's *subsequently being the case*, where P may not be about a at all. It makes exposition easier if I stick to the special case where P is of the form Ga, and in the meantime that narrowing is harmless. I shall later move from the special case (Ga) back to the general one (P).

Here is an example of how to use instrumental predicates. My rose-bush (a) will be alive tomorrow (Ga) if, but only if, it is watered (Fa) today. So the bush has an instrumental property which can be expressed in my stroke-notation by 'F/Ga' or, in English-with-stroke, by 'My rose-bush is watered/alive'. This reports on the bush's present structure and situation, and implies nothing about needs or demands or aims or goals. Everything has instrumental properties all the time, not only where goals are involved. As well as 'The snake is kills-mouse/ eats-protein' we have 'The window is struck/broken'.

Every statement of the form 'F/Gx at T' means 'x is so situated and structured at T that the truth of Gx at a later time requires and would be secured by the truth of Fx at an intermediate time'. Strictly, each instrumental predicate should put limits on the 'later time': watering my rose-bush now is not required for it to survive the next hour, and would not suffice to get it through the next month. Such details are left for the reader to supply: it will usually be clear what time-span is needed for a given example to be realistic, and writing it into the formulae would only clutter the exposition.

As well as the monadic predicate F we have the monadic predicate-variable f, which could be used in statements of the form $(\exists f)fx$, meaning that x has some property. With the aid of this we can construct instrumental-predicate variables, such as f/G, which could be used in statements like $(\exists f)f/Gx$, meaning roughly that there is something such that x's doing it is required for and sufficient for x's shortly becoming G.

With the modest machinery so far assembled, we can introduce the notion of a teleological law.[6] As a start, I count as a teleological law any lawlike statement of the form

$$(x)(f)(t)((Rx \text{ at } t \ \& \ f/Gx \text{ at } t) \ \rightarrow \ fx \text{ at } t+d).$$

Informally: any R thing will do whatever is required for and sufficient for its becoming or remaining G. As a mnemonic, think of 'Rx' as meaning 'x is ready'; but really R is a complex predicate with long-standing components ('is a wolf') as well as episodic ones ('is hungry').

Let 'Rx' stand for 'x is a healthy adult polar bear with a low blood-sugar level', and let 'Gx' be 'x eats protein'. The above law-formula, thus interpreted, says roughly that any healthy adult polar bear, when its blood-sugar level is low, will do whatever is required for and sufficient for its subsequently having a protein meal. If the bear is killing/eating it will kill; if it is running/eating it will run; if it is digging/eating it will dig; and so on.

It is important that R does not include any mentalistic components

<hr>

[6] Following Taylor, pp. 9–10.

such as 'wants food'. The aim of the enterprise is to lay behavioural foundations for such statements as 'The bear wants food', and so the latter must not enter unannounced. Nor should R include 'is hungry', unless that is understood purely in terms of the bear's physiological state.

Our law must not imply that if the bear can get protein only by singing an aria it will sing an aria. So let us construe each teleological law as meaning only that a thing which is R will do anything *which it can do* which is necessary and sufficient for its being G, the qualification being built into the meaning of the stroke notation.

There are more troubles to come, demanding further changes in the form of teleological law I have introduced. But already we can answer Spinoza, by showing how an event can be explained in terms which mention a later time without our implying that causes can follow their effects.

In an explanation using the above form of teleological law, an event is explained in terms of *earlier* states of affairs. Look at it schematically, first. Suppose that an organism a does F at a certain time $T+d$, and we want to explain this event. Suppose further that it is a fact that

(1) Ra at T

and that

(2) F/Ga at T,

and that it is a law that

(3) $(x)(f)(t)((Rx$ at t & f/Gx at $t) \rightarrow fx$ at $t+d)$.

From this material – two particular facts and one law – it follows by logic that

(4) Fa at $T+d$,

which is what we wanted to explain.

For example, suppose that (1) the thing is a polar bear with low blood-sugar etc., and (2) it could eat protein by killing a seal but in no other way; and suppose it is a law that (3) such a bear does anything it can which is required for and sufficient for its getting a protein meal. By adducing those materials, we explain (4) the bear's killing the seal.

Explanations of all sorts can be abbreviated, and the above one might be cut back to 'The bear killed the seal so as to get food'. That is not truly explanatory, though, unless it is backed by a law to the effect that

R items always do whatever they need to that will bring them food, the given bear being R and being so situated that it was killing/eating.

Does the adducing of all this material really *explain* the bear's killing the seal? I think so. It could remove puzzlement about the killing of the seal; it brackets the killing together with other events which, though unlike it in many ways, resemble it in one crucial respect; and it shows how the killing could have been predicted by someone who knew the facts and the relevant law. That surely makes it genuinely explanatory.

We can now answer Spinoza. The foregoing explanation, which shows how the bear's killing the seal arose from *earlier* states of affairs, does not 'completely reverse the order of nature'. Yet the explanation is truly teleological, in that it refers non-idly to a time later than that of the event being explained. It reaches forward in time, not for anything so absurd as a later cause, but for a possible later event which is mentioned in the description of the earlier cause.

I need not insist that the earlier circumstances *are* the cause of the event. If they are, that answers Spinoza in one way. If they are not, an explanation of an event need not adduce its cause; which would answer him in another way.

It may be thought that this account of teleology is too limited because it allows us to explain behaviour only if it is required for, as well as sufficient for, the achievement of some end. Don't we explain an animal's climbing, say, if the animal is hungry and climbing is sufficient for its getting food? Does it matter if it could also have got food in some other way?

Well, suppose that the animal could get food if it climbed or if it swam, but not otherwise. Although it was neither climbing/eating nor swimming/eating, it was climbing-or-swimming/eating; and so, on the basis of the above account of teleology, we can explain the fact that the animal *climbed or swam*. As for the fact that it *climbed rather than swam*, we cannot explain that until we know something about its goals which differentiates climbing from swimming. In §§18–20 below I shall show how we can get such knowledge, and extend the theory to incorporate it. The 'required for' half of the concept of an instrumental property will then become a hindrance rather than a help, and near the end of §20 it will be dropped. But while we cannot explain why the animal climbed rather than swam, it is better to admit that we cannot do so, by underlining the difference between 'It climbed or swam because . . .' and 'It climbed because . . .' That is what our teleological theory does, by its use of the concept of what is required for as well as sufficient for some state of affairs; and so that aspect of the theory is not a defect but a virtue.[7]

§13. Some earlier theories of teleology

The foregoing treatment of teleology yields an account of what it is for an organism to have a goal: *a* has coming-to-be-G as a goal at a certain time if at that time *a* would do anything it could which was required for and sufficient for its becoming G. That, I repeat, still needs qualification; but even as it stands it improves on all accounts of teleological concepts before Nagel's. Two of its features, in particular, look good when one inspects theories which lack them.

One is that it makes basic the notion of a teleological *law*, or of something's being teleologically explainable; whereas many earlier accounts try to start with a purely descriptive use of teleological concepts, giving explanation a secondary role or none at all. Here, for example, is the pith of Bertrand Russell's treatment of teleology:

A 'behaviour-cycle' is a series of voluntary or reflex movements of an animal, tending to cause a certain result, and continuing until that result is caused, unless they are interrupted by death, accident, or some new behaviour-cycle. . . . The 'purpose' of a behaviour-cycle is the result which brings it to an end, normally by a condition of temporary quiescence – provided there is no interruption.[8]

How, on this account, could one explain an organism's behaviour by reference to its 'purposes'? Russell gives no answer, and seems not to offer a workable basis for one.

Russell might say that what he sought was not a theory of teleological explanation, but only an account of the behavioural criteria which govern ordinary descriptive statements about the goals of organisms. But his account is inadequate to even this limited objective. If weight is rested on the remark about 'temporary quiescence', an organism's 'purposes' are just its states at the beginnings of periods of quiescence; so that its 'purposes' will probably include the achievement of fatigue, and exclude the finding of food or of sexual partners. And if we do not rely on 'temporary quiescence' we are left with nothing at all. To identify a 'purpose' we must be able to tell when a behaviour-cycle has ended; so we must know what counts as a behaviour-cycle; but Russell's account in terms of something 'tending to cause a certain result' is vacuous. We can segment an animal's behaviour-sequences

---

[7] This matter is discussed by Taylor, p. 9 n.
[8] Bertrand Russell, *The Analysis of Mind* (London, 1921), pp. 65–6.

into 'cycles' and 'episodes between cycles', and on that basis identify its 'purposes', in any arbitrary way we like.

Russell gets the descriptive use of teleological concepts wrong *because* he gives them primacy rather than basing his account of teleology on the notion of teleological explanation and/or law.

There is a similar failure in the attempt of the psychologist Tolman to lay a behavioural foundation for the notion of purpose, in a seminal work which was first published in 1932.[9] Many psychologists are now coming to share Tolman's commendable desire to introduce a rich mentalistic vocabulary into psychology by giving it firm behavioural foundations, but they seem to have improved little on his poor execution of this programme.[10]

Tolman presents three 'descriptive properties' of behaviour which, he says, show that it is 'purposive'. One is the tendency to seek the easiest route to the goal; but this, as Tolman admits, presupposes that we can already identify goals. For his basic account of how purposes 'are defined by characters and relationships which we observe out there in the behavior'[11] we must look to the other two 'descriptive properties'.

One is that the behaviour 'seems to have the character of getting-to ... a specific goal-object, or goal-situation'. For example, 'the rat's behavior of "running the maze" has as its first and perhaps most important identifying feature the fact that it is a getting to food'.[12] This treats as a 'goal' any state which the animal is 'getting to' or which it comes to be in: not just its getting food but its drying its fur, disturbing dust in the maze, and so on. If Tolman says that these are not 'first' or 'important' features of the situation, he should explain what that means.

The remaining 'descriptive property' is the fact that the behaviour manifests 'persistence' in getting to the goal. Given what Tolman has said about the goal, this is vacuous. It means only that the animal goes on doing something until it starts doing something else. Tolman brackets with 'persistence' the fact that the behaviour 'involves a specific pattern of commerce ... with such and such intervening

[9] E. C. Tolman, *Purposive Behavior in Men and Animals* (New York and London, 1932). Similarly defective work by McDougall is described in Margaret A. Boden, *Purposive Explanation in Psychology* (Cambridge, Mass., 1972), ch. 2.

[10] This impression is confirmed by the discussions of psychologists in Taylor; by the treatment of Tolman and others in Alvin I. Goldman, *A Theory of Human Action* (Englewood Cliffs, N.J., 1970), ch. 5, §2; and by what is shown of the state of the art in the opening chapter of T. A. Ryan, *Intentional Behavior: an Approach to Human Motivation* (New York, 1970).

[11] Tolman, *op. cit.*, p. 13.   [12] *Ibid.*, p. 10.

means-objects, as the way to get [to the goal]'. This could mean merely that the behaviour relates in certain ways to certain objects, and that this aids progress towards the goal; and that would inherit the vacuity of 'goal'. There is another reading of 'as the way to get [to the goal]', however: Tolman may mean that the animal relates itself to certain objects *in order to* achieve the goal. That is not vacuous, but nor is it purely 'descriptive' of behaviour.

Tolman says: 'These descriptions in terms of gettings to or from, selections of routes and patterns of commerces-with imply and define immediate, immanent purpose and cognition aspects in the behavior.'[13] I have shown, though, that they do not 'imply and define' purposiveness but, at best, presuppose it.

Tolman failed because he did not cast his net wide enough. Trying to base teleological concepts on single items of behaviour, taken singly, he had to try such weak offerings as that an item of behaviour 'seems to have the character of a getting-to'. He needed what Taylor and Nagel have, namely the notion of a teleological *law*; and so he should have been looking for 'descriptive properties' of *histories* of behaviour or of behavioural *regularities*.

The second glowing feature of the Nagel–Taylor approach is its use of the concept of an instrumental property. The power which this generates is best seen by examining a theory which is defective only in lacking it. I choose the teleological theory of Braithwaite.[14] This gives primacy to statements which say what an animal would have done if the circumstances had differed in certain ways; and, because such statements rest on laws, Braithwaite does perhaps give laws their due place in his account of teleology. But the account fails because it lacks the concept of an instrumental property.

Here is Braithwaite's account, slightly simplified. An animal *a* is so structured and situated that it will eventually become G. Some changes in its environment would still lead to its becoming G, whereas others would not. Braithwaite uses the label 'the variancy' for the class of states-of-the-environment which would still lead to *a*'s becoming G, and he says: the larger the variancy, the more 'plasticity' *a* has in respect of becoming G; and the greater that plasticity, the truer it is that *a* has becoming-G as a goal.

The notion of a large variancy is supposed to capture the idea of an

13 Tolman, *op. cit.*, p. 21.
14 R. B. Braithwaite, *Scientific Explanation* (Cambridge, 1953), ch. 10.

animal which could overcome many different *prima facie* obstacles to its becoming G. That this is Braithwaite's aim is shown by his approving quotation of this criticism of Bertrand Russell's account:

> Coming to a definite end or terminus is not *per se* distinctive of directive activity, for inorganic processes also move towards a natural terminus. . . . What is distinctive is the active persistence of directive activity towards its goal, the use of alternative means towards the same end, the achievement of results in the face of difficulties.[15]

But Braithwaite's theory does not perform as he intends it to. It fails to express the idea of persistence in the face of difficulties, and it counts as teleological many items which really are not. The most striking of these is an animal's relation to its own death. Every animal is tremendously plastic in respect of becoming dead: throw up what obstacles you may, and death will still be achieved. Yet animals seldom have their deaths as a goal.

Taylor identifies the central trouble in Braithwaite's theory: 'Braithwaite . . . speaks of a variety of [causal] chains which, starting from different points, all end in the same final state. But the point of teleological explanation is not the co-incidence of different antecedents having the same consequent, but the type of antecedent involved.'[16] Perhaps it would be better to say 'not *just* the co-incidence of different antecedents etc.', but the main thrust of Taylor's remark is right: Braithwaite needs some reference to how *a* behaves *when it has a certain instrumental property*. That would eliminate the 'death' counter-example and its like; for most things an organism does are not necessary and sufficient for its subsequent death. 'But going on living is required for and sufficient for subsequent death' – very well, I stipulate that for purposes of my theory an instrumental property is one which the animal sometimes has and, during its lifetime, sometimes lacks. That manoeuvre could not help Braithwaite much, for his theory must count among an animal's goals at any given time anything which it can hardly avoid at that time.

Braithwaite has another difficulty. He relies on the notion of the size of the variancy, that is the class of possible environmental states of affairs in which *a* would still become G. But how do we count possible states of affairs? This bird will eat that worm; and it would still do so if the temperature were .005° warmer, or if there were two more leaves on that tree or five fewer dandelions on the lawn or . . . We can go on

[15] E. S. Russell, *The Directiveness of Organic Activities* (Cambridge, 1945), p. 144.
[16] Taylor, p. 14 n.

45

indefinitely like this without increasing our sense of the bird's plasticity or adaptability in respect of worm-getting. So differences like those must be declared irrelevant when we are counting the members of the variancy; but on what principle can this be done? Not on the ground that those differences would not affect the bird's getting the worm; for we are trying, *within* the class of differences which would not affect its getting the worm, to locate the sub-class which are not relevant to the plasticity of its behaviour. Nor can we say that an environmental difference increases the size of the variancy only if it would alter the causal route to the goal; for Braithwaite emphatically distinguishes 'the size of the variancy' from 'the number of possible causal chains' leading to the goal.[17] And in any case, do we know how to count causal chains?

This problem also vanishes when the concept of an instrumental property is used. For then we do not need the notion of the size of the variancy: what matters is just that the orgadism does whatever it needs to do, and can effectively do, to become G. In this context, it is interesting to look at Nagel: 'The characteristic feature of [goal-directed] systems is that they continue to manifest a certain state or property G (or that they exhibit a persistence of development "in the direction" of attaining G) in the face of a relatively extensive class of changes in their external environments . . .'[18] That fits Braithwaite's theory, but the next bit does not: '. . . – changes which, if not compensated for by internal modification in the system, would result in the disappearance of G'. That introduces something which Braithwaite aspires to but, as we have seen, fails to work into his theory – namely the notion of an instrumental property. Nagel does build it into his theory, though not very perspicaciously. Of Taylor's various contributions to the subject, I think that the most important is his isolating and highlighting the concept of an instrumental property.

§14. The concept of registration

It is time to admit that there are no true laws of the form I have presented as teleological. Given any purported law of that form, we can always contrive a situation where an R animal which is F/G nevertheless fails to do F because – to put it roughly – the facts which make it F/G are not epistemically available to it. For example a laboratory assistant is told to feed a hungry rat if and only if it walks seventeen inches and then lies down for seventeen seconds; and the rat, not being

[17] Braithwaite, *op. cit.*, pp. 332–3.   [18] Nagel, p. 411.

apprised of this requirement, goes on starving. That would refute any purported law to the effect that the rat, when hungry enough, will do anything which *is* required for and sufficient for its getting food. Similar trouble could be made for any 'law' of the suggested form.

Things could be otherwise. It could be a basic fact about some physical system that its mere possession of an instrumental property F/G was always enough to get it to do F. But although this is conceptually possible, I am sure that it never happens; and I want a theory of teleology which is applicable in the actual world.

What is needed is not piecemeal repair but systematic rebuilding of the theory. We need a form of law which does not imply that the animal performs a suitable action unless the fact that it is suitable is somehow registered upon the animal. Analogously, a self-guiding missile will make the swerve which keeps it tracking its target only if some state of the missile, perhaps caused by a radio echo bounced back from the target, registers or records the need for the swerve. So we need to replace statements about what a will do when F/Ga by ones about what it will do when it registers that F/Ga. So the form of law that we need is this:

$$(x)(f)(t)((Rx \text{ at } t \ \& \ x \text{ registers that } f/Gx \text{ at } t) \to fx \text{ at } t+d).$$

The form 'x registers that P' is just short for 'it is registered upon x that P': registration may be something which happens to the agent rather than something he actively does. I dislike inventing technical terms; but if I used the more idiomatic word 'perception' I might introduce unnoticed and uncontrolled implications; whereas I can control the meaning of 'registration' just because it has little life of its own in daily English, and none which bears much on my present use of the term. I shall say more about this in my next section.

In what follows, I shall use 'P' to stand for any proposition which a might register. It will stand for propositions such as that a has a certain instrumental property, is in the presence of a certain kind of object, is suffering a certain kind of weather, and so on. Those examples reflect the assumption that we shall initially be able to cope only with a's registrations of propositions which concern relational or monadic features of itself, that is, ones about the present state of a or a's present environment. Later on, we shall be able to do better.

There must be no entailment-relation between P and 'a registers that P'. The former must not imply the latter, because the original point of introducing the concept of registration was, precisely, to allow for cases where *P* is true and yet *a* does not register that *P*. Nor should '*a* registers that *P*' entail *P*. That is because our teleological laws should be strong enough to cover various cases where an animal acts on misinformation, doing *F* because it registers that it is *F/G* although really it is not. For example, a bear lopes across the ice towards what looks like a seal but is really a rock: to explain that teleologically we need a law whose antecedent implies not that the explained behaviour will further any of the bear's goals but only that the bear registers that it will. In brief: because there can be ignorance, *P* must not entail '*a* registers that *P*', and because there can be error there must be no entailment running the other way.

We do not even want *P* to make it fairly probable that *a* registers that *P*; for *a* can be ignorant of most of the truths about itself – animals usually are. Massive error is different: an animal which frequently registers that *P* when in fact not-*P* will not survive long, and so '*a* registers that *P*' should render *P* probable. But its doing so can be a contingent fact about the animal, required by the law of the jungle; it need not be inherent in the concept of registration as such.

Still, there must be some systematic connection between *P* and '*a* registers that *P*'. The former must occur in the latter as a constituent, something which contributes its own meaning to the total meaning, and not as a meaningless accident like the occurrence of 'cat' in 'catastrophe'. Broadly speaking, a successful theory of registration must enable one to *derive* an understanding of anything of the form '*x* registers that *P*' from one's understanding of the relevant *P* and one's understanding of registration in general.

My account of registration will make that possible, though not in a simple and mechanical way. At the end of §15 I shall explain what, according to the account I shall by then have given, is the fundamental systematic connection between *P* and '*a* registers that *P*'.

§15. Registration: the pure theory

The best way of explaining what registration is is to explain how statements using the concept can be tested. Such tests must concern the animal's behaviour, and immediately a problem arises. An animal's behaviour does not show what it registers unless we know what it seeks; but how can we learn what it seeks before we know what it registers? Its climbing the tree shows that it saw the nest only if it has egg-eating as a goal, and shows that it seeks eggs only if it saw the nest.

It is a commonplace in epistemology that someone's behaviour manifests his beliefs only on assumptions about his intentions, and manifests his intentions only on assumptions about his beliefs. (See the end of §10 above.) I am now maintaining what is hardly less of a commonplace, namely that an analogous structure exists down at levels where there are goals but not intentions, and registrations but not beliefs.

What an animal registers is partly a matter of what it sees and hears and feels. Cannot we find out about that without knowing what its goals are? Not really. The fundamental way of learning how an animal is epistematically related to its environments is by observing how environmental changes correlate with changes in the animal's pursuit of its goals. Other evidence should be treated circumspectly unless it is confirmed through goal-pursuing behaviour. If a beetle, when suspended in the air, moves its legs in different ways under different kinds of light-stimulus, it is certainly affected by those stimuli but perhaps it does not perceive them. If its food-seeking behaviour, say, cannot be modified by light-stimuli, then its being affected by light is not a perceptual or epistemic matter; and so I do not count it as a matter of registration.

I can now explain further why I persist with 'register', when my topic is admittedly perception. It is clear that the behaviour of even quite lowly animals may be modified by some environmental fact which somehow impresses itself upon them. For example, something a frog does may be explained partly through its somehow taking in that it is swimming/eating. If the intake is purely visual, then I could say that the frog sees that it is swimming/eating; but many thoughtful people hear this as meaning that the frog thinks, going by what it sees, that it is swimming/eating; and they are naturally reluctant to credit a mere frog with *thinking* that P, for any P. To avoid the dispute about this reading of 'sees that P', I choose a term of art which is to be read as I direct.

So much for my avoidance of '*a* perceives that P', but what about '*a* perceives O'? I contend that statements about what objects an animal perceives rest on ones about what propositions, and ultimately what instrumental propositions, it registers. Thus, we can know that the frog sees the fly only because we know that it registers that there is a fly on the lily-pad, which in turn rests on our knowing that the frog registers that it is swimming/eating. It is tempting to suppose that an animal which could not register instrumental propositions might

49

nevertheless manage simpler feats such as seeing flies; but this, I contend, stands the truth on its head.

So: we want to learn about the registrations and the goals of animal a, and each inquiry needs help from the other. The solution is to develop the two theories together.

We need some sort of start, however wild. Let it be the naive assumption that a has our goals and perceives the world just as we do. Given some sort of registration-plus-goal theory, we can use it to predict a's behaviour; many of our predictions will be wrong, requiring amendment to our joint theory; and *we can have reason to attribute some failures specifically to errors in the goal-theory, and others specifically to errors in the epistemic theory.* That is what gives the two their separate identities. If every wrong prediction bore equally on both parts of the theory, the latter would not really have two parts – or anyway there would be no reason to say that one concerned goals and the other registrations. I now explain why this fate need not befall our theories about an animal's goals and registrations.

Any sane guess about what instrumental propositions a registers must be supported by conjectures about what other registrations the former ones are based upon – the 'basing' being causal rather than logical. For example, in a given environment the conjecture that a bear registers that it is swimming/eating generates the further guess that it registers that there is a seal on the ice-floe. We could err about this: the bear might register that it is swimming/eating because of some feature of the environment, imperceptible to us, which does not involve the seal. Still, such mistakes can in principle be corrected. All I need is that we have reasonable, disciplined, corrigible ways of moving from conjectures about what instrumental propositions an animal registers to conjectures about what else it registers, the latter registrations being conjectured to be the basis for the former.

Now, suppose that our joint theory implies that whenever animal a is R, if it registers that F/Ga it will proceed to do F; and suppose that a does something which we regard as refuting this. We might suspect that the antecedent of the law should have R^* rather than R, and we can check this by observing how a behaves under variations of the background conditions embodied in R: if some relevant difference in a's behaviour is correlated with the difference between Ra and R^*a, and not with anything else that we can discover, then probably our initial trouble arose from the R component of the original law. Let us suppose that it didn't, and see what other possible sources of error we can find.

My examples will be strained and unrealistic, because of a lack which will be made good in §18. But I wish only to demonstrate the abstract form of a solution to our present difficulty, not to add plausible details.

Suppose we have hypothesized that whenever a is R and registers that it is climbing/eating-eggs, it will climb; and suppose that on a certain occasion it does not climb although we expected it to register that it was climbing/eating-eggs – the nest is clearly visible, this is the season for eggs, and so on. Perhaps (1) we are wrong in our goal-theory: a does not seek eggs, but rather seeks food in pieces within certain size-limits, and on the troublesome occasion the eggs in question were too small. Perhaps on the other hand (2) our epistemic theory is wrong: this nest is black, and the others whose presence a has registered were all brown, and that difference may from a's point of view be a disqualifyingly large one, so that its visual intake from this nest did not give it a basis for registering that it was climbing/eating. We could test (1) by observing what a does when these latest eggs are simply laid at its feet, thus checking on the goal component of the theory in a context which does not involve how a sees a nest (though it does involve other assumptions about a's registrations). And we could test (2) by observing a's behaviour when threatened by a predator which is just like ones it has frequently hidden from except that they are brown and this one is black. This would give us evidence about what a makes of the black–brown difference in a context which does not involve egg-eating (though it does involve another of a's goals, namely predator-escaping).

Every test of the theory involves its epistemic and its goal components; but we can combine a given epistemic element with different goal elements, and vice versa, and this provides leverage on each element separately. It is as though we had to test the freedom from distortion of a collection of panes of glass, under the restriction that we must always look through two panes at once. Although we may not look through any pane singly, we can still discover what each is like because we can see what happens when we combine it with various others; and in particular we can identify a distorted pane because it will carry distortion with it through all or most combinations. Similarly, we can identify a false epistemic or goal element in our joint behavioural theory, because it will carry falsehood with it through all combinations, except perhaps for a tiny number where it happens to compensate exactly for an error in the other part of the theory.

I used an example where *a* was in fact climbing/eating-eggs, and we were puzzled because it did not then climb. Our theory about *a*'s goals and registrations might also lead us to predict that it would climb for eggs on a certain occasion when it was not in fact climbing/eating-eggs. If at that time *a*'s environment was relevantly similar to – and not relevantly dissimilar from – ones where climbing would lead to eggs, then we could predict that in that environment also *a* would register that it was climbing/eating-eggs. The question of what counts as a 'relevant (dis)similarity' is of course to be settled by our overall theory about *a*'s registrations. The theory will include hypotheses about the aspects of *a*'s environment to which *a* is most sensitive, and those to which it is least sensitive; and these will generate hypotheses not only about cases of '*P* and *a* does not register that *P*', but also about cases of 'not-*P* and *a* registers that *P*'. All of these hypotheses are testable in the manner adumbrated above.

What, according to all this, *is* registration? It is whatever will do the theoretic work associated with 'registration' in the account I have given. That amounts to introducing 'registration' as a theoretical term, standing for whatever-it-is about the given animal which validates predictions of its behaviour from facts about its environment; comparable to introducing 'gene' to stand for whatever-it-is about organisms which validates predictions about offspring from facts about their parents.

If the behaviour depended on the condition and orientation of certain parts of the animal's body-surface, these parts would count as sense-organs, and so we might say that the animal's registrations involve sensory states. But the word 'sensory', in its ordinary acceptation, seems to exclude plants and non-organic systems, and even the lowest animals. My treatment of 'registration', on the other hand, should apply just as well to the quasi-sensory states of grass and self-guiding missiles, *if* the behaviour of these is a fit subject for teleological explanation. I shall sometimes use 'sensory state' and shall generally be thinking of animals higher than arthropods, but nothing in my conceptual inquiry requires this limitation.

Much later, I shall broaden the concept of registration so that it facilitates predictions of behaviour on the basis of *a*'s past environments as well as its present ones (see the opening of §31 below). I choose to delay that development until I am dealing with a species of registration which I call 'belief'; but it could in principle be introduced right here.

At the end of §14 above, I pointed out that there must be no entailment relation, either way, between P and '*a* registers that P'. Nor is there one in the account I have given. With a given animal we might be able always to move in one direction or the other: such an animal would be either omniscient (forwards) or infallible (backwards) about its opportunities for achieving its goals. My account can easily cope with either possibility. Each would simplify the work that the concept of registration had to do, leaving it doing just half of its job – handling the ignorance of the animal which never errs, or the errors of the animal which is never just ignorant. For an omniscient and infallible creature, of course, the concept of registration would be idle: the antecedents of our teleological laws about such a creature could contain '*a* is *f/G*' without a preceding '*a* registers that . . .', which is just to say that we could predict its behaviour on the basis of the state of its environment without mediating help from the concept of registration.

My account also refrains from implying that there is a probabilifying relation, either way, between P and '*a* registers that P'. But it nicely prepares the ground for the empirical argument, sketched in §14 above, for saying that with actual, surviving animals we can expect that usually P will be true if *a* registers that P.

So much for negatives. What systematic connection *does* my account establish between P and '*a* registers that P'? No defensible theory of registration (or of belief) could yield a compact answer to this question, I suspect; but my theory yields an answer. That is, it contains the materials for deriving an understanding of '*a* registers that P' from an understanding of P, for any value of P. In showing how, I shall be giving an abstract answer to an extremely abstract question; so I shall skip details, such as the relevance of *a*'s sense-organs to what *a* registers.

My account connects P with '*a* registers that P' by implying things of this form: If *a* is in an environment which is *relevantly similar* to some environment where P is *conspicuously* the case, then *a* registers that P. The italicized expressions are shorthand jargon: each must be defined through our combined goal and registration theory for *a*. That theory contains hypotheses about which features of its environments *a* is sensitive to, and those hypotheses enable us, for many values of P, to pick out a certain class of environments which is made up as follows:

(i) a core of environments where P is the case, and where the features because of which P is the case are ones to which a is sensitive;

and

(ii) a surrounding ring of environments where P is not the case but which do not differ, in any respects to which a is sensitive, from some members of the core.

In each member of (i), P is 'conspicuously' the case; while each member of (ii) is 'relevantly similar' to some members of (i) – as the latter are, trivially, to themselves. So (ii) is explained by reference to (i), and (i) is defined with the aid of 'P is the case'. It is thus possible in principle, given some value of P, to investigate the world to see what sorts of environments are ones where P is the case; then to scrutinize the theory about a's goals and registrations to find out what sorts of environmental features a is sensitive to; and from all of that to derive an account of the class of environments in which a can be expected to register that P. So the occurrence of P in 'a registers that P' is more like the occurrence of 'Plato' in 'Platonic' than like the occurrence of 'cat' in 'catastrophe'.

The concept of registration must be anchored on one side in epistemic input and on the other in behavioural output. It might seem that the preceding paragraph is concerned with the former of these to the exclusion of the latter, but really it is not. I have chosen, for a special purpose, to present 'a registers that P' in terms of the kinds of environment where a will have the right intake for registering that P. But those *kinds* are defined through environmental features which are selected because of their utility in a theory for predicting a's behaviour. I have focussed on the epistemic-intake side, but have used concepts ('conspicuous' and 'relevantly similar') which utterly depend upon a theory in which we link a's epistemic intake with a's behavioural output through the concept of registration.

§16. Registration in practice

I have discussed how empirical evidence can be brought to bear upon a registration-plus-goal theory, once we have one. I make no apology for presenting the theory in terms of how it can be tested, but I sympathize with anyone who feels entitled to be told how to get the theory going in the first place. This demand might also reflect a desire to know more about registration than merely that it is whatever-it-is about the animal that makes the theory of registration true. In the present section I shall try to satisfy this desire by sketching one way in which a registration-plus-goal theory might be launched. The section can safely be omitted by those who feel no need for it.

Before we have any theory of registration for a, we can still tentatively identify some of a's goals: for we can identify certain values of G for each of which a significantly often does something which is required for and sufficient for the achievement of G; and so for each value we can conjecture that achieving G is one of its goals. This requires no limits on how ignorant a is. It does assume that a is not extravagantly prone to error, and if that assumption is wrong the present procedure will fail.

If G is one of a's goals, then I shall say that *a acts on the fact that F/Ga* on any occasion where F/Ga and Fa are both true. For example, if eating is one of a's goals, and on an occasion when a is swimming/eating it swims, then on that occasion it acts on the fact that it is swimming/ eating. It is also possible to act upon non-instrumental facts. If a acts on the fact that F/Ga, and in that situation F/Ga is true only because Ha is true, then a acts also on the fact that Ha. For instance, if it is swimming/ eating only because there is a fish in the pond, then in swimming it acts on the fact that there is a fish in the pond. This whole use of 'acts on the fact that' is purely stipulative.

Given our tentative identification of some of a's goals, then, we can amass data about the facts which a acts upon at various times. Our next task is to isolate the large sub-class of cases where *a non-coincidentally acts upon some fact*. In any such case, a acts on the fact that P, and the explanation of its behaviour requires some mention of the fact that P. (The idea is that the fact that P must somehow have influenced or been registered upon a; but that is to anticipate.) To sort out these cases, we shall need some general theory about what sorts of features of its environments a is sensitive to. This can be launched through attention to the data about facts which a has acted on, just so long as we can assume that most cases are not coincidental. For then we can get some leverage on a's sensory capacities by comparing, for instance, environments where it is swimming/eating and does swim with ones where it is swimming/eating and does not swim. These two classes of environment will differ in how they are sensorily presented to a, if we are right that eating is one of a's goals. Alongside these environmental differences we must set any facts we know about the condition and orientation of a's sense-organs; and our task is to devise a theory which will let us

adduce these facts – about the sense-organs and the states of the environments – to explain why a swam in the first set of situations and not in
the second. If it was sometimes a sheer coincidence that a swam when it
was swimming/eating, our theory does not explain those cases. But its
failure there, together with its success in the other cases, will be evidence that the former cases are indeed coincidences.

Here is an example of the kind of theorizing I have in mind. S is a
sub-set of occasions when a acts on the fact that it is swimming/eating,
and S^* is a sub-set when it is swimming/eating but does not swim; the
two sets are very alike in respect of the condition and orientation of a's
sense-organs, and they differ environmentally only in that in each member of S there was a red fish on a grey background while in each member of S^* there was a red fish on a blue background. This suggests that
a is sensitive to the red–grey but not to the red–blue difference, and that
conjecture can be tested against further environmental–behavioural data.

In this manner, we can assemble well-tested hypotheses about what
aspects of its environments a is sensitive to; they in turn will entitle us
to predict when it will swim and when it will not (except for a minority
of cases where it does so coincidentally). And so we can become entitled to say that on this or that occasion when a acted on the fact that
P it did so non-coincidentally – because we can explain a's behaviour
in terms of (its sensitivity to some aspect of) the fact that P.

Now, if a acts on the fact that P and the question arises 'Was this
coincidental?', the answer must depend upon what state a was in at the
time. If P is the fact that a was swimming/eating, and a was in receipt
of visual stimuli from a red fish on a grey pool-bottom, our theory may
imply that the case was a non-coincidental one; whereas if a had no
visual stimuli, and only olfactory stimuli of such and such a kind, that
might suffice under our theory to make the case one of mere coincidence. For any given proposition P and any state S, I shall say that S is
a *P-operative* kind of state if a's being in state S would, according to our
theory, imply that its acting upon P was non-coincidental. Note that by
this definition a is in a P-operative state only if P is true and a is acting
upon P.

At last, I introduce the concept of registration. I say that a registers
that P if a is in a sensory state which is *sufficiently like* some P-operative
state. It follows that if a is actually in a P-operative state then it registers
that P; but it may also register that P when its state is not P-operative
but bears to some P-operative state the relation, not yet explained, of
'sufficient similarity'.

Ways of registering that P can vary as much as can P-operative states: a might register that it is swimming/eating by being in a state sufficiently like its state when it sees a red fish against a grey background, or hears a beaver swimming on the other side of a log, or smells fresh blood across the water. And it might register that there is a fish in the pond on the sensory basis of something sufficiently like a clear view of the fish through still water, or the plopping sound as the fish rises to take a fly, or the feel of a tiny movement in the water, and so on.

What makes a state 'sufficiently like' another one? In answering this we must avoid sliding into vacuity. Suppose that we conjecture that this is a law.

$$(f)(t)((Ra \ \& \ a \text{ registers that } f/Ga) \to fa),$$

and at a certain time T we want to know whether a registers that F/Ga for a certain value of F, i.e. whether a's state at T is sufficiently like some state which is F/Ga-operative. One might answer that if a does F at $T+d$ then its state at T was sufficiently like ... etc., and that otherwise it was not. But if that were our only leverage on 'sufficient likeness' between sensory states, and thus on 'registration', our laws would have no predictive value and little explanatory power.

So we need some other way of deciding whether a's state at one time is 'sufficiently like' its state at another – one which will let us say what a's state is like at T without our knowing how a will behave at $T+d$. But we already have the materials that we need; for we have some theory about a's sensory relationships to its environments, this being based on facts about how situations where $(F/Ga \ \& \ Fa)$ differed from ones where $(F/Ga \ \& \sim Fa)$. This will put us in a position to say things like this: 'In ten seconds from now a will be in a state S^*, which is somewhat like a kind of state S which is P-operative; and S^* differs from S only in a respect which we have never found to affect a's behaviour. So we classify S^* as "sufficiently like" S, and therefore predict that in ten seconds' time a will register that P.' If we are working with the hypothesis that when a registers that P a will do F, our prediction about what a will register generates one about what it will do. So our claim about a's registration has predictive value, and thus is not vacuous.

The whole account given in this section depends upon our roughly identifying some of a's goals before having any hard data about a's registrations. We can subsequently refine our account of its goals; but if they are too difficult to get an initial line on by the method I have indicated, then this approach is doomed. We may then have to start in a more haphazard manner, starting with a blind guess as to a's goals and its registrations and then gradually improving this double theory in the fashion indicated in §15 above. If the initial guess is too far from the mark, the technique of gradual improvement may fail altogether, and so some further stabs in the dark will be needed. We might never hit on a conjecture which enables us to progress, and thus never understand the springs of a's actions. My account does not promise understanding of the goals and registrations of a given animal, and there would be something wrong if it did.

I have assumed that a's goals and sensory capacities are in general fairly constant through time, for otherwise I could not bring evidence to bear separately on goal- and registration-theory. I accept this, as a point for rather than against my approach. If an organism had a very erratic sensory relationship to its environments, we could not know that the latter were registering upon it at all. Nor, it seems, could we discover its goals if they changed rapidly and arbitrarily.

'But surely we can make sense of the idea of an animal's briefly pursuing a goal which didn't enter into its value-system at any other time.' Yes, but this poses no problem for my Taylorian theory, because we can also make sense of the idea of a law's applying to something at a time or for a very short period. To say that (Ja at $T \rightarrow Ka$ at T) is a law about a is just to say that at T a had some property H such that it is a law that *anything* which at *any* time satisfies both Hx and Jx also satisfies Kx. (Some constraints must be laid upon H, such as that it is not merely the property of being if-J-then-K; for the latter would trivialize any use of the purported 'law' about a, like the famous 'explanation' that opium puts people to sleep because of its dormitive virtue. I shall not discuss what those constraints should be.)

Applying this to the special case of teleological laws, we get the following. To say that at T it was a law about a that

$$(f)(a \text{ registers that } f/Ga \text{ at } T \rightarrow fa \text{ at } T+d)$$

is just to say that at T a had some complex property H which satisfies certain triviality-blocking conditions and which is also such that the following is a law:

$$(x)(f)(t)((Hx \text{ at } t \ \& \ x \text{ registers that } f/Gx \text{ at } t) \rightarrow fx \text{ at } t+d).$$

So if we could know that at T a registered that F/Ga, and if we knew that at T a had a property H satisfying the above conditions, then we could explain a's doing F at T by reference to this teleological law which applied to a at T and at no other time at all.

In the light of this, consider the following often-criticized and strikingly Taylorian analysis of Ryle's:

The statement 'he boasted from vanity' ... is to be construed as saying 'he boasted on meeting the stranger and his doing so satisfies the law-like proposition that whenever he finds a chance of securing the admiration and envy of others, he does whatever he thinks will produce this admiration and envy'.[19]

It is often objected that this 'law-like proposition' entails that the man is generally vain, whereas 'He boasted from vanity' does not, for he might have had a sudden thrust of vanity which was right out of character. But Ryle need not say that the 'law-like proposition' holds throughout the man's lifetime, or even for a week or an hour. He needs to say only that at the time of the boasting the man was in a state such that it is a law that *whenever anyone is in that state* he will do whatever he thinks will produce admiration and envy. Though, as I said above, constraints must be laid on the 'state' – e.g. it must not be merely 'being vain' or 'being prone to do whatever one thinks will produce admiration and envy'.

So one can make sense of extremely short-term goals. The only problem is to discover them when they exist. If a does F on a given occasion when we know that it registers that F/Ga, we may – for want of a better 'explanation' – conjecture that it momentarily has G as a goal; but that is not very interesting. What we want is something more explanatory – something which says *what* the H is which brought a briefly under the relevant teleological law, or at least something which could have enabled us to predict that at that time a would do F. Such discoveries will be hard to make, and will probably be impossible unless we know a good deal about a's more long-lasting goals. That is my justification for presenting a heuristic which relies upon steady sensory relationships and durable goals.

§17. Negative feed-back

In my sketch of some earlier theories of teleology in §13 I might have mentioned one by Norbert Wiener and others.[20] I have saved it until

[19] Gilbert Ryle, *The Concept of Mind* (London, 1949), p. 89.
[20] A. Rosenblueth, Norbert Wiener and J. Bigelow, 'Behavior, Purpose and Teleology', *Philosophy of Science*, vol. 10 (1943).

now, because I need the concept of registration to help me to focus sharply on one aspect of Wiener's thought, namely the important concept of 'negative feed-back'.

Wiener and his collaborators introduce a weak concept of purposeful behaviour and a stronger one of teleological behaviour. The former is weak indeed: 'The term purposeful is meant to denote that the act or behavior may be interpreted as directed to the attainment of a goal – i.e., to a final condition in which the behaving object reaches a definite correlation in time or in space with respect to another object or event.'[21] As Richard Taylor has pointed out, this definition is so broad as to be vacuous.[22] Nor is Wiener's reply convincing. About one of Taylor's proposed counter-examples he says: 'We consider the behavior of a weighted roulette purposeful, [like] the behavior of a magnetic compass . . . By this we mean that the analysis of the motions of the wheel or of the needle should include the fact that they end in a definite relationship to a specific characteristic in the environment in which they occur.'[23] This shares the crucial defect of Bertrand Russell's theory, namely that it tries to define the purposes of systems in terms of where 'they end' rather than in terms of how they get there.

Things improve when Wiener turns to what he calls teleological behaviour. Purposeful behaviour is teleological, he says, if it involves 'negative feed-back', i.e. if 'the behavior of [the agent] is controlled by the margin of error at which the [agent] stands at a given time with reference to a . . . goal', and if this behaviour-control is caused by 'signals from the goal' which the agent receives *in the course of the behavior*.[24] For instance, a 'self-guiding' missile may stay on the track of its dodging target because it is sometimes caused to swerve by radio signals reaching it from the target.

The phrase 'signals from the goal' is poor; for the goal is always a state of affairs, not an object. It may involve reaching some object, but even that is not necessary. However, Wiener could have used 'signals from the environment', or just 'signals'; so I shall not press the point.

Wiener's concept of feed-back implicitly involves that of an instru-

---

[21] Rosenblueth *et al.*, *Philosophy of Science*, p. 18.

[22] Richard Taylor, 'Comments on a Mechanistic Conception of Purposefulness', *Philosophy of Science*, vol. 17 (1950), pp. 311–13.

[23] A. Rosenblueth and N. Wiener, 'Purposeful and Non-purposeful Behavior', *Ibid.*, p. 319. See also Richard Taylor, 'Purposeful and Non-purposeful Behavior: a Rejoinder', *Ibid.*

[24] Rosenblueth, Wiener and Bigelow, 'Behavior, Purpose and Teleology', pp. 19–20.

mental property. The agent receives signals indicating its present 'margin of error' with respect to attaining the goal, which is to say that it registers facts about what is currently required for and sufficient for the attainment of the goal. Wiener's account, then, could be said to include the theory of Nagel and Charles Taylor. But his is much stronger, for it restricts the concept of teleology to cases where *changing* facts about the agent's instrumental properties are registered on it 'in the course of the behavior'. Much behaviour which does not meet this condition, and so does not involve 'feed-back' in Wiener's sense, would still be counted as teleological by Nagel and Taylor and, I suggest, by common sense. Wiener himself gives examples: 'A snake may strike at a frog, or a frog at a fly, with no visual or other report from the prey after the movement has started. Indeed, the movement is in these cases so fast that it is not likely that nerve impulses would have time to . . . modify the movement effectively.'[25] Even there, the frog's striking at the fly may be partly explained by its registering that it missed the fly last time, and is thus still hungry; but that is not an instance of 'negative feedback' in Wiener's sense.

Negative feed-back is valuable because it enables an agent to handle an environment which is, so to speak, changing faster than it can act. But it is not required for teleological behaviour as such. All that is essential to the concept of teleology is the notion of an agent's being disposed to do whatever it registers as conducive to and needed for its becoming G; and negative feed-back is merely one way in which such 'registrations' can occur. There is no conceptual obstacle to there being a rich domain of goal-pursuing behaviour with no occurrences whatsoever of negative feed-back in Wiener's sense.

So Wiener's account of 'teleological behaviour' is too strong. On the other hand, his weaker account of 'purposeful behaviour' covers too much logical space to be useful. When Wiener moves from the too-weak to the too-strong, through the concept of negative feed-back, it is as though in trying to understand dogs he had slipped straight from a theory about mammals to one about spaniels. What he needed was the concept of an instrumental property.

§18. Competing goals

Even if an animal often seeks to become G, it may sometimes instead pursue some more attractive goal. If our teleological laws are not

[25] *Ibid.*, p. 20.

modified to deal with that eventuality, we shall be in trouble. Suppose we apply to organism a a law implying (for short) that it is a G-seeker and another implying that it is a G^*-seeker, and then on one occasion a registers that it is F/G and that it is F^*/G^*, and it cannot do both F and F^*. For example, a generally seeks food and generally seeks shelter; and right now it is digging/eating and climbing/getting-shelter, and the relevant laws do not give it time to climb as well as dig. If our theory is to avoid implying that a will, impossibly, dig while climbing, it must retreat into a sulky silence about the case.

This silence is intolerable: a decent theory of teleological explanation must say something useful about competing goals. I have been pretending that a's opportunities will always present themselves one at a time, but that is so grossly unrealistic as to constitute a serious defect in the account. In remedying it, I shall be much indebted to the work, mentioned in §11 above, of Ann MacKenzie.

What I have presented so far is the theory of what Ann MacKenzie calls an organism's 'highest goals'. This lacks generality because not all goals are highest ones, and indeed an organism might have no highest goal. (Note that highest goals are the 'pathological preference functions' of §10 above. They are not to be equated with the organism's *needs*; and the latter concept is one which the theory of teleology does not need.) To increase the theory's scope, we must find some way of saying that a will do any f for which it registers that f/Ga unless it registers that f^*/g^* for some f^* and some g^* which it prefers to G. So we must establish theses about a's preferences.

The items in the G position in our teleological laws, which specify a's goals, may have to be complex and specific. If we stay with simple items like 'eating' and 'getting sex' we may find a sometimes preferring the former and sometimes the latter, leaving us with no general thesis about a's preference as between the two. But dependable preferences might emerge if we considered such goals as 'getting food but no shelter, while becoming wet and cold but not exerting much physical effort' and 'getting sex while running into considerable danger from a predator', and so on. Ann MacKenzie calls these items 'goal-complexes', but I call them *goals*, with a reminder of how complex goals can be.

Another complexity is needed. Suppose that on one occasion a seeks food rather than sex, and on another sex rather than food; there are no relevant differences in physiological states (sexual satiety, blood-sugar, etc.) at the two times; and the discrepancy resists treatment in terms of goal-complexes, e.g. by saying that *a* preferred food-and-shelter to sex-without-shelter, and sex-and-drink to food-without-drink. The behaviour might still be explained, if on the first occasion *a* could get food by taking a short walk and could not get sex without climbing a tree, whereas on the second it could get sex just by rolling over and could not get food without swimming a river. Such explanations ought to be provided for in our theory.

Provision is made in Ann MacKenzie's account, where 'goal complex' is stretched to cover what might be called 'means-and-goal complex'. An animal may have general preferences amongst means-and-goal complexes. For example, on one occasion *a* did *F* in order to achieve *G*, rather than doing *F** in order to achieve *G**, because *a* prefers doing-*F*-and-becoming-*G* to doing-*F**-and-becoming-*G**. For brevity, I shall use the form '*F-G*' to abbreviate 'doing-*F*-and-becoming-*G*', and I shall replace the clumsy 'means-and-goal complex' by the technical term *course*. So *a* did *F* in order to achieve *G*, rather than doing *F** to achieve *G**, because it preferred the course *F-G* to the course *F*-G**. We are interested in cases where the first part of the course is a means to the second part, but that is not part of the meaning of 'course' or of my hyphen notation.

If *F-G* is a course, then an animal which does *F* and becomes *G* can be said to *follow* the course. And I shall say that *a* registers that *F-G* is *open* to it if *a* registers that it can follow *F-G*. Our evidence that it does so may be evidence that it registers that *F/Ga*, i.e. that its doing *F* is required for and sufficient for its becoming *G*; but all that is meant by 'It registers that *F-G* is open to it' is that it registers that a certain two-stage event can occur.

One last preliminary explanation. In my formulae from now on I shall omit temporal details. Each law is to be understood as universally quantified with respect to *t*, each conjunct in the antecedent is to be expanded to '... at *t*', and the consequent expanded to '... at *t+d*'. We can safely omit all this clutter, now that we have survived Spinoza's accusation that teleology 'reverses the order of nature'.

Now, at last, I can say what form of teleological law we need if we are to cope with non-highest goals. It must be something of the form

$$(x)(f)((Rx \ \& \ x \text{ registers that } f/Gx \ \& \ f\text{-}G \text{ is most preferred by } x)$$
$$\rightarrow fx).$$

That introduces the notion of 'most preferred by *x*', for which no behavioural grounding has yet been supplied. And that is all it introduces. (I have expressed various forms of teleological law in a formal way so as to make it easier to identify any new elements, in sharp separation from materials which have already been behaviourally grounded.) I define 'most preferred' as follows. To say that F-G is most preferred by x at T is to say

$$(f)(g)((f\text{-}g \neq F\text{-}G \ \& \ x \text{ registers that } f\text{-}g \text{ is open to } x \text{ at } t) \ \rightarrow$$
$$x \text{ prefers } F\text{-}G \text{ to } f\text{-}g \text{ at } T).$$

So the original law-formula, expanded by means of that definition, says that when an animal is R it does whatever it registers as required for and sufficient for its becoming G, as long as that involves its following a course which it prefers to any other course which it registers as open to it at that time.

A simple inspection of the above expansion of 'F-G is most preferred by x at T' shows that it involves just one element which has not yet been properly grounded in behavioural evidence, namely the notion of preference for one course over another. All we need now is to become able to discover things of the form 'a prefers F-G to F^*-G^* at T'; for if we have enough facts of this form, we can discover that a prefers F-G to every other course which it registers as open to it at T.

Obviously, we discover what a prefers by observing what a does; but if we could know what a prefers at T only through observing what a does at T our whole enterprise would collapse into vacuity, for our laws then could neither predict nor explain. We must become able to judge what a prefers at T on the basis of what a does at other times; then we can predict its preferences, and thus its behaviour, at T. So we need some general truths about a's enduring preferences – meaning ones which last long enough to yield behavioural evidence as to what they are. If a acts on a preference which it has just acquired and which it immediately loses again, then that behaviour may well not be explicable by the sort of theory I am describing. See the last part of §16.

We need not insist upon establishing results of the form: throughout this period of time a regularly prefers F_1-G_1 to F_2-G_2. Our needs can be met by statements recording preferences which a has *when such and such conditions obtain*, e.g. when a is wet, or when a is hungry, or at night, and so on. Such preference-rules, as I shall call them, may be less general than we should like; but they are still general, and so they may support predictions about how a will behave on given occasions.

The evidence for each preference-rule will come, in an obvious way, from our observations of a's behaviour. (There is no circularity in this.

Every empirical theory is supported by the very facts which it can predict and explain.) A little more specifically, the situation is as follows. Our teleological laws covertly use preference-rules, because the latter are needed to generate things of the form 'at T, a prefers c to c^*', which in their turn are covertly involved in things of the form 'at T, c is a's most preferred course'. The task of establishing preference-rules is just the task of finding ones which, when fed into the teleological laws in that way, yield true predictions about a's behaviour. If a certain prediction is falsified, the source of the error must be located within our total theory; and the question of whether it lies in one of the preference-rules or rather in some other aspect of the teleological law is a matter for empirical investigation. The logical structure of that investigation can easily enough be worked out from the discussion of comparable problems in §15 above.

Objection: 'You are now offering a form of teleological law which says that a will do so-and-so if that is its most preferred course at the time. Isn't that an empty banality?' No. For in the teleological laws I am proposing, any overt or covert reference to what a prefers is a reference to *what our preference-rules say* that a prefers. Thus, any clause of the form

At T, a's most preferred course is F-G

can be taken as shorthand for, or at least as decisively testable against, the corresponding statement of the form

For any course c which a registers as open to it at T, *there is a true preference-rule* of the form 'When P obtains, a prefers F-G to c' for some P which is true at T.

Thus construed, the teleological laws are not banalities at all: they could turn out to be false because one of the preference-rules was wrong. As for the preference-rules themselves: it is best to think of them as theoretical items which have no meaning except what they get from their employment in the teleological laws. There is an alternative reading of them, which gives them all the content of the theory and renders the original teleological laws idle; but the theory in that form of it is hard to manage.

§19. Theory about preferences

There is a difficulty about establishing the preference-rules. We know how in principle any one of them can be (dis)confirmed by behavioural data, but it is not practically possible to establish each needed preference-rule by observing behaviour which bears upon it alone. Recall that a preference-rule relates a single course to a single other course (and perhaps only subject to some condition P, but I shall now ignore that further complexity). Since the identity of a course is constituted by every feature of it which ever affects whether a will follow the course, the number of them for a given animal may be enormous; so if we must separately establish a preference-rule for each pair of courses, our endeavour is doomed. Our only hope is to establish a small set of more general items of preference-theory for a, from which the multitude of specific preference-rules for a could be derived. Let us consider how this might be done.

It would help if the relation 'a prefers . . . to . . .' turned out to be transitive, so that if a prefers c to c^*, and prefers c^* to c^{**}, it will prefer c to c^{**}. There is no necessity about this. The basic notion of preference has to do with what a does in a situation where it registers certain courses as open to it; and it could happen that although it would choose c out of the pair c and c^*, and would choose c^* out of the pair c^* and c^{**}, it would nevertheless choose c^{**} out of the pair c and c^{**}. As for the situation where it registers all three courses as open to it: there are different things we might discover about that, and none of them is determined by our findings in situations where a registers only two courses as open to it.

If a's preference relation is transitive, the number of independent general theses about its preferences can be usefully reduced. Suppose there are a hundred different courses which figure in the teleological explanation of a's behaviour. If a's preference relation is not transitive, the complete facts about its preferences require nearly five thousand separate preference-rules, one for each pair of courses; but if a's preference relation is transitive we need only one hundred separate preference-theses, one for each course. For it would then suffice to say which course(s) came top, which came second, which came third, and so on down.

In Ann MacKenzie's ground-breaking treatment of competing goals, the basic concept is that of a *ranking* of courses. She supposes that relative to a we can assign an overall rank to each course, so that which course a chooses out of any given pair is a simple function of which has the higher rank. This clearly presupposes that a has a transitive preference relation. I have chosen to reach this stage through a less developed one (§18 above) at which we can, in principle, handle competing goals, but not with anything as strong as a system of all-purpose rankings. Even if the preference relation of most animals is approximately transitive, this is at best a contingent truth, and I wanted to see where we could get without it.

Transitivity, I pointed out, would let us divide by about fifty the number of separate preference-theses needed for a if there were a hundred different courses which sometimes figured in the explanation of a's behaviour. But that would still leave a hundred theses to be established, which is bad enough; and for most animals the number of relevant courses would doubtless be much higher even than that. How might we simplify our preference-theory material still further?

The most powerful simplification I can think of is the following. We form a set of *kinds* (or *features*) of states of affairs $\{K_1, \ldots, K_m\}$ such that each course is of one or more of those kinds; to each K_i we assign a value-measure, expressed by a positive or negative integer; then each course is assigned a value-measure by summing all the value-measures of the kinds to which it belongs; and then, finally, the rank of any course is a simple function of its value-measure: the higher the measure, the higher the rank.

For example, at T there are just two courses open to a: getting food and becoming warm by expending a lot of muscular effort and risking some pain, and getting shelter with little effort but remaining cold; and these are the only features of the two courses which are relevant to what a will do, and thus the only ones in our value-measured set $\{K_1, \ldots, K_m\}$. Now, we have a value-measure for getting food, another for getting warm, a third for risking pain, and so on; we sum these to get a value-measure for each course; and then we predict that at $T + d$ a will follow the course which has the higher value-measure.

If we could find something like this for a, it would vastly simplify our account of its preferences. The transitivity of preference reduced the number of independent theses to the number of courses; but this latest simplification, if we had it, would carry us much further; we could get about five hundred distinct ranking theses, corresponding to five hundred distinct courses, on the basis of just nine distinct value-measured kinds.

It is a purely empirical question whether a given animal does admit of any theory along these lines. We must look for a way of resolving courses into kinds, and assigning value-measures to the kinds, such that the simple algorithm I have described yields only true predictions about what a will do. But we might fail, finding that our best endeavours led mainly to false predictions; and this could be because we had not yet found the right resolution into kinds, or because there was none to be found since a's value-system did not have this kind of structure.

The latter reason for failure is the more likely, for this simple addition of values is surely inapplicable to most actual organisms. It will not fit any animal for which the contribution which a given feature makes to a course's value depends upon what its other features are. In the human sphere, for example, the difference in value between x-ing-and-reading and x-ing-and-not-reading cannot be computed from a single value-measure for reading; for the size of that difference depends on what x-ing is. A book may enhance one's pleasure in soaking in a warm bath but not one's pleasure in climbing a mountain.

Still, one could no doubt usually find some simplifications of the material. For most animals the value of a given course varies directly with the brevity and ease of its 'means' component, and that fact alone spares us much enumeration of separate rankings. There may even be animals which conform to something like the simple-addition system, with just a few kinds of non-additiveness which would have to be separately specified in our theory.

From now on I shall assume that we are dealing with organisms whose value-systems can be described in a tolerably small set of independent laws; but that assumption will not be a load-bearing part of the account.

§20. Subjective probability

All this is to prepare the way for the special case where the animal's registering that it is F/G is its *believing* that it is F/G. We know perfectly well that an agent often acts on his belief not that his doing F *is*, but just that it has some chance of being, required for and sufficient for his becoming G. Let us prepare for that right away, by introducing the more general notion of a's registering that probably F/Ga. This is not an essential part of a basic theory of teleology: there can be animals whose behaviour admits of teleological explanations but to which the concept of subjective probability is irrelevant. I introduce that concept at the present stage just to show that it can be properly grounded long before we reach the level where registrations are beliefs.

To give the concept of subjective probability a grip on a's behaviour, we need a metric for a's value-sytem, that is, a way of saying by how much a ranks one course over another. The ruling idea behind subjective probability is that when a has two courses c and c^* open to it, which one it follows depends upon two independent aspects of the situation: which course it ranks higher (and by how much), and which one it registers as having the greater chance of success (and how much greater). For example, taking a case where the registration is a belief: what a does depends not only upon which means-and-goal it finds more attractive, but also upon whether it believes that one goal has a better chance – and, if so, how much better a chance – of being reached by the available means.

For brevity, I shall write 'a registers$_n$ that P', meaning that a registers that it is probable in degree n that P.

Then the fundamental relation between subjective probability and value-measures is as follows. If a registers$_n$ that F/Ga, and registers$_m$ that F^*/G^*a; and if it ranks F-G higher than F^*-G^* by amount k; then whether it does F or F^* depends upon how the difference between the two probabilities (m and n) compares with the difference (k) between the two value-measures.

With a finely graded value-metric, we may be able to have a finely graded system of subjective probabilities. But even the crudest possible value-metric, which merely distinguishes 'a ranks c slightly higher than c^*' from 'a ranks c much higher than c^*', could support a working concept of subjective probability; though the latter would be equally crude, serving to distinguish only two levels of probability. How are we to establish any value-metric, fine or crude?

It might seem that everything is plain sailing. 'We have introduced non-probabilistic registration, and, in connection with that, preference-rules; we know how the latter might yield a value-metric for a; and with that at our disposal we can proceed to establish what its subjective probabilities are.' But that is all wrong. If we are going to have probabilistic registration$_n$, as well as the notion of outright registration with which I started, the latter should be treated as a special case of the former, namely as registration$_1$. So we should introduce registration$_n$ without relying on non-probabilistic registration, or, therefore, on anything so far established about preferences, value-measures and so on. In short, we must start again.

Still, what mainly needs to be said runs so closely parallel to the treatment of non-probabilistic registration (§§15, 18) that a sketch will suffice.

The crucial problem is just a variant on the one discussed in §15.

Each item of behaviour manifests facts about a's registrations$_n$ and a's value-measures, but we must find some way of giving these two concepts separate lives of their own. Otherwise there will be nothing to stop us from setting a's value-measure for F-G arbitrarily high, and then explaining a's not doing F at T by saying that at T a registered$_n$ that F/Ga for only an extremely small value of n. The point is not that we shall behave perversely unless we are stopped; rather, it is that we need standards for judging what *is* perverse.

The solution, like that in §15, fits the metaphor in which we test panes of glass in pairs and learn which ones are distorted by changing the pairings. To explain any given item of behaviour we must invoke measures of subjective probability (P) and of value (V); but we can get a purchase on these measures independently of one another, for we can test P against behaviour where it combines with value measures other than V, and we can test V against behaviour which involves probability measures other than P. Since we can thus have evidence against individual measures of subjective probability, and individual measures of value, these two notions have separate lives within the overall theory.

If we are to use some items of behaviour to correct our diagnosis of others, both sides of our theory must contain fairly durable truths about a. On the value side, there is no problem: one expects statements about the amount by which a prefers F-G to F^*-G^* (under such-and-such conditions) to remain true for considerable periods of time. But the same does not hold for specific statements about a's registrations$_i$: for example, we cannot expect a to spend a week registering that probably the way to get food is to dig. What we need here (as in §15) is some theory about the relatively durable epistemic principles which, in combination with data about a's environment and sense-organs at specific times, let us predict what a registers$_i$ at those times. Such principles might do their work in a single sweep: state of environment and sense-organs in the antecedent, registration$_i$ of instrumental proposition in the consequent. But they might instead proceed in two stages: from environment and sense-organs to registration$_i$ of propositions other than instrumental ones, and then a second step to the registration$_i$ of instrumental propositions. To illustrate the two-step procedure: from data about a's environment and sense-organs we infer, through our general theory, that it registers$_j$ that there is a seal on the rock and registers$_k$ that it can climb the rock; and from these results plus some more theory we infer that a registers$_{(j \times k)}$ that it is climbing/eating. Of course this is drastically over-simplified.

How do we discover what links there are between the state of a's environment and sense-organs at T and what a registers$_i$ at T? Well, something like the heuristic procedure described in §16 above might work here too, but I shall not go through that again. The crucial thing is just to see how, once we have somehow possessed ourselves of some theory about registration$_i$ and value-measures for a, we can effectively test it against a's behaviour; and I have said enough about that.

It may be that subjective probabilities actually occur only high up in the animal kingdom; but they could occur very low down. An animal which has subjective probabilities need not have a theory of probability, or a concept of or thoughts about probability. All it needs are behaviour-patterns which support a theory with the structure I have presented in this section.

Late in §12 I sketched a case where an animal is climbing-or-swimming/eating and we cannot explain its climbing rather than swimming. Perhaps now we can explain this, in any of three distinct ways. (1) It prefers climbing-eating to swimming-eating. (2) It registers$_j$ that it is climbing/eating and registers$_k$ that it is swimming/eating, where $j > k$. (3) Or the explanation may combine elements from the first two.

To make any such explanation work, we must re-define '/' so that F/Ga means only that Fa is sufficient for Ga. If we leave in the clause 'Fa is necessary for Ga' then we cannot after all have cases where F/Ga and $F*/Ga$ at the same time, for although Fa and $F*a$ may each be sufficient for Ga, just because either would suffice for Ga neither can be required for Ga. I hereby adopt that weakening of the stroke notation, and the corresponding weakening of the terminology of 'instrumental property [predicate, proposition]'. The clause which I am now dropping had important work to do, namely in reminding us of certain things we could not explain. Now that we have a theory of preferences and subjective probabilities, we are well placed to explain them, and so the reminder is now inappropriate. Furthermore, the dropped clause would, if it were retained, positively prevent us from using our theory of preferences in cases where a chooses between two courses which relate as $F-G$ and $F*-G$.

It is no part of my theory that there must always be an explanation. I do not think that an ass would starve to death when equidistant from two equally attractive bales of hay; and, moving up the intellectual ladder, Leibniz was wrong when he said that no one can act without a reason to act in some absolutely specific manner, as though a reason to scratch my nose must be a reason to scratch it with just that curvature of my finger and this tilt of my head.[26] All I am saying is that the notions of preference (and value-measure) and of subjective probability may enlarge the range of behaviour which we can explain completely.

As well as the possibility that some of *a*'s behaviour is not covered by our best teleological theory, there is the possibility that the best theory we can find is refuted by some of *a*'s behaviour. There is no reason inherent in teleology as such why there should not be strong, exceptionless teleological laws; but we might well find in practice that we always had to settle for less, i.e. that we could keep our generalizations true only by qualifying them with 'Usually . . .' or 'Except in very special circumstances . . .' Still, even a theory of that kind could support (tentative) predictions and (imperfectly satisfying) explanations of behaviour.

§21. Teleology and mechanism

If there is a teleological explanation of some item of behaviour, does it follow that that item cannot or should not be explained mechanistically, that is, explained in terms of earlier events and without reference to any later time? The view that this does follow – which I call the 'rivalry thesis' – has been used both to argue that because animals have goals mechanism does not cover all events, and, contrapositively, that because mechanism does cover all events we should never explain an event teleologically. I shall not choose between those directions of argument, because I want to confute the rivalry thesis and argue that 'There is no necessary incompatibility between our describing and explaining behaviour by purpose in ordinary life or in the context of scientific theories of teleological-intentional type . . . on the one hand, and our being able to give a mechanistic neurophysiological account of them on the other.'[27]

Because I agree with that, I cannot argue that there is no choice to be made because the two sorts of explanations must cover different sorts of events. It used to be commonly said that mentalistic explanations occupy a different arena from physicalistic ones, since the former explain actions while the latter explain bodily movements; and one might

[26] H. G. Alexander (ed.), *The Leibniz–Clarke Correspondence* (Manchester, 1956), Leibniz's fifth letter, §17.

[27] Charles Taylor, 'Reply [to Robert Borger]', in R. Borger and F. Cioffi (eds.), *Explanation in the Behavioural Sciences* (Cambridge, 1970), at p. 89. Taylor seemed to accept the rivalry thesis in *The Explanation of Behaviour*.

adapt that line of thought and say that teleological explanations apply to events of a different kind from those which can be mechanistically explained. But the fallacy in the original line of thought is now fairly widely recognized, and its suggested analogue is equally untenable. If an organism moves, one can ask 'Was that movement teleologically explicable?' If it was, one may then apply some description which is proper only to a teleologically explicable event (perhaps: 'The animal didn't just move – it acted'); but no such nuance as that can rule out the initial question, and it is *there* that teleological and mechanistic explanations do meet and might be thought to conflict.

One might argue that they must conflict because any good explanation of an event assigns a cause to it, so that explaining an event in two different ways would involve assigning two different causes, one of which must be wrong. This could be countered in any of three ways. (1) Some good explanations do not assign causes, and teleological explanations might be among them. (2) An event can be over-determined, having more than one sufficient cause. (3) Anyway, it could be that the two explanations assign the same cause: a's coming to register that F/Ga might be the very same biochemical event which is mentioned in the mechanistic explanation of a's doing F. This identity-claim, as Davidson has shown, need not involve any of the problems which confront those who maintain the contingent identity of *properties*.[28] It is not suggested that coming-to-register-that-F/Gx is (always) identical with undergoing-chemical-process-C; but only that when a came to register that F/Ga at T, that particular event was just a's undergoing process C at T.

With all those defences available, we need not consider that basis for the rivalry thesis any further. But a different basis, not using the concept of cause, should be discussed: –

Mechanistic explanations of animal movements will presumably be chemical ones: the animal was structured thus, these processes were occurring in those parts of its central nervous system, and all this led by pure chemistry to the movement in question. It seems that such an explanation exhausts the material, covers all the facts, leaves nothing to be said; so a teleological explanation of the same movement must, it seems, be idle.

Granted, we usually do not have the chemical explanation. But can we defend teleological explanations only as being acceptable *faute de mieux*?

[28] Davidson (1970).

No, we can do better than that, even if all animal movements are purely chemically explicable. Every explanation of an event implicitly groups it with other events which can be similarly explained; so a chemical explanation of an animal's movement implicitly classes it with other events of the same chemical kind. But the best teleological explanation of it might group it quite differently, e.g. classifying it with other movements which, like it, were made in order to get food. If that grouping is the best for our purposes, say because we are study- ing how the animal relates to its ecological niche or trying to protect our crops from it, then we need not apologise for the teleological explanation which yields it.

Charles Taylor, apparently endorsing the rivalry thesis, implies that replacing a teleological explanation by a chemical one (if one exists) will always bring sheer gain: we can substitute chemistry for teleology, he says, 'without losing at all, but on the contrary gaining, in explanatory or predictive power or the capacity to control [the behaviour]'.[29] Even if that were right, the teleological explanation might bring some advantage, by giving us a grouping which we wanted and which the chemical explanation did not provide. But Taylor's remark about prediction and control is not quite true in itself, for a reason which connects with my point about 'grouping'. Let us take prediction first.

Suppose that mechanism is comprehensively true. Then if we knew everything about their chemical causes, we could predict an animal's movements with perfect accuracy and in full detail. In practice, though, we must settle for approximate predictions – ones involving slight error and slight incompleteness. What sort of approximation will satisfy us depends upon what our interests are; what sort we can hope to get depends on what our basis for prediction is; and the two might fail to coincide.

For example, even if we have a chemical basis for a *fairly* accurate and complete account of how an animal will move, our interest in its movements may be unsatisfied by this knowledge. Although in chemical terms we have an impressively detailed prediction, we may have left wide open the question of whether the animal will pursue prey or flee from a predator; and this may be the very question we want answered. Conversely, we might have a teleological basis for predicting that the animal will seek food, without being able to come anywhere near saying what chemical mechanisms will be involved.

[29] Taylor, p. 29.

(Analogously: one might know fairly exactly how someone will move his fingers, yet not know whether he will validly sign the cheque; and one might know that he will pay his debt somehow, without knowing how he will move his fingers. This seems to be the truth underlying the once-popular error that the concepts of action and of bodily movement are immiscible.)

Those points about approximate prediction can obviously be re-applied, *mutatis mutandis*, to the notion of partial control. The latter involves keeping what happens within certain limits: if the desired limits are statable in terms of 'food-seeking' or the like, then the basis for control had better be teleological rather than chemical.

The foregoing argument presupposes that the teleological explanation does not simply model over into the chemical one, that is, that no one chemical law covers precisely the facts which the teleological law covers. I have been working with a picture in which some of the animal's food-seeking movements involve biochemical events of kind K_1, others involve ones of kind K_2, others kind K_3, and so on; and in which events of each of those kinds are involved sometimes in shelter-seeking, sometimes in predator-escaping, sometimes in sex-pursuing, and so on. If that picture were wrong, then teleological explanations might sometimes be useful *faute de mieux*, but I can find no deeper justification for them. If anyone thinks there is one, let him produce it. (The deepest justification would come if some teleologically explicable event could not be mechanistically explained at all; but I doubt if there are any such events.) My next section illustrates the force of the question whether a given teleological explanation can be simply matched with a single mechanistic explanation of the same range of facts.

§22. A fraudulent teleological explanation

Stable Lake is a body of water occupying an extinct volcanic crater in the Yukon. Around its edges, above the water-line, alpine lilies grow; and rocks beneath the water harbour a population of fresh-water shell-fish. The lake loses water only by evaporation, and gains it only through rainfall. The lilies cannot survive immersion, nor can the shellfish survive exposure to the air; but one is not surprised to learn that the water-level never rises above the lilies nor falls below the shellfish – for if it did they would have vanished by now. However, one may be surprised to learn of evidence that Stable Lake *protects* its flora and fauna from the disasters I have mentioned. In any normal year, the water-level sometimes nearly reaches the lilies and sometimes falls almost to the level of the shellfish; but in an abnormally rainy year the flowers are still not drowned, nor are the shellfish desiccated in an abnormally dry one. In fact, Stable Lake conforms to two teleological laws: (1) Whenever the lake registers that it is f/not-drowning-the-lilies, it does f. (2) Whenever the lake registers that it is f/not-desiccating-the-shellfish, it does f. Combining the two: whenever the lake registers that it is f/saving-the-wildlife, it does f. (Because there is not even an apparent place here for preferences, I temporarily revert to the old, strong meaning of '/' in which it expresses requirement as well as sufficiency.)

I confess that the concept of registration is idle in the foregoing; for in fact the lake registers that it is f/saving-the-wildlife when and only when it *is* f/saving-the-wildlife. This may seem to make the story even stranger, presenting the lake as not just ecologically minded but also omniscient and infallible.

Everyone will be sure that my teleological account of the lake must be wrong or gravely misleading. Why? 'Because a lake cannot intend to protect its flora and fauna, cannot want them to flourish or care about their welfare.' That is a poor reason; for it is certainly wrong to restrict teleological explanations to systems which *intend* or *want* or *care*. What makes my teleological account of the lake's behaviour suspect is the suspicion that the very same facts can be covered by a single mechanistic explanation. And so indeed they can: —

All around the lake, the meeting of bed and bank has a cross-section like this:

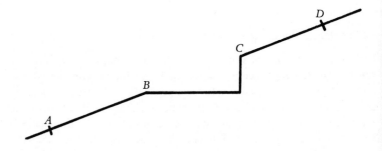

with the shellfish all below A and the lilies all above D. The surface of the water is usually between B and C. If rainfall brings the water above

C, the lake's surface-area increases and, therefore, so does the rate of evaporation. The higher the water rises above C, the greater the evaporation-rate, and so the water never passes D and drowns the lilies. Similarly, if the water-level falls below B, the surface area is reduced and so evaporation slows down; so that the shellfish are protected.

That mechanistic explanation disqualifies the teleological one – not because each thing Stable Lake does can be explained mechanistically, but because a single mechanistic explanation covers exactly what the teleological explanation covers. We do not even have a *faute de mieux* defence of the latter, for the mechanistic explanation is known and is easy to apply: it is no harder to notice that the lake's surface-area has altered than to notice that if the rate of evaporation does not alter the wildlife will suffer.

The inadequacy of the teleological explanation can be seen as the upshot of the following sequence of facts about it. Firstly, the concept of registration was idle, so that instead of

(1) $(f)(a$ registers that $f/Ga \rightarrow fa)$

we could as well have used

(2) $(f)(f/Ga \rightarrow fa)$.

Next, although the explanation purported to generalize over classes of instrumental property, saying that *for any f* when the lake is f/saving-the-wildlife it does f, in fact only one value of f ever comes into play, namely undergoing a change in evaporation-rate. So the form of the law could as well have been not (2) but

(3) $F/Ga \rightarrow Fa$.

Finally, the instrumental property F/G is in each case co-extensive with an intrinsic property (i.e. one other than an instrumental property), namely that of undergoing a certain change in surface-area; and so the law could just as well have the form

(4) $Ha \rightarrow Fa$.

And so at last we reach something which is not teleological at all.

We have moved from (1) 'The lake does whatever it registers as required for and sufficient for saving the wildlife' to (2) 'The lake does whatever is required for and sufficient for saving the wildlife' and then to (3) 'The lake changes its evaporation-rate whenever that is required for and sufficient for saving the wildlife', and from that finally to (4)

'The lake changes its evaporation-rate whenever its surface-area changes'. This last is a law, whose antecedent and consequent are linked by the physics which explains how evaporation-rate depends on surface-area. They are not linked by the evident connection that obtains between *F/Ga* and *Fa*, but that connection, we can now see, was fraudulent.

Suppose that we could get to (3) but not right down to (4)? That would be less interesting than having to use (1) or (2), but it would still be a case of teleology, I think. I count as 'teleological' any law whose antecedent uses an instrumental predicate (or predicate-variable), with the part of it on the left of the stroke being used also in the consequent. If a given range of events can be covered by a law which is teleological in that sense, and not by any other law, then those events constitute a genuine case of teleology, even if not a very rich or interesting one, and even if they do not involve the concept of registration. But, as I said early in §14 above, I believe that in fact any events which are legitimately explicable in teleological terms do give work to the concept of registration.

§23. Three corollaries

Three somewhat disparate issues, all about teleology and mechanism, will now be discussed.

(1) 'Even if an animal's behaviour can be explained through an honest teleological law, should not we explain *why it falls under such a law*?' Yes, I should like to, but let us be careful about what we are looking for. Even if for each teleologically explicable event we have a mechanistic explanation, which is more basic than the teleological one in the sense that it involves wider and deeper laws; that still does not explain why the animal conforms to a teleological law. To explain *that* in mechanistic terms, one must assemble the facts about the mechanisms which were involved in all the instances of the teleological law, and explain why those mechanisms co-exist in that animal. The explanation would presumably be an evolutionary one: mechanisms are hereditary, new ones occur through random mutation, those which make for survival will tend to spread through the species, and the particular set of mechanisms which add up to the animal's conforming to a teleological law have had survival value for their possessors.

(2) People sometimes give 'functional' accounts of parts and features

of organisms: the function of the heart is to pump blood, the function of the grass's bending towards the window is to catch sunlight. These will figure in §62 below, but they will not be important in my book. Still, I shall briefly relate them to my theory of teleology.

I contend that functional statements need not involve anything which is 'teleological' in my sense. The grass bends towards the window so as to get more sunlight; but since this behaviour is controlled by one unitary mechanism, it ought not to be explained teleologically, except perhaps in a *faute de mieux* spirit. Indeed, I prefer not to say that the grass moves 'so as to' achieve a result. But certainly the gathering of more sunlight is in some sense the *function* of the grass's movement, and I want to explain what that sense is.

I suggest that the functional statement about the grass means something like this: (a) By bending towards the window, the grass does receive more sunlight than it otherwise would; and (b) The fact that the grass contains a mechanism which causes it to bend towards sources of sunlight is explained by the fact that this mechanism enables the grass to receive more sunlight than it otherwise would.[30]

Similarly, 'The function of the mammalian heart is to pump blood throughout the body' means: (a) The mammalian heart does pump blood throughout the body, and (b) The fact that mammals have hearts is explained by the fact that hearts pump blood throughout the body (a mutant which lacked a heart would not survive because its blood would not circulate).

In this account of functional statements, they always say something about what *explains* a certain fact. Where the functional statement concerns an organism, I believe that the explanation will always be an evolutionary one, but that is no part of the meaning of the functional statement. Someone who says 'The function of the grass's movement is to get sunlight' might think that the relevant explanation is theological: God implanted the requisite mechanism in grass because He wanted it to get sunlight. Or he might have some other sort of explanation in mind; or, indeed, he may have no opinion about the explanation except that there is one.

This account of functional statements has the merit of covering also statements about the functions of parts and features of artefacts. 'The function of the fan is to cool the engine' means, roughly, that (a) the fan does cool the engine, and (b) that is why the fan is there; and this time

---

[30] This view of functional statements is due to Larry Wright, 'A Comment on Ruse's Analysis of Function Statements', *Philosophy of Science*, vol. 39 (1972).

the 'why' is backed by an explanation involving the purposes of the manufacturers. It can also be made to cover statements about the functions of members of a society, organization, team etc.; though there may be factors here which cannot be applied to artefacts and parts of organisms, for a person's 'function' may be definable partly in terms of what he is told to do or paid for doing or the like.

No doubt the account needs further refining, to deal with the difference between 'the function' and 'a function'. Also, one does not want to assign a function to a part of an organism or member of a team on the strength of a role which it shares with every other part of the organism or member of the team, even if its playing that role does help to explain its presence.[31] But the details are unimportant if the general direction is right.

(3) Donald Davidson has argued for what he calls 'the autonomy of the mental', meaning that there is no general, systematic way of expressing mental facts in a physicalistic vocabulary, although he thinks that each mental event is a physical event. One of his arguments for this uses Quine's thesis about the indeterminacy of translation (see §78 below) in a manner which I find unconvincing.[32] Another reason for it involves Davidson's doctrine of the 'anomalous character of the mental' – meaning not just that there are no physicalistic laws of the mind but that there are no laws of the mind. He says: 'Beliefs and desires issue in behaviour only as modified and mediated by further beliefs and desires, attitudes and attendings, without limit. Clearly this holism of the mental realm is a clue both to the autonomy and to the anomalous character of the mental.'[33] I cannot see any warrant for the phrase 'without limit', and this makes me doubt Davidson's thesis about the anomalousness of the mental, and also doubt whether he has argued convincingly for the autonomy of the mental.

If one thinks (as I am inclined to) that the mental realm is not lawless, but is autonomous, its autonomy may be expressed by saying that *the laws of the mental realm are not systematically reducible to those of the physical realm.* And one can argue for this in a manner which is perhaps stronger and deeper than Davidson's arguments for his version of the

[31] Something like that is needed to neutralize a counter-example in Peter Achinstein's instructive review of Ruse's *The Philosophy of Biology*, in *The Canadian Journal of Philosophy*, vol. 4 (1975).

[32] Davidson (1970), pp. 97–8.

[33] *Ibid.*, p. 92; see also p. 98, and Donald Davidson, 'The Material Mind', in P. Suppes *et al.* (eds.), *Logic, Methodology and Philosophy of Science IV* (Amsterdam, 1973), pp. 717–22.

autonomy thesis. I introduce this matter here because the argument I have in mind rests on the premisses that *teleogical laws cannot be systematically reduced to mechanistic ones.*

I am assuming that Davidson reasonably thinks of physicalistic laws as all being mechanistic, that is, as having antecedents which use only intrinsic predicates and never instrumental ones. And I adduce the discussion in §15 above as some evidence that whatever is mental must be teleological, in the sense that any system of mentalistic concepts must ultimately rest on teleological notions.[34] If that is right, then any theory of the mental realm must be based upon and structured around teleological laws; by my argument of §§21–2 these laws are fully legitimate only if they cannot be systematically replaced by mechanistic ones; and so, *a fortiori*, no legitimate theory of the mental realm can be captured in a mechanistic or, therefore, in a physicalistic theory.

In a nutshell: mentalistic→teleological (by §15 above); teleological→ non-mechanistic (by §§21–2 above); but also non-mechanistic→non-physicalistic (by common assumption about the actual content of physics); therefore mentalist→non-physicalistic.

Davidson's challenging views in the philosophy of mind deserve more attention than this, of course. I have merely sought to suggest how one of his doctrines might be strengthened by input from the theory of teleological explanation.

[34] I do not assert, conversely, that whatever is teleological must be mental; for that is true only on intolerably weak accounts of mentality. See Section II of Ausonio Marras, 'Introduction', *Intentionality, Mind, and Language* (Urbana, Ill., 1972). My argument assumes 'All physical laws are mechanistic' as something which is true and generally accepted, but not as in any degree conceptually necessary.

BELIEF AND INTENTION: FORM

§24. Introducing intention and belief

I have presented a minimal account of teleological explanation, focussing on behaviour which can be explained through laws of the form

$(x)(f)((Rx$ & x registers that f/Gx & f-G is most preferred by $x)$
$\rightarrow fx)$.

That omits subjective probabilities, because they are not essential to teleological explanation as such. Perhaps there could be cases which did not involve preferences, or did not need the concept of registration; but they would be so marginal and peculiar that a paradigm of basic teleology can safely exclude them.

Now we come to a teleological concept which I have not yet discussed, namely that of *intention*. In §11 above I praised Taylor's treatment for showing us how to identify a genus of teleologically explicable behaviour and then to mark off intentional behaviour as a species within it. Taylor himself, though, represents them as two species with no overlap, one involving laws of the form

(1) $(x)(f)((Rx$ & $f/Gx) \rightarrow fx)$

and the other involving laws of the form

(2) $(x)(f)((Rx$ & x believes that $f/Gx) \rightarrow fx)$.

Like many other philosophers, I agree that intentional behaviour is essentially behaviour which is explained by what the agent thinks he must do to achieve some goal. For lower-level teleology, however, (1) is inadequate. It omits course-rankings, but never mind that. My main complaint against (1) is that as well as (rightly) saying nothing about what the agent thinks, it (wrongly) says nothing about any epistemic state of the agent, i.e. about what propositions are registered upon him. Taylor sees the move to intentions as a move from lower to higher; I see it as a move from general to special. In this chapter I shall argue that belief is a species of registration, that intentional behaviour is a species of teleologically explicable behaviour, and that the two species coincide just as the two genera do.

That 'intend' and 'believe' are applicable in the same behavioural areas is confirmed by how they are used by literate speakers of English; and many philosophers agree that intention and belief are conceptually inter-linked. But there is nothing like a consensus, among philosophers or others, about *what* the behavioural area is in which 'intend' and 'believe' are both at home; and so my view about this may be controversial. I shall not defend it as supported by 'ordinary language', for on this matter ordinary language speaks with an uncertain voice. My defence will be that my account withstands attack better than its two chief rivals.

(1) Some people use '*x* thinks that *P*' more generously than my account permits. I object that they cannot explain why they would deny that a westward-oozing amoeba thinks there is acid to the east of it. On my account there is a continuum between organisms which can think that *P* and ones which cannot; but I can explain what the continuum is, and why I draw the line well above the amoeba.

(2) Others prefer to use '*x* thinks that *P*' less generously than I do, because they think that beliefs require language. I can find no cogent arguments for their view (see §9 above). It might be argued, negatively, that unless we use language-possession to delimit the cases where *x* can think that *P*, we cannot delimit them at all; but I shall show that we can. Of course no theory can fit everyone's usage, but mine fits one way of using 'believe' which is prevalent enough in polite circles.

Even if some other account of belief and intention were viable, I would still pursue my own, *stipulating* that in my work 'believe' and 'intend' mean what my theory says they do. For I really care not about those two words but about the conceptual structures which I associate with them.

Through the next three sections I shall defend a view about the conditions under which registrations count as beliefs. Then in §§28–9 I shall turn to the concept of intention. But I do not suggest, and indeed I deny, that one could become entitled to credit a creature with beliefs before being entitled to credit it with intentions. Like the general notions of registration and goal, the more special notions of belief and intention stand or fall together.

To move from the genus registration to the species belief, I need the help of the concept of educability, and perhaps also of that of inquisitiveness. I give these a section each.

§25. Educability

Back in §§15–16 I assumed that we could establish durable truths to the effect that whenever animal a is in an environment of physical kind K it registers that P – where P might be an instrumental proposition or some part of a's basis for registering such a proposition. (Similarly with a's registering$_i$ that P, in §20, but I shall keep things simple by ignoring subjective probabilities.) This was to assume that a is frozen in its epistemic relationship to the physical world. That assumption could be false because a changed in respect of its fundamental sensory capacities, say by becoming red–green colour-blind or by acquiring a sense of smell. But my concern is with a different way in which the assumption might be false, namely the occurrence of changes in how a *bases* its various registrations – that is, changes in the patterns which associate some of its registrations with others. If for a while a registers P whenever it registers that its environment is of kind K, and then later it does not register P in those circumstances because it has learned better, then a manifests *educability*. I must now replace 'learned better' by something respectable.

Suppose that a registers that F/Ga *whenever* it registers that it is an environment of one of the kinds $K_1, \ldots, K_n$. For example, suppose that a registers that it is digging/eating whenever it sees newly dug earth, or smells but does not see meat, or hears rabbits moving in their burrow. These bases for registering that F/Ga could lead to error, for a may encounter environments of kind K_n where F/Ga is manifestly false. For example, a sometimes smells but does not see meat, digs, and does not find food. For a while a will still dig in K_n environments; but the more educable it is, the sooner it will stop doing so. If it is educable, it can be *educated out of* using an environment's being K_n as a basis for registering that F/Ga – perhaps dropping K_n altogether, or perhaps merely replacing it by something more specific.

Conversely, suppose that a registers that F/Ga *only when* it registers that it is in an environment of one of the kinds $K_1, \ldots, K_n$. Those bases for registering that F/Ga could prove unsatisfactory because they turned out to lack scope; for a may encounter environments which are of kind K_{n+1}, not of any of the kinds $K_1, \ldots, K_n$, where it becomes evident that it was the case that F/Ga. For example, on several occasions a sees a shovel sticking into the ground and soon thereafter sees edible meat being dug up from right under where the shovel was. If a is educable, it will come to be disposed to dig when it sees a shovel etc. – that is, it will be *educated into* using its environment's being K_{n+1} as a basis for registering that F/Ga.

Educability is concerned only with the links through which some registrations are causally based on others. In a situation where a registers that a certain dark patch is a shadow, on that basis registers that there is a seal on the rock, and on that basis registers that a is climbing/eating, there are two links which might be changed by education. For a could learn that the presence of such dark patches does not guarantee the presence of a seal, or that seals sometimes escape while their predators are climbing towards them.

In short, any registration for which a has a basis could be the focus of education, but registrations with no basis could not. Thus, for example, we might have grounds for saying that a registers that a is warm, and that this is not based upon any other registration. (It may be caused by a certain neural state of a, but that sort of item does not enter into our kind of epistemic theory, and so is not a matter of registration.) In that case that registration can owe nothing to the animal's education; but education may affect what a bases on its registering that it is warm.

Clearly, an animal may be educable also in respect of its probabilistic registrations$_i$ – for example learning from experience that in a K environment it is suitable to register$_n$ that P rather than registering$_m$ that P. Indeed, educability gives subjective probabilities an altogether healthier look; for it lets us connect an animal's subjective probabilities with facts about relative frequencies in its past experience.

An animal might be adept at picking up new sensory clues yet slow at dropping bad ones, or vice versa. But in real organisms the two go together, and I use 'educability' to cover the ability to relinquish and to acquire.

Although educability – or *intelligence*, as it is often called – can be indispensable to its possessor, many animal species manage with little of it. This could be because their environments remain steady, giving them no need to change their bases for registrations; but the explanation is sometimes more interesting than that. A species of relatively unintelligent animals may undergo enough environmental change to give them a high pre-maturity death-rate. If this is not accompanied by a high rate of reproduction, the species will die out by simple arithmetic, as it were. But if the rates of reproduction and of infantile death are both high, then the species has a high rate of genetic turn-over; and that increases its chances of developing, through random variation and natural selection, behaviour-patterns which continue to suit its changing environment. These new forms of behaviour may be just as inflexible as the old, considered as facts about individual animals, but they reflect a sort of educability of the species as a whole. The theory of natural selection describes the substitute which species have for individual intelligence.

Intelligence itself presumably evolved, and there is no mystery about why it did so on such a scale, for intelligence obviously brings biological advantage. The advantage is that a species with intelligent members can adapt to relatively *rapid* changes in its circumstances. Education is the emergency rewiring of one's behavioural programme, and it lets one cope with changes for which evolutionary adaptation would be too slow. But the capacity for education, viz. intelligence, presumably arose like everything else in the biological realm through chance mutations and natural selection.

§26. Inquisitiveness

Inquisitiveness is a disposition to seek information; but that must be explained in terms of concepts that have been properly grounded in behaviour. I shall do that rather carefully, taking care not to base anything on anthropomorphic impressionism – e.g. attributing inquisitiveness on the grounds that the animal 'seems to be exploring' or 'has an air of wondering whether P'.

First, I need the concept of epistemic enrichment. This occurs when a comes to register as open to it some course with a combined probability-and-value measure which is higher than any course which a previously registered as open to it. This could happen through a's finding a more attractive course (value), a more practicable course (probability), or an overall more satisfactory course (probability-and-value). In each case a adds something to its epistemic store, i.e. to what it registers; and in each case the change is for the better, given a's rankings and/or subjective probabilities. So 'epistemic enrichment' is a fair phrase for it.

The materials I have already introduced enable us to know that a has been epistemically enriched during a given period. Also, we can know that at a given time a is F/enriched for a particular F. That is, we can know that its doing F is sufficient for its acquiring some epistemic enrichment,[1] e.g. that if it walks around that rock it will discover

[1] Not 'required for and sufficient for', because I have now halved the concept of an instrumental property and the force of the stroke notation which expresses it; see §20 above.

either prey or predator. Our evidence for this could be available to a as well; so a can register, or register$_i$, that it is F/enriched.

Furthermore, a's registering something like that might help to explain its behaviour. We might be entitled to say: 'At T, a registered that it was F/enriched, and the course F-enrichment was at T ranked top by a; and that is why a did F at $T+d$'. Or the explanation might be that a registered$_i$ that it was F/enriched for a suitably high value of i. Behaviour which is best explained in one of those ways, i.e. as engaged in with the goal of acquiring epistemic enrichment, is what I call *inquisitive* behaviour.

We can often identify some question towards which an animal's inquisitiveness is directed: 'It did F so as to register what was the case with respect to such and such a matter – what was behind the rock, or whether the animal behind the rock was a predator.' This will be important in my next chapter.

There could be an inquisitive animal which was not very educable. It would often act in order to get useful registrations, but would be rigid about what it registered upon what basis. Conversely, a highly intelligent animal might wholly lack inquisitiveness, being flexible in its handling of its epistemic resources but passive in relation to its epistemic opportunities. I guess that the two usually go together, but that is a contingent matter which has not affected my accounts of what intelligence and educability are. Similarly, although inquisitiveness looks better when linked with subjective probabilities, and the latter are helped by educability, I have not given any of these three concepts a role in my basic introduction of the other two.

§27. Two theses about belief

I shall offer two conjectures about the concept of belief: first, a strong thesis which I am not sure of, and then a weaker one which may well be right.

The strong thesis is that *a believes that P* is true if a registers that P and a is highly educable with regard to many kinds of propositions which do not exclude any important kind to which P belongs.[2] On this account, a registration-that-P counts as a belief if the animal is in a general way educable, and its educability is not systematically walled off from P.

[2] My only source for this account of belief is Bennett (1964), where it is mishandled in ways I shall correct in chapter 4 below.

That allows that *a* might for some special reason not be educable with respect to *P*. *A fortiori*, it allows that *a*'s registration that *P* did not actually arise from education. 'The bear thinks that there is a seal nearby' – this implies nothing about how the bear came to think this; but it does imply something about the bear's disposition to revise its set of bases for registering such things as the proximity of seals. So this account lets us say 'The bear thinks there is a seal nearby' even when it has the seal in plain view. For if the bear sees the seal, then it registers that the seal is nearby; and if it is also educ*able* about the proximity of seals, then according to my strong thesis it thinks that there is a seal nearby.

'If the bear has the seal in plain view, one would not ordinarily say that it *thinks* there is a seal on the rock, but rather that it sees or knows or is aware that there is a seal on the rock.' Agreed; but many things that would not ordinarily be said are still true. One would not ordinarily describe a mountain as 'bigger than a thimble' or as 'harder to carry than a billiard-ball', but these descriptions fit it none the less. As for the difference between 'believes that', 'knows that', 'sees that', 'is aware that' and so on: my present inquiry stands to gain nothing from attending to them, and so I lump all those expressions together under 'believe' and the more humdrum 'think'. In the same spirit, I shall later be careful not to distinguish acting *with an intention* from acting *intentionally* or *intending to achieve something*. Also, I shall casually use 'want', 'desire' etc., for occasional relief from 'intention' etc. This will presumably trample on several nuances; but where '*x* intended to achieve G' is correct, '*x* wanted (or desired) to achieve G' cannot be *very* wrong.

According to my strong thesis, belief shades off smoothly into mere registration. That seems satisfactory. It suggests that when people differ about what sorts of animals can 'think that *P*', they merely exhibit preferences for introducing 'thinks that' at different points on the scale. I suggest that the disagreement seems to have that sort of structure.

What can I say directly in defence of my strong thesis about belief? Well, we have an animal *a* whose behaviour can be teleologically explained only by reference to a certain proposition's being registered on *a*; and this mode of registration is such that what is registered on *a* (i) depends upon *a*'s present perceptions, (ii) may depend also upon its past experience, (iii) can be altered by its future experience, and (iv) is manifested in behaviour which is usually suitable to *a*'s goals, though it can be unsuitable because *a* has bad luck or because it has not properly adjusted its registrations in the light of its past experience. Doesn't that sound like a description of *belief*?

If the reader says 'No', perhaps that is because he thinks that beliefs are states[3] whereas registrations are events or episodes. That would be a mistake about registrations. On my account, for *a* to register something is for *a* to fall under a law of a certain kind, and thus to be in a certain state. For good reasons I have focussed on registrations of propositions about fast-changing features of the environment; and so I have emphasized the sorts of registrations which come and go quickly. But they have been short-lived states – as though I were discussing how something can be rapidly changed from being brittle to being ductile and then to being elastic, or from being spherical to being cubic and then to being ovoid.

My weaker thesis about belief says that *a believes that P* is true if *a* registers that *P*, and *a* is highly educable about many kinds of propositions including ones like *P*, and *a* is inquisitive with regard to many kinds of propositions which do not exclude any important kind to which *P* belongs. Perhaps *a*'s registering that *P* did not result from inquiry, but *a* must be generally disposed to inquire into classes of matters which do not systematically exclude *P*.

The general idea, then, is that belief is registration as it occurs in animals which are extensively and intensively educable and inquisitive. I think that registration plus educability may be sufficient for belief; but the claim that registration plus educability plus inquisitiveness is sufficient for belief, though weaker, will still serve my purposes. For that triple condition is still general enough to obtain in a large and basic class of beliefs. I chiefly aim to illustrate an aspect – the linguistic aspect – of the human condition, and humans are highly educable and inquisitive right across their epistemic range. It would also be relevant to some investigations, though not my present one, to note the high degree of educability and inquisitiveness of the apes.

My main defence of the weak thesis is that it looks right. If we were actually studying animals which we found to be highly educable and inquisitive, I am sure we would unhesitatingly credit them with 'thinking that *P*' for any *P* which we knew them to register. Even adherents of the view that belief requires language would talk like that unless they were careful not to.

---

[3] That would include the view that beliefs are dispositions. See Armstrong (1973), pp. 16–21.

§28. Introducing intention

In conformity with the common view that intention and belief belong together, I propose that we take

a did F intending thereby to become G

as always being grounded in the corresponding statement of the form

In doing F, a was conforming to a law of the form:

$(f)((Ra \ \& \ a \text{ thinks that } f/Ga) \rightarrow fa).$

That is, behaviour for which a has an intention is behaviour which is best teleologically explained by reference to a's believing that the behaviour will produce a certain upshot. The temporal details can be supplied by the reader.

The above formula, through its use of the form 'f/Ga', restricts the agent's intentions to upshots involving himself. It is time to remove that restriction. In showing how a can register that F/Ga, I have laid a basis for saying that a registers that its doing F is sufficient for the subsequent truth of P, for values of P which are not about a. And the shift from registration to belief was perfectly general. So we can make sense of saying that a can believe that Fa/P – meaning that a's doing F would bring about the truth of P – even where P is not about a. Accordingly, we can handle statements of the general form 'a did F intending thereby to bring it about that P'.

Another broadening of the theory is also needed. The beliefs of humans heavily involve subjective probabilities, and I want my account to capture this aspect of the human condition. So I need the notion of what an agent thinks$_i$ for various values of i. There is no difficulty about that: one simply applies my earlier treatment of belief to the enriched kind of registration which involves subjective probabilities and value-measures. It is then easy to re-phrase the account of intention so that what an agent intends depends upon what he thinks$_i$ rather than merely upon what he thinks. Let us assume that the whole account is now before us in that broadened form.

Now, if a did F intending to achieve P, then a must have thought$_n$ that doing F would bring about P, for a value of n high enough to make F-P a's best course; but n could still be close to zero. For example, if a is hungry enough, he may dig because he thinks there is a tiny chance that digging might uncover food. In that case one would ordinarily say that a digs *in the hope*, rather than *with the intention*, of finding food; and that fact about colloquial English seems to require a lower limit on the n in 'a thinks$_n$ that doing F will achieve P'.

I shall not trouble myself with it. A basic theory of intention does not need to represent shades of meaning like that between 'with the intention of' and 'in the hope of'. When I base 'what a means by . . .' on 'what a intends by . . .', it will not matter much whether we set that lower limit on n. If we do not, we must count as 'meaning' some cases where one would ordinarily say that the speaker hopes, rather than intends, to communicate;[4] but since these cases will be structurally just like examples of 'meaning', more strictly so-called, it will do no harm to admit them. On the other hand, the hope-to-communicate cases are peculiar, and our confident intuitions would not be violated if those cases were excluded from the province of meaning. So dispose of them as you will.

I shall assume, however, that whatever beliefs$_i$ a's intentions are based upon are themselves supported by a's past experience. They must not strongly conflict with it, because a is fairly highly educable: if he were not, his registrations would not be *beliefs* at all. Sometimes, perhaps, a's belief$_i$ that by doing F he will achieve P is neither in conflict with his experience nor supported by it – the belief might be drug-induced, innate, miraculous, speculative, impudent, or whatever. But such beliefs must be in the minority. If an educable animal is to believe *in vacuo* (as it were) that his doing F will achieve P, this must be the first time he has confronted this question or any which bears directly on it. Such 'first times' must occur; but we are studying long stretches of a's behaviour, and presumably most of our data will not concern 'first times'. Also – a deeper point – our best way of predicting a's beliefs is through their sources in epistemic input into a; so any belief of his which is not traceable to such input may be unpredictable in advance of the behaviour which manifests it, in which case it cannot help to explain the behaviour. Perhaps on rare occasions we can predict a belief on some other basis – e.g. because a has taken a certain drug – but such occasions must be in the minority. If there were a kind of behaviour-modifying state which a often acquired through taking drugs, and seldom as a result of sensory intake, that kind of state could not properly be called 'belief'.

[4] Armstrong would say that the speaker has the 'objective' of communicating; and he reserves 'intend' for the case where the agent 'believes that the thing aimed at is within his power'. But he ties 'meaning' to the 'objective' of communicating, thus including the 'hopes to communicate' cases in the province of meaning. Armstrong (1971), p. 432 n.

So Grice's theory of meaning is not seriously threatened by an alleged counter-example of Searle's in which someone utters a certain German sentence to a non-German-understanding audience, in the *groundless hope* that they will think it means that the speaker is a German officer.[5] Something similar applies to Ziff's attempt to embarrass Grice's theory by appealing to what a madman thinks he can communicate by certain utterances.[6]

§29. Defending the intention doctrine

Acting intentionally, on my account, is acting under the guidance of the thought of what will ensue if one acts (and, perhaps, what will ensue if one does not). Objection: 'Your analysis of intention does not involve the concept of thought, but only a purely behavioural concept of *so-called* thought or belief.' If you like, then, take it that I am dealing not with belief (which is a kind of thought), but rather with belief* (which is a kind of thought*), these starred concepts being the nearest purely behavioural relatives of the unstarred ones. The rest of my account holds up on that basis, and I can get on with my work without being side-tracked into arguments about dualism, philosophical behaviourism, and so on.

The given analysis of intention might be criticized as providing only for intentions which are in character, or explicable in terms of the agent's durable goals. My answer to that is implied at the end of §16 above: the account admittedly relies upon the laws which explain the agent's behaviour, but a given law may be applicable for just a few seconds to a given individual. It will be hard in such a case to discover the law; and it is a merit in my account that it brings that difficulty to the surface.

Another objection: 'Intentional actions often arise from decisions which are preceded by indecision and deliberation. Where does that appear in your analysis?' Nowhere; because deliberation is not essential to intention. There could be creatures to which the concepts of belief and intention were richly and helpfully applicable but which did not ever hesitate, deliberate, or the like. My analysis would be faulty if it resisted the addition of these activities, but it does not. A realistic

---

[5] See Searle, pp. 44–5; criticized by Grice (1969), pp. 160–6, by Armstrong (1971), pp. 440–1, and by Bennett (1973), p. 164.
[6] Paul Ziff, 'On H. P. Grice's Theory of Meaning', *Analysis*, vol. 28 (1967–8), p. 5; criticized by Dennis W. Stampe, 'Toward a Grammar of Meaning', *Philosophical Review*, vol. 77 (1968), pp. 173–4.

treatment of practical indecision, hesitation and deliberation mainly needs materials which my account contains: in the background, educability and inquisitiveness; and, temporarily set aside for ease of exposition, value measures and subjective probabilities. A theory with those four concepts at its disposal can easily provide for hesitation and deliberation.

My account of belief and intention yields a theorem which is independently plausible, namely that intentional behaviour is *more* teleological than any kind of non-intentional behaviour. I argued in §21 that behaviour which could be explained mechanistically might also admit of legitimate teleological explanation, and I defended a view about the source of that legitimacy. That view, I shall now argue, implies that the legitimacy is greatest if the behaviour is intentional.[7]

The point was that a teleological explanation is legitimate in proportion as it cannot be modelled over into a mechanistic explanation which covers the same range of facts: the behaviour of Stable Lake should not be explained teleologically because there is a single mechanistic explanation covering that very same behaviour. The two explanations cover the same ground because their crucial predicates are co-extensive: the lake has the instrumental property 'changes-evaporation-rate/saves-the-wildlife' when and only when it has the intrinsic property 'changes surface-area'. Quite generally, a teleological explanation of a's behaviour is safe from mechanistic challenge if it involves something of the form 'a registers that . . .' which cannot be simply replaced by 'a is in a state of kind K' where K is definable in purely intrinsic terms. Whenever a does register that Fa/P for some F, its state on that occasion will be exhaustively describable in intrinsic terms; and those are the terms which would appear in a mechanistic explanation of the behaviour. But there could be many different intrinsic kinds of state which had in common only that each of them constitutes a's registering that Fa/P for some F. If that were so, then the range of behaviour which can be teleologically explained in terms of P-seeking must be explained mechanistically in various different ways, corresponding to the different intrinsic kinds of state which are involved.

That does not require that a be educable. For a might be inflexibly wired up to behave in ways which conform to the law:

---

[7] I use 'intentional' in the sense of 'pertaining to [or explained by] intentions', not in the technical sense in which 'a registers that P' is 'intentional' simply because it does not entail either that P or that $\sim P$.

$$(f)(Ra \ \& \ a \text{ registers that } fa/P \ \rightarrow \ fa),$$

where a mechanistic account of the same behaviour would have to say that a does a P-producing thing when it is in a state of intrinsic kind K_1 or K_2 or ... or K_n. That gives us a choice between a unitary teleological explanation and an n-part mechanistic one, and the former choice is legitimate in proportion as n is large. (In fact, 'does a P-producing thing' should also be unpacked into a disjunction of kinds of movement, but let that go.) Even if a is ineducable, n could be large.

If a is educable and 'educated', however, the value of n goes soaring. For then the conditions under which a does P-producing things, though still covered by the single characterization 'a registers that fa/P for some f', are not covered by any permanent list, however long, of intrinsic kinds of sensory state. For K states may for a while lead a to register that fa/P and then cease to do so; or not lead a to register that fa/P and then come to do so; or join a's set of bases for registering that fa/P, then leave it, then rejoin it. Any of these might occur through a's experiencing changes in the world or coming to notice features which were there all along. In any of these eventualities, should K be included in or excluded from the list of intrinsic kinds of sensory state which lead to a's doing a P-producing thing? There is no answer, so there cannot be such a list. A mechanistic account now needs a list of lists of intrinsic kinds of sensory state which lead a to do P-producing things – listing the kinds which were appropriate last week, then those which are appropriate today, then those which will be appropriate until next Thursday, and so on.

Alternatively, one might seek a mechanistic account of the process of 'education', generating claims of the form: 'a did, does or will do a P-producing thing on any occasion when it is in a state of kind k for any k which at that time satisfies condition C', where C is a mechanistic equivalent of 'k is a kind of sensory state which a has learned to be a good basis for registering that it is f/P for some f'. Perhaps this is possible; but I suspect that C would be so complex as to make this approach little better than the 'list of lists' referred to above.

Yet we can easily say in teleological terms when a did, does or will do P-producing things, namely when it did, does or will register that Fa/P for some value of f.

The upshot is not that intentional behaviour cannot be explained mechanistically. For all my argument has shown to the contrary, such explanations might be easy to find. What my argument does conclude is that the range of facts which are covered by a single intentional explanation, of the form 'It did those things because in each case it intended to achieve P', could be accounted for mechanistically only through an enormous number of partly different explanations.

That argument assumes that if an item of behaviour is somehow based on a's being in a sensory state of intrinsic kind K, a mechanistic explanation of the behaviour must refer to K or to something law-connected with it; so that if one item is based on K_i and another on K_j, where $i \neq j$, then their mechanistic explanations must differ. That assumption is needed for the move from (1) the changing list of intrinsic kinds of sensory state which constitute a's registering that fa/P to (2) the impossibility of a unitary mechanistic explanation of all of a's P-seeking behaviour. The assumption seems fairly safe. It merely denies that any single mechanism could fully explain all of a's P-seeking behaviour in such a way as to render irrelevant the differences in the kinds of sensory state that a is in when seeking P.

Finally, what *are* intentions? I decline to answer that question. I need truth-conditions for sentences of the form 'He did F intending to bring it about that P', and I have tried to give those in my theory. But I do not need – and so shall not labour to discover – application-conditions for the substantive 'intention'. This is an incompleteness in my account, but not a superficiality; for the substantive must be based upon the sentence, not vice versa. To reverse the order, one must (i) explain what an intention is, (ii) explain what it is to do something with some-thing, and then (iii) *derive* an account of doing something with an intention – as distinct from doing it with a knife, with great energy, with a fiendish grin, with regret, and so on. That order of explanation seems to be impossible.

4

BELIEF AND INTENTION: CONTENT

§30. Beliefs about the environment

When I shall speak of non-linguistic beliefs and intentions, I mean ones which can be properly attributed to creatures which do not have language and are not being compared with creatures which do have language. Thus, if we say that a languageless deaf-mute thinks that *P*, our only reason being that he behaves just like people who say that *P*, we are not attributing a non-linguistic belief.

This chapter will investigate what main species of non-linguistic beliefs and intentions there can be. The foregoing general theory of beliefs and intentions will be used in answering this, but the answers will not come through routine mechanical applications of the general theory.

The question is important, because some answers to it would kill my programme of founding a theory of language on an account of meaning-intention-belief which does not itself presuppose that the subjects have language. The programme must not be seen as bolder than it is. It does not imply that for any value of *P* if a language could express *P* then a languageless creature could believe that *P*. On the contrary, I can comfortably admit that languageless creatures could not believe that $e = mc^2$, or that if it rains less than twice a week for the next month the corn harvest will be almost the best for three or four years. I want to start with propositions which can be non-linguistically believed, show how these can be meant, on that basis develop a repertoire of conventionally meaningful utterance-types, then show how these can have significant structure, enabling new ones to be constructed and their meanings calculated; and *then* I can exploit those structures to build sentences expressing new sorts of propositions. Some of these may be beyond the reach of languageless creatures, yet they will all be expressed by a language which is firmly grounded on the behaviour and beliefs of such creatures.

So I need not introduce at the present level every *P* which I shall want to be expressible in the final language. But I need a good stock of propositions which can be non-linguistically believed, and it is important to see what that stock can contain. I want to get clear about the scope of non-linguistic beliefs, also, because in my book *Rationality* I published a thesis about this which I now see to be wrong and which I shall refute in §33 below.

I shall discuss non-linguistic beliefs for seven sections, taking up non-linguistic intentions in §37. The final section of this chapter will discuss one way of interlocking the two concepts.

Any account of what non-linguistic beliefs a can have must start with what propositions he can register. I have done my best to show how we can be entitled to credit him with registering propositions of the form Fa/P and, *associated* with those, propositions about perceptible features of his environment – that there is water in front of him, that there is a predator on the rock, that there is food under the newly dug soil, and so on. These associations between instrumental and other propositions are the heart of the whole theory of registration: they are what let us test one bit of epistemic theory against a's behaviour in pursuit of different goals.

I take it that there is no difficulty about non-linguistic beliefs concerning a's instrumental properties and concerning perceptible features of his environment.

Furthermore, a can be discovered to have *singular conditional* beliefs about his environment, that is beliefs to the effect that a certain kind of event will occur if (or only if) another kind of event occurs. From the outset, we have had registrations of biconditionals of the form F/Ga, meaning that Fa is required for and sufficient for Ga. I then weakened F/Ga to mean only the one-way conditional that Fa suffices for Ga; and I could also have allowed a to register the converse conditional that Fa is required for Ga. Later I moved to the broader form Fa/P, meaning that Fa suffices for the subsequent truth of something which may not be about a at all; and here again the converse form would have given no more difficulty. All I need now is a's registering that the truth of Q is required and/or sufficient for the truth of P, where neither Q nor P need be about a. It seems clear that this can easily be accounted for on the basis of materials already introduced. For instance, we might have evidence that a registers that he is waiting/eating partly because he registers that *if everything is quiet for a while the prey will move within reach*. This is the registration of a singular conditional which does not count as an 'instrumental' by any of the criteria I have successively given. But it seems to be as legitimate – as capable of being integrated into the theory and tested by the evidence – as any of its instrumental forebears. To credit *a* with registering a singular conditional of this new kind, where neither the antecedent nor the consequent is about *a*, we need evidence that what *a* registers is not merely that if *he* is quiet the prey will approach; but with a little ingenuity one can describe a case which supports '. . . if everything is quiet . . .' etc.

And if there can be singular conditional registrations, there can be singular conditional beliefs.

These singular conditionals need not have anything general backing them up. When *a* thinks that if he shakes the tree the bear-cub will fall out of it, he need not support this by a general belief about what results from any shaking of any tree of a certain kind. One result of insisting that where there is a conditional belief there must be a general one underlying it is that the notion of languageless general belief becomes boringly weak. For I contend that conditional beliefs, and especially instrumental ones, are the cornerstones of any possible behavioural evidence for *a*'s beliefs; so that if they automatically carry general beliefs with them we must accept that if *a*'s behaviour manifests any beliefs at all then it manifests general ones. I shall contend in §§32–3 below that if we are more demanding than this, interesting questions arise and can be answered.

§31. Beyond the here and now: epistemic input

Can *a* have beliefs about something lying beyond his present environment? All the beliefs discussed so far have concerned particular items which are present to *a* at the time of the belief; so his repertoire might be extended by adding beliefs whose content is not particular but general, and/or by adding beliefs about matters which are not present but absent.

Indeed, these extensions could have occurred back at the level of registrations which were not beliefs. It is an expository accident, not a conceptual necessity, that most of the 'mere registrations' I have discussed were of propositions about *a*'s present environment. Before he reached the level of belief, we could still have found ways – like those I shall display in §§31–3 – of crediting him with registering propositions about absent matters.

There are three sorts of absence. An absent matter may be temporally removed, in either the past or the future, or it may be spatially absent – i.e. lying beyond the present range of the believer's senses. I shall deal first with beliefs about the past ('past beliefs', for short) and general beliefs. The future and the spatially absent will be briefly touched upon at the end of the section.

From the outset, the concept of registration – and thus that of belief – has had two anchors. Each claim about what a registers has (1) been grounded in epistemic theory which enabled us to predict what a would register on the basis of certain facts about its environments, and has (2) helped us to predict and explain a's behaviour. (See §§15–16 above.) The epistemic theory (1) has involved sensory input into a from its environments, and the behavioural output (2) was easily found because a's behaviour is always primarily an operation on the present environment. But if a is to have beliefs about any other topics, we must find (1) epistemic input and (2) behavioural output which are appropriate to them. These two must stand or fall together, but I introduce them *seriatim*.

The epistemic theory for a's past beliefs must be a theory of memory. This will state the general principles governing a's recall of its past perceptions and thus of states of its past environments. (Some people credit animals with 'memory' merely because they are causally affected by their past experiences, but I confine 'memory' to the capacity for having beliefs about the past. The difference between these will be discussed in §32 below.) If the concept of a's memory is to be a working one, a must sometimes forget, and our theory of a's memory should tell us what a will remember and for how long. Presumably a's chance of remembering a past event will depend upon how long ago he experienced it, and perhaps also upon internal features of the experience – its degree of vividness, its having a visual component, its involving at least two sense-modalities, or whatever. It would be an empirical matter to discover which of these features of an experience increased its memorableness for a.

I am assuming that memory is an essentially intra-mural affair. That is, a remembers a past event by being in an epistemic state which is causally derived from his earlier perception of the event.[1] Memory stretches back to a past inner state, from which the senses stretch to the outer circumstance. Thus our total theory of memory has our sensory theory as a working part.

[1] C. B. Martin and M. Deutscher, 'Remembering', *Philosophical Review*, vol. 75 (1966).

This is all up in the air, though, unless we can find (2) behaviour-explaining work for the attribution of past beliefs to do. Without that, we cannot test our hypotheses about the workings of a's memory. That will come in my next section.

Now for the epistemic input into general beliefs. This requires some theory about a's propensities for generalizing (i.e. forming general beliefs; I do not here use the word, as I shall in §49 below, in its normal sense in which an animal 'generalizes' if it learns something about one stimulus and then automatically applies it to further ones). We shall no doubt eventually be able to predict that a will have certain general beliefs on the basis of our knowledge that he has others; but that cannot be the basic story, so I set it aside. So we are left only with facts about particular events and circumstances which a has experienced. We must predict that a will believe that *All Fs are G* on the basis of some facts about Fs which he has experienced.

The needed theory might be a simple adaptation of our theory of a's memory; for we might find that (for any F and G) a can be relied on to think that *All Fs are G* just so long as he remembers many Fs which were G and none which were not G. But we might instead find that more than the theory of memory was required: for instance, it might turn out that if the experience of an F involves the same sense-modality as that of a G – both auditory, or both visual, etc. – then a is much more likely to believe that *All Fs are G* than if different sense-modalities were involved. Facts like that could be sheerly additional to anything in the theory of a's memory; for a feature of F–G pairs which reduces the likelihood of a's coming to think that *All Fs are G* might be irrelevant to his chances of remembering any particular F–G pair. Alternatively, the theory about a's generalizing propensities might differ from the theory of his memory not merely by addition but also by subtraction; for there might be circumstances in which a will predictably believe that *All Fs are G* although he has forgotten ever having encountered an F which was G. I have no plausible examples of features of F–G pairs which would make an animal likely to remember them but not to generalize over them, or likely to generalize over them but not to remember them. But the abstract point still stands: general beliefs need their own kind of epistemic input, and if that turns out to be just what memory also needs, that is a contingent fact.

The question of what sorts of experience-pairs are generalizable by a must be settled by testing conjectures against a's behaviour. And that is a reminder that our (1) theory about epistemic input into a's general beliefs cannot be tested unless it collaborates with (2) a theory of behavioural output which displays the sorts of behaviour which are to be explained by a's having general beliefs. Just what sorts of behaviour those are will be my topic in the next two sections.

Beliefs about what is spatially absent – beliefs about other places – are epistemic parasites. In the only sturdy sense I can find for the phrase, 'the environment which a is in at T' covers the whole area which a can know about just through the exercise of his senses at T; so it is not logically possible that a should have some special sense which enables him to perceive the present state of an environment other than the one he is in (as distinct from acquiring a new sense which enlarges the environment he is in). I do not deny that a can have a belief about another environment which is based *partly* upon the present deliverances of his senses: if a finds the village burned down and blood on the ground, this may lead him to believe that his wife and children are now captives in the next valley; and it would be absurd to say that this pulls the next valley into the ambit of his 'present environment'. What stops it from being pulled in is the fact that the belief about 'blood and ashes here' relates to the one about 'captives in the next valley' through the mediation of general beliefs to effect that blood and ashes always betoken raids, that raiding parties always take captives, and so on; so that in this case the belief about the 'other environment' is not based just upon present sensory evidence but also upon general beliefs.

A belief about what is spatially absent might also be based, with the mediating help of general beliefs, upon past beliefs. For instance, a's reasons for thinking that his wife is now in the next valley might include his belief that a scream occurred about an hour ago.

In my next two sections I shall discuss the role of general beliefs in mediating between pairs of non-general beliefs, and that discussion will apply *mutatis mutandis* to the basing of a belief about another place on beliefs about the present environment or about the past. It would take too long to go into all that in detail, however; so from now on I shall leave beliefs about the spatially absent to take care of themselves.

Beliefs about the future can, like beliefs about what is spatially absent, be based upon beliefs about the present or past, mediated by general beliefs. Sometimes, indeed, it may be unclear whether a given belief of a's is primarily about the present state of another place (who is now in the next valley?) or about his own future (what will he find on reaching the next valley?). In so far as the epistemic input into beliefs about the future is like that into beliefs about other places, it will be implicitly covered by my subsequent discussion of the role of general beliefs as mediators; and I shall say no more about it than that.

However, it seems that we must allow that beliefs about the future are not always based upon other beliefs with the mediating help of general beliefs. Our whole theory about a, just because it is teleological, is oriented towards the future from the outset: as soon as it becomes a theory of belief at all it credits a with believing that he has certain instrumental properties, i.e. that if he does so-and-so the upshot *will* be such-and-such. Furthermore, if we can credit a with believing such future-pointing conditionals, we must also be able to credit him with believing future-pointing categoricals. For example, his thinking that he is climbing/eating may be inexplicable unless he thinks that the prey *will* fly to its nest.

If the latter belief is not based upon a bit of general theory – the prey will fly to its nest because (a) it is F, and (b) whenever a bird is F it flies to its nest – what is it based upon? A faculty of precognition? No, for the fact is that we cannot draw a really sharp line between beliefs about the present and beliefs about the short-term future: for instance, if a's belief that x is a predator has any real content, it must include some beliefs about how x *will* behave. For that reason, any theory which credits a with contentful beliefs about his present environment must credit him also with some beliefs about the short-term future, these being based upon the same epistemic input as goes into the beliefs about the present.

How can we distinguish future beliefs which are inextricably involved in present beliefs from future beliefs which are based upon present or past ones with the mediating help of general beliefs? I have, I am afraid, no systematic answer to this. That is one of my reasons for not going at length into the mediating role of general beliefs in cases where one of the terms of the mediating relation is a belief about the future.

The line I have taken on future beliefs might be resisted on the grounds that even in those very basic cases where the future belief seems to be immediately and inevitably involved in a present one, it may in fact be supported partly by a general belief. The trouble with that is that it results in an indiscriminately generous treatment of general beliefs, according to which they occur whenever beliefs of any kind occur. Similar points will arise over certain other matters which I now proceed to discuss.

§32. Beyond the here and now: behavioural output

How can a's non-linguistic behaviour manifest his past beliefs and his general beliefs? This can be answered in either of two ways, a demanding and an undemanding one.

The undemanding line on past beliefs says, roughly, that if a has any beliefs which result from some of his past experiences, then he also has beliefs about those experiences, or about the outer events to which they pertained. By this standard, past beliefs would inevitably be involved when an animal *recognizes* something, and would also have to be involved in the exercise of educability.

I prefer to be more demanding than this, as part of a general policy of being as grudging as possible in the making of mental attributions on behavioural evidence. If a dog's giving me a welcome because it recognizes me as its friend and master is to be explained in terms of its past beliefs, we must say that it thinks that I have been good to it in the past and also, presumably, that it believes something about the durability of human character. As against that, we can credit the dog with just one relevant belief, namely that I will be good to it in the immediate future, this being caused in the dog by some of its past experiences of me. No doubt past beliefs are also caused by past experience; but what I am denying is the converse claim that any belief which is caused by the past must be or involve a belief about the past. It seems to me clear that sometimes, as in the above example, the attribution of a past belief can be effectively challenged by a lower-level, more economical attribution in which the past is introduced only causally and not epistemically. That is why I prefer more demanding standards for what it is to count as a behavioural manifestation of a past belief.

Where general beliefs are in question, the undemanding line says that if a is disposed to think, of any F it encounters, that it is G, then a thinks that *All Fs are G*. This view has had support, for instance Braithwaite: 'Action appropriate to a belief in a general proposition does not present any special problems. "I am disposed to act appropriately to every P being Q" means that, whenever I am disposed to act appropriately to a thing's being P, I am disposed to act appropriately to its being Q.'[2] This clearly yields one defensible construal of attributions

[2] R. B. Braithwaite, 'The Nature of Believing' (1933), as reprinted in A. P. Griffiths (ed.),

of general beliefs, but a different and stronger construal is possible. The difference between the two is perhaps that between 'All *F*s are *G*' taken distributively and the same sentence taken collectively.[3] In our present context, the distributive construal has a sadly flattening effect. Any animal that has beliefs at all must have certain 'habits of singular belief' (to use Ramsey's phrase), and so must have general beliefs construed distributively. So general beliefs, thus construed, can be attributed as widely as can beliefs of any kind at all. As well as being an implausible view of the scope of occurrence of general beliefs, this is an unprofitable view. If we demand more, and ask for evidence that an animal believes that *All Fs are G* when this is taken collectively, the capacity for general beliefs becomes an intellectual possession which can be less widespread than the capacity for beliefs as such; and in exploring how far it does spread we encounter some interesting questions and instructive answers.

With neither past nor general beliefs have I been able to find any coherent way of saying, in advance of my analytic inquiry, just what the force is of the stronger construal, the 'more demanding' approach, which I shall be following. I can say only that I want a defensible notion of 'belief about the past' which amounts to more than merely that of 'belief which causally arises from past experiences', and one of 'general belief' which amounts to more than that of 'general disposition to acquire singular beliefs' or the like. That, unsatisfactory though it is, is strong enough to sustain some results.

Any non-linguistic manifestation of past beliefs must also manifest general beliefs. Non-linguistic behaviour is essentially a manipulation of a present environment, and the immediately relevant beliefs must be ones about the present. If an item of behaviour of this kind is also to show that the agent has a certain belief about the past, this must presumably be because the attribution of the past belief helps to explain the present one. But that requires that the two be somehow linked by the agent, and I do not see how they can be linked except through a general belief. In that argument I rely on my 'more demanding line'

Knowledge and Belief (Oxford, 1967), pp. 39–40. See also Armstrong (1973), pp. 89–93. Armstrong says he is 'following F. P. Ramsey', presumably referring to Ramsey's 'General Propositions and Causality', in *The Foundations of Mathematics* (London, 1931); but what Ramsey says (p. 240) is that a general belief 'consists in (a) A general enunciation and (b) A habit of singular belief'; and (a) makes a difference.

[3] See Lewis, pp. 64 ff., where the matter is handled in terms of Abelard's distinction between generality *in sensu diviso* and generality *in sensu composito*.

about past beliefs. For an animal which has no general beliefs may still manifest a present belief which is *caused* by some past experience which it has had; and if we undemandingly take that causal relation to justify attributing a past belief to the animal, we have a case of behaviour which manifests a past belief but not a general one. But I want a more strenuous notion of 'past belief' than that; and that seems to require behaviour which also manifests general beliefs.

For example, suppose that *a* chases a victim *v* up a tree, guards the foot of the tree for a while, and then climbs up after *v*. We could discover, in ways I have described, that *a* climbs the tree because he believes that *v* is in the tree. Can that belief be explained as arising from the belief that *v* was earlier in the tree? Only, I suggest, if *a* is also credited with the linking belief that *v*-like animals leave trees only by climbing down them (or that *v*-like animals never fly, or some such). As a matter of abstract logic, the past and present beliefs could be linked by the non-general conditional proposition that if *v* was in the tree then *v* is still in the tree; but I submit that a non-linguistic manifestation of *that* would have to manifest a general belief from which the non-general conditional followed.

In my book *Rationality* I also maintained conversely that behaviour which non-linguistically manifests general beliefs must also manifest past ones. Those two kinds of beliefs do indeed sometimes collaborate, as in the case last given: *a*'s climbing shows that he thinks that *v*-like animals never fly only if it also shows that he thinks that *v* was earlier in the tree. But still the thesis is not true as it stands. I now replace it by the weaker claim that *a* can non-linguistically manifest a general belief only through behaviour which also manifests a pair of other beliefs as well; but I do not now say that one of the pair must be a past one.

My argument for the weaker thesis is as follows. All the beliefs which are most immediately relevant to *a*'s non-linguistic behaviour must concern the present state of the particular environment he is in. If work is to be done by the attribution to him of any general beliefs, the latter must help to explain what *a* believes about his particular environment. But the only explanatory role they can have is in providing a link between *a*'s beliefs about his environment's present, on the one hand, and some other beliefs of *a*'s on the other. Anyway, if this is false, it should be easy to counter-instantiate.

If it is true, the question arises of what sorts of beliefs might be linked with the present through general beliefs. The answer is that *a*'s beliefs about his present environment might be explained, with the aid of a general belief, through some other belief about (a) his present environment, (b) the present state of some other environment, (c) the past, or (d) the future. Also, once we have introduced beliefs of kinds (b), (c) and (d) into the picture, they in turn may be based on yet other beliefs, again with the help of general beliefs; thus, general beliefs might help to base a past belief on a present one, a future belief on a past one, and so on.

Out of this plethora of possibilities, I select just one. The others could be discussed, but they are in various ways tricky, without apparently being notably illuminating. The one I choose to concentrate on is the (a)–(c) case, where a belief about the present is based upon one about the past, with the mediating help of a general belief. That was the locus of a central argument in my book *Rationality*; and although the conclusion was not widely accepted the argument was good enough to deserve rebuttal. I now proceed to rebut it.

§33. Separating past from general

The argument in question used the true premiss that any non-linguistic behaviour which manifests a belief about the past must also manifest a general belief. Its other premiss was the converse thesis that non-linguistic behaviour which manifests a general belief must also manifest one about the past. This, as I have already noted, is false. But the difficulty which it led to in *Rationality* is not solved, merely rendered more complex, if we replace the second premiss by the related truth that the manifestation of a general belief requires the manifestation of *some* other beliefs. So I shall pretend that both premisses of the original argument are true, i.e. that when we are looking for behavioural manifestations of general beliefs and past beliefs, neither can be found except in the presence of the other.

Nothing like that would be true if linguistic behaviour were taken into account, for that involves producing actions which map systematically onto true propositions, and someone can show that he thinks that P – for any P – by doing something which correlates with P in some accepted system of mapping. The same would hold for any mode of behaviour whose point was to correlate actions with propositions, even if it was not intended to communicate and therefore was not linguistic. But I cannot think of any motivation that there could be for such a mode of behaviour.[4] So I shall take it that the separate manifestation

4 See Strawson (1969), p. 185.

of past and general beliefs is the prerogative of, specifically, linguistic behaviour.

From that basic premiss, I inferred in *Rationality* that languageless creatures ought never to be credited with having general or past beliefs. The basic idea was that a creature which cannot manifest two sorts of belief separately cannot manifest them at all. Some of my argumentative moves were simply bad,[5] but my present concern is with a systematic error which underlay my whole line of thought.

For a clue to it, consider my demonstration in §15 above of how we can separate the concepts of registration and goal, even though they do all their explanatory work, and thus all their work, in collaboration with one another. The point was that one item of epistemic theory could be made to collaborate with different items of goal theory, and vice versa; thus we could get evidence to tell more heavily against one side of the total theory than against the other, and so each side could have a life of its own. Similarly with past and general beliefs: we should seek ways of combining one past belief with different general ones, and vice versa, so that recalcitrant behavioural evidence can bear with different weights on the two sorts of belief.

Here is how this can be achieved. Suppose that a dog saw a bone being buried under a tree yesterday, and that its behaviour today shows that it does not think there is a bone under the tree – e.g. it is hungry, yet does not dig. Somehow, the dog has failed; but how? Perhaps it has failed to recognize the place where the bone was buried; and that might not be a memory-failure, in my sense in which 'memory' covers only the capacity for beliefs about the past. But suppose that we think that the failure lies elsewhere, and we want to know where: has the dog forgotten that a bone was buried here, or does it rather think that in general buried bones dissolve or somehow fail to stay put? Contrary to what I assumed in *Rationality*, we could find evidence supporting one or other specific answer to this.

On the one hand, we could discover that the trouble lay in the dog's memory and not its generalizing capacities. For the belief that the bone was buried there might, given the dog's goals, dictate other behaviour to it as well, involving other general beliefs; and we might find that the dog did indeed behave in those other ways. For instance: bone-burying loosens the soil, and our dog shows that it thinks this soil is loose, by trying to uproot a sapling which in normal soil it could not budge. The example is fanciful, but it makes the vital point that a single past belief

---

[5] For example, Bennett (1964), pp. 89–91.

may connect with different items of present behaviour, through different general beliefs; and so we can test the conjecture that an animal has a given past belief.

The evidence could be much strengthened by data which invoke our epistemic theory for the dog. For example, our theory about its memory might say that its chances of remembering a given event depend upon how protracted and conspicuous its experience of the event was, how many sense-modalities it involved, how long ago it occurred, and how eventful the dog's life has been in the interim; and all this would let us predict some of the dog's memory-failures. Now, on the occasion when the dog could have dug for the bone but did not do so, our diagnosis of its failure as pertaining to memory rather than to a generalization about buried bones would be immeasurably strengthened if we knew things about the dog which would, through our theory about its memory, have supported a prediction that it would forget the burying of the bone.

Just as a single past belief may issue in action through different general beliefs, so a single general belief may lead to action through different past ones. For example, the belief that buried bones stay put may lead to bone-excavations on different occasions through the mediation of distinct beliefs about the earlier interment of bones. (Each could be expressed in the form 'A bone has been buried here', but they should count as genuinely different for all that. They would involve different times and places and bones, and would run different risks from memory-impediments.) If the dog often digs for bones it has seen buried, that tends to confirm that today's trouble was just that it had forgotten the burying or failed to recognize the site.

Here too we could be helped by our epistemic theory, if we had any, about the dog's generalizing capacities. Suppose we have evidence that if the dog experiences many Fs which are G and none which are not, it will come to think that *All Fs are G* if and only if C is satisfied – where C is some condition on the dog's experiences of Fs. An hypothesis of that form might put us in a position to predict that the dog would have a given general belief on a given occasion, or to predict that it would not; and these predictions, combined with conjectures about what the dog will remember, will generate predictions about how it will behave. The successes and failures of these last predictions could provide strong evidence for or against specific conjectures about the animal's past and general beliefs.

In *Rationality* I insisted that one should never credit an animal with a belief except on the strength of a single item of behaviour. That was a mistake.[6] In making it I was declining, as I still do decline, to infer '*a* thinks that all *F*s are *G*' just from the fact that *a* thinks, of each *F* that it encounters, that it is *G*. In my present treatment of general beliefs, however, I do not rely on that simplistic inference but rather on arguments against which the objections posed in *Rationality* are powerless.

Robert Kirk has persuasively argued that we can also get leverage on languageless past and general beliefs through animals' inquiries.[7] Thus, behaviour which perhaps manifests the past belief *P* and the general belief *G* may be preceded by behaviour which is best explained as an inquiry into *P* alone. This could hardly happen if memory were the sole epistemic basis for past beliefs, for the ransacking of one's memory is too private a matter. But memory is not the only basis: our animal might base some past beliefs on present beliefs together with general ones, and so it might visibly inquire into a question about the past – that is, behave in ways which are best explained as a scrutiny of present evidence, other than memory-traces, for or against a proposition about the past.

There can also be behaviour which is best explained as aimed at getting general knowledge. For example, an animal might walk and wait and stalk and watch so as to discover what is generally the case with wolves after they have been attacked. I first introduced inquisitiveness as manifested only at the time of need. But if there is a proposition which an animal can usefully believe throughout a substantial period of time, then we should allow that the animal could inquire into it even when there is no immediate prospect of its opening up a new and better course. So it might inquire whether *P* – where *P* is a general proposition – with a view to storing the answer for possible later use.

But we must be careful about how the general belief is used. Suppose that our animal is thought to have learned that attacked wolves become savage. If it uses this only in a simple forward-looking way, attacking wolves so as to make them savage (perhaps so as to make trouble for other predators), then it is not clear that the animal acquires a general belief at all. For we have the option of attributing to it the seemingly humbler discovery of *how to make a wolf savage*. To be fully entitled to

---

[6] As is pointed out by Robert Kirk, 'Rationality without Language', *Mind*, vol. 76 (1967), p. 378.
[7] *Ibid.*, pp. 375–6.

the general-belief diagnosis, I suggest, we must see the general belief employed in a manner which does not collapse into a mere 'how-to', and the best prospect for that is for the belief to be employed in a retrospective way, e.g. avoiding a wolf which our animal thinks has recently been attacked. Kirk's examples involve 'general beliefs' which do collapse into 'how-to's'. Kirk gives the contrary impression by implying that each inquiry points unequivocally to a single general proposition: specifically, his languageless creatures make 'toys' which we are to understand as devised to test physical theories; each toy is 'so constructed as to work only if some proposition of mechanics were true which is in fact false'; and the implication is that we can identify 'the proposition' just by examining the 'toy'.[8] But the phrase 'toy which would work only if some false proposition of mechanics were true' is logically equivalent to 'toy which doesn't work'; and if a toy does not work, there are infinitely many falsehoods whose truth would suffice for its working. Still, Kirk's conclusion is right, and I owe him thanks for pointing me towards it.

§34. Beliefs about beliefs

There can also be languageless beliefs about beliefs. We human observers can get plenty of evidence as to what animal b believed on various occasions, and can establish and test theories which support predictions about what he will believe on some further occasion; and all our data for this consist in behaviour of b's which is perceptible by a as well. So a can have all the epistemic intake that would be needed for beliefs about b's beliefs.

Could a do the necessary theorizing? Well, all I have stipulated about him is that he lacks a language, and *that* certainly does not prevent him from having theories about b's beliefs, goals and so on.

A more serious question is this: what can a do which will manifest his beliefs about b's beliefs, that is, give us evidence that he has beliefs about b's beliefs? Granted that a can have suitable epistemic input for such beliefs, there remains the question of what, if anything, would constitute suitable behavioural output.

This could be an intolerably long story, but the essential core of it is simple. Suppose that we know that a has had epistemic input suitable to a mainly true theory about b's beliefs, goals etc. Suppose further- more that at time T a does something for which our best explanation

[8] *Ibid.*, p. 372.

includes the conjecture that a has just come to believe that b is going to dive into the water. (There are plenty of ways of filling in the details, specifying a's behaviour and his value-system and his other relevant beliefs so as to make 'a thought that b would swim' helpful in explaining a's behaviour.) That is a belief about what b will do, not about what he believes; but we might be unable to explain a's coming to think that b *will swim* except by supposing that a has just come to think that b *believes there is a predator nearby*. For example: some event has just occurred, perceptible to a, which would be apt to make b think there was a predator nearby, and nothing else has happened which bears in any way on the likelihood of b's swimming. In such a case, we could reasonably conjecture that a reached his belief that b would swim via a belief that b believed that he was threatened by a predator.

This must be handled with care, though. If the crucial event was an ursine roar, and if b dives into water when and only when he hears such a roar, then the notion of a *belief* of b's is out of place. If we and a are to be entitled to think that b enters the water because he *believes* there is a predator nearby, various conditions must be satisfied which make the behaviour genuinely teleologically explicable and, more than that, intentional. But I shall not repeat my account in chapters 2 and 3 of what those conditions are; and my present point is just that if they are satisfied, and if a has observed enough of b's behaviour which satisfies them, then we may on a given occasion be entitled to suppose that a's expectation about how b would behave was backed by a conjecture about what b believed.

It hardly needs saying that if a can thus have beliefs about b's beliefs, then he can also have beliefs about b's intentions. In fact, a cannot pull those two concepts apart any more than we can.

All of this can be taken further, for we could learn that a had a belief about b's beliefs about a's beliefs. This requires a situation where some behaviour of a's is best explained by something including

a thinks that b will do x;

which in turn is best explained by

a thinks that b believes that a will do y;

which is best explained by

a thinks that b believes that a believes that P,

where P is some proposition with regard to which a has just received epistemic input, or *b* thinks he has, or *a* thinks that *b* thinks that he (*a*) has. All of this differs only in complexity from the '*a* thinks that *b* thinks that *P*' case dealt with above. Nor is there any obstacle in principle, though there might be insuperable ones in practice, to discovering that *a* thinks that *b* thinks that *a* thinks that *b* thinks that *P*, and so on upwards.

If *a* can think that *b* thinks that *a* thinks that *P*, as I have contended, then a languageless creature can manifest a belief about his own beliefs. This conflicts with the quite common view that self-consciousness, or the capacity for beliefs about one's own inner states, is possible only to creatures with language. I once argued badly for this view,[9] and more recently I have hoped to support it through my present account of belief. According to this, *a* can believe *P* only if he is educable with respect to the bases upon which he registers *P*; which seems to imply that some of the things which *a* can register he nevertheless cannot believe, because they are themselves basic and are not registered upon any basis at all. For example, *a* could believe he is in danger, because experience could lead him to improve his reading of signs of danger; but he could not believe he is in pain, because nothing could count as his learning to make a more accurate reading of the signs of his own pain – there are no such signs. That line of argument still seems to me to have some force. But now it collides with the fact that languageless *a* can manifest a belief about *b*'s beliefs about *a*'s beliefs; and clearly we could also have *a* believing something about what *b* believes about *a*'s pain, say, or about any other of *a*'s behaviourally manifested inner states. I am not sure what to say about this.

We might have it both ways, conceding that *a* can think that *b* thinks that *a* is in pain, while denying that *a* can think simply that he is in pain. That is not an exercise in mindless peace-making: there is something to be said for it. The difficulty about beliefs about one's own inner states is that *a* can have a belief about *x* only if *x* is far enough away from him, so to speak, for educability to have some play; and by that standard *a*'s inner states are too close. But distance is achieved when *a* thinks about *b*'s thought about *a*'s inner states, and so there belief is possible. Another kind of distancing is involved when *a* thinks about his own future inner states – and so he can believe that he soon will be in pain, or that if such-and-such occurs he will be in pain. It seems intuitively plausible to suppose that a languageless creature can have

[9] J. Bennett, *Kant's Analytic* (Cambridge, 1966), pp. 105–6, 116–17.

beliefs about its future or possible inner states; and my theory of belief permits this, for *a* can be educable with regard to the signs that pain, say, is impending, as distinct from the signs that he is in pain.

If one persists in denying that *a* can have self-consciousness in the sense of having beliefs directly about his own inner states, one must explain how such beliefs become possible when there is language. That is not hard. If someone has a language which includes an element which lets him refer to himself in sentences meaning that he is wet, is dirty, is going fishing etc., and has the use of predicates meaning '. . . feels warm', '. . . is in pain' etc. for use in sentences meaning that others feel warm, are in pain etc., then he has the materials for sentences which mean that *he* is warm, in pain, etc. If he uses such sentences appropriately, we have reason to say that he can believe he is warm, in pain and so on. I have so far offered only sufficient conditions for belief, leaving the way open for further sufficient conditions, such as linguistic ones, later in the inquiry.

Objection: 'It is not especially plausible to suppose that there is a kind of self-consciousness which languageless creatures lack. And if *a* can think that it will be the case that *P*, or that if *Q* then *P*, or that *b* thinks that *P*, then *a* must be able also to think that *P*.' If someone says this, I have neither the resources nor the will to oppose him strenuously. As I said, I am not sure.

§35. Why logic needs language

This section and the next will tackle some problems centring on the general question: Can we say *exactly* what a languageless creature believes? For a start, consider a question about the beliefs of those who *do* have a language. For what sorts of proposition-pairs can *L* be true?

(*L*) *x* believes that *P* and *x* believes that ∼*Q*.

Clearly, *L* can be true where *P* has the same truth-value as *Q*; for people often believe falsehoods. *L* can also be true where *P* is scientifically attested as having the same truth-value as *Q*, for people can accept one proposition and reject another which is equivalent to it in the securest parts of physics, say. And *L* need not fail even when *P* logically entails *Q*, for people do sometimes disbelieve logical consequences of their beliefs.

However, *L* must fail where *P* and *Q* are expressed by synonymous sentences. Someone might sincerely *say* 'I think that . . ., and I do not think that . . .' with the gaps filled by synonymous sentences; but he would be misreporting his beliefs, presumably through error about meanings. That is because the notion of sentence-synonymy, such as it is, rests on the idea of sentences which are inter-substitutable *salva veritate* in the context '*x* believes that . . .'

Now, how does *L* fare when the beliefs in question are entirely non-linguistic?

Obviously, *L* could be true even if *P* and *Q* had the same truth-value. Non-linguistic beliefs, like linguistic ones, can be false.

Less obviously, *L* can be true even if *P* is equivalent to *Q* within well-tested scientific theory. For even then we could have evidence that *a* believes one and not the other: there might be a time when *P* is already true and *Q* is not yet true, and *a* could encounter an environment during its *P* stage and leave it before the *Q* sequel; or if *P* and *Q* involve different sense-modalities, *a* could register one and not the other.

Can *L* be true, for non-linguistic beliefs, if *P* logically entails *Q*? I say No. Since every logical mistake consists in believing some *P* and disbelieving a *Q* which it entails, this implies that we should never attribute logical mistakes to languageless creatures. This follows from the prevalent view that language is the source of logical truth, but I can defend it on other grounds as well.

If *P* entails *Q*, then any environment in which *P* is also one in which *Q*, and there cannot be any saving differences of time or of sense-modality which would let us connect *a* with *P* but not with *Q*. In brief, wherever my epistemic theory lets us say '*a* registers *P*' it will also warrant '*a* registers *Q*' if *Q* is entailed by *P* – subject only to a qualification which I shall present in my next section.

My theory apart, how could an animal's behaviour suggest that it thinks that *P* and that ∼*Q*, where *P* entails *Q*? Clearly, no one thing a dog could do would suggest that it thinks that the cat is in the tree and that the cat is on the ground. It could act sequentially on the two beliefs; but that would show only that at *T* it thinks the cat is then in the tree and that at *T** it thinks the cat is *then* on the ground – and that contains no logical error. Or the dog might show at *T* that it thought the cat was then in the tree at *T* and show at *T** that it thought the cat had been on the ground at *T*; but that would prove only a change of mind, perhaps through faulty memory, and not a logical mistake.

People who try to describe non-linguistic evidence for logical error usually fall into describing evidence for memory-failure. The animal saw two pairs of men enter the barn, has seen four men leave, and awaits a fifth: it thinks that two plus two make five! Is it not better to suppose that it has forgotten that only two pairs went in?

If languageless creatures could make logical mistakes, all their mistakes could be logical ones. The dog wrongly thinks the cat is in the tree – or perhaps rightly thinks the cat is on the ground and wrongly thinks that to approach a thing one must move away from it! This kind of absurdity would be present, sometimes in lesser degree, in any attempt to diagnose the dog's epistemic failures in terms of logical error.

Then does a languageless creature believe everything that is entailed by any of its beliefs? No; if *a* believes *P*, and *P* is stronger than *Q*, then whether *a* believes *Q* is a further question which must be settled by further empirical evidence. Let us consider what is at issue in the decision whether to attribute to *a* the belief at *T* that *there is a cat in the tree*, or the belief at *T* that *there is an animal in the tree*, or both.

(1) Suppose that *a*'s behaviour at *T* is sufficiently explained by the weaker belief; *a* would have acted in the same way if the treed animal had resembled a raccoon or a monkey or ... etc. In that case the attribution of the stronger belief ('cat') is seriously in doubt, since *ex hypothesi* it is too strong to yield the best explanation of *a*'s behaviour at *T*. If we are to justify it, that must be because we know from other behaviour of *a*'s that he is capable of the belief that there is a cat, specifically, in the tree; and we know that he can have that belief on the basis of epistemic input just like his input at *T*. In that case we may attribute the stronger belief as well as the weaker one, but only because the former is supported by behavioural data gathered on other occasions.

(2) Suppose that *a*'s behaviour at *T* is best explained by the attribution of the stronger belief that there is a cat in the tree: had it been a raccoon or a bear in the tree, *a* would have behaved differently. In that case, the attribution of the weaker belief is too weak to yield a complete explanation of *a*'s behaviour at *T*; and so it is justified only if we can support it by behavioural data drawn from other occasions which are, so far as epistemic input is concerned, sufficiently like the one at *T*.

(3) Here is another kind of stronger–weaker case: *a* believes that *Attacked wolves are savage* and that *This wolf has been attacked* and that *This wolf is savage* (see §33 above). Yet the third of these is a logical consequence of the first and second. But the sort of evidence which could entitle us to attribute all three of these beliefs to *a* would be evidence that he has inquired into the first two, and perhaps has acted on the first on many occasions, together with evidence that at *T* he has

acted on the third. What we must not do is to credit *a* with the first two beliefs because we have behavioural evidence that he has them, and then credit him with the third on the grounds that even he must have enough logical power to perform that deduction. We cannot have grounds for crediting a languageless creature with moderate logical acumen: either it can make no inferences, or it can make every inference; and in the latter case it believes everything which is entailed by any of its beliefs, which seems clearly to be absurd.

§36. What exactly does he think?

If *P* and *Q* are logically equivalent, and *a* believes *P*, must *a* also believe *Q*? Nothing I have said rules out the view that in attributing any non-linguistic belief we are really attributing the set of all beliefs which are inter-deducible with it. But I do want to rule that out, on the ground that if *P* is inter-deducible with *Q*, and is structurally simpler than *Q*, then one should not say that *a* believes *Q*. So we should prefer '*a* thinks that (*P*) there is a cat in the tree' to '*a* thinks that (*Q*) either there is a cat in the tree or if there is not a cat in the tree then there is a cat in the tree'. The attribution of *Q* is objectionable because *Q* is longer yet does no extra work, and because listeners might think that its complexities help to explain *a*'s behaviour, which they cannot do if *a* has no language. Those two reasons for not attributing *Q* to *a*, although strong enough, fall short of saying that that attribution would imply falsehoods about *a*'s behaviour. For any languageless animal *a*, it seems, if *a* thinks that *P* then its behaviour cannot positively conflict with the attribution to it of the belief that *Q* where *Q* is logically equivalent to *P*.

There remains the question of whether to explain a bit of *a*'s behaviour through the belief that *P* or the belief that *Q*, in cases where neither entails the other. This must be settled by discovering what differences in the environment would have altered *a*'s behaviour. Did *a* think the stuff in the basket was *grass*, or did he think it was *green organic material*? Well, would he have behaved in the same way if it had been any other green organic material but not if it had been either not-green or inorganic? If so, the second attribution is better. But the first would be preferable if *a* would have behaved in the same way if the stuff had been brown grass, but not if it had been anything other than grass. And chapters 2 and 3 above show how one should investigate the truth-value of those counterfactual conditionals.

(Strictly, what counts is not the nature of the environment but rather how it is registered upon *a*. But we know about that only through our epistemic theory for *a*, which is a theory for sorting out the kinds of environment-differences which do affect *a*'s behaviour from the kinds which do not.)

Suppose we have evidence that *a* thinks the stuff in the basket is green organic material, and someone says 'So *a* thinks that the stuff contains chlorophyll?' This cannot be ruled out as being weaker than the originally attributed belief, or as pointlessly complex. Nor can we arbitrate between '... is green organic material' and '... contains chlorophyll' by discovering which changes in the environment produce changes in *a*'s behaviour; for the two predicates are just about co-extensive, so that whatever falls under either must also fall under the other.

Still, no one will accept '*a* thinks that the stuff contains chlorophyll'. Presumably that is because 'chlorophyll' is a heavily theory-laden term, and no one would expect *a* to know the requisite theory. Although there can be non-linguistic general beliefs, it seems unlikely that a languageless creature could know the kind of theory in which the chemical formula for chlorophyll might be stated. But I need not insist on that. My present point is just that *if a* knows nothing like that theory, we ought not to say that he thinks the stuff in the basket contains chlorophyll. Humans who do not know chemistry can think that something contains chlorophyll, but that is a belief based on hearsay; whereas for languageless *a* there can be no hearsay.

We cannot, by avoiding unduly theory-laden terms, express *a*'s beliefs in terms which exactly capture his epistemic state. In fact, our belief-attributions will usually credit him with too much; as when we say that he thinks the stuff in the basket is green organic material, although he has no delicate distinction between the organic and the inorganic. But we allow ourselves such inaccuracies in attributing beliefs to one another, so why should we struggle heroically to avoid them in attributing non-linguistic beliefs? Let us rather do what we *conveniently* can to avoid inflating these attributions, always remembering that we are still giving them more content than we strictly ought to. For example, let us say 'The dog thinks there is a cat in the tree' rather than 'The dog thinks there is a fairly cat-like object in the tree', but let us not *automatically* infer that the dog's belief includes the whole biological load which the word 'cat' might carry.[10]

[10] This matter is usefully discussed in Armstrong (1973), pp. 25–31, and Williams, pp. 138–9.

The slight vagueness of most of the predicates in our language can bring inaccuracy into our belief-attributions, but it does not always do so. When I attribute a belief to someone who has a language, *he* might be prepared to express his belief in just my words, so that their vagueness unites us rather than coming between us. Something similar can obtain in the attribution of non-linguistic beliefs: I used to think that in those attributions any vagueness in the words must be an imperfection, even if only a slight one; but Michael Beebe has shown me that even a languageless creature can have a state of mind which is exactly captured by vague language. Suppose that F is a somewhat vague predicate: most things are clearly F or clearly not F, but there is a boundary region of things which we cannot firmly classify in either way although we know all the facts about them. It could happen that a's doing x on a certain occasion is *perfectly* explained by something which includes the hypothesis that he believed that Fb, with the vagueness of F contributing to the perfection of the explanation. For we might discover that if Fb had been clearly false a would not have done x, so long as Fb was clearly true a would have done x, and if b had been neither clearly true nor clearly false the probability of a's doing x would have been high in proportion as b came close to being clearly F.

Still, vagueness may bring imperfection into our attributions of beliefs. This, like the theory-load difficulty, should be met by our doing our reasonable best and then treating the results circumspectly. The modest measure of inaccuracy which this allows is theoretically avoidable, for we could discover exactly what features of the environment are relevant to the animal's behaviour, and then devise a belief-report which incorporates those features and no others. We are not doomed to inaccuracy in our attributions of non-linguistic beliefs. In particular, do not think that those attributions must be inaccurate because they use language whereas a is languageless. If that were valid, then we could not even be perfectly accurate in a language-using account of a's digestive system.

§37. What exactly does he intend?

What a intends by a bit of behaviour depends upon which of his beliefs explain the behaviour. That question can go very deep. Intention rests on belief, which rests in turn on educability; the latter is a capacity suitable to modify the 'basing' relationships between some registrations and others; and so we must learn about a's basic sensory capacities if we are to discover whether and how he is educable, and thus to know what he believes and intends. Otherwise, we might credit him with impressive flexibility when really he is following a single sensory clue of which we were unaware.[11]

Conversely, we may under-rate a's educability, counting him as relatively unintelligent because he has not learned from something of which, in fact, he was never sensorily aware. This could lead to our withholding justified attributions of intentions to him. For example, some species of dolphins have this charming behavioural trait: when one of their number has been injured so that it risks drowning, others will support its head above the water until it recovers. This suggests an intention to achieve the survival of the injured dolphin. But a dolphin has been observed to kill a leopard-shark and then support its head above water for five whole days, from which one might infer that we are 'obliged to conclude that the attribution of intention to these actions was groundless'.[12] The inference would probably be correct; but notice that a different account is *prima facie* possible, namely that dolphins are *perceptually* unable to tell dead sharks from wounded dolphins, and that their head-supporting behaviour is after all intended to enable their fellows to survive. Admittedly, if dolphins were bad at distinguishing dolphins from others, and dead from wounded, it could not be quite correct to say that a dolphin thinks that it is helping a *wounded dolphin* to survive. But that mild inaccuracy, of the sort discussed above, does not imply that this pattern of behaviour is not intentional at all.

In saying that we shall not get a's intellectual level right unless we are well informed about his perceptual capacities, I do not mean to imply that in this matter the sky is the limit. It makes no sense to suppose that a has very highly developed intentions which never show up in his behaviour because he cannot make any perceptual discriminations, or, conversely, that a has highly tuned senses which do him no good because of the crudity and inflexibility of his goal-structure. But within these limits, one can ask whether the sources of an individual behavioural failure are perceptual or intellectual; and answers are findable.

Even if we know what a believes, however, we can have problems

[11] See Bennett (1964), pp. 32 f.
[12] W. E. Evans and J. Bastian, 'Marine Mammal Communication: Social and Ecological Factors', in H. T. Andersen (ed.), *The Biology of Marine Mammals* (New York, 1968), p. 431.

about what he intends. Suppose that he does F, *expecting* to achieve both G and G^*: whether he *intended* to achieve both ends depends upon which of his beliefs explain his doing F. Roughly speaking, if a would have done F even if he had not believed that this would achieve G^*, but would not have done F unless he believed that that would achieve G, then he did F intending to achieve G, not G^*. Thus my theory; and thus also common sense, which distinguishes what an agent intends to achieve from what upshots he foresees but does not intend.

When we say that a intended to produce G, we must ensure that his behaviour is not as well explained by some less complex intention: for example, we should not say 'a intended to make b brittle' if the facts are as well covered by 'a intended to make b break'. Let us explore this example.

We could say that a intended to make b brittle if we learned that a attaches little value to b's breaking but a high value to its breaking-if-struck, i.e. a large negative value to its being struck and not breaking. The example is implausible, though. When b is likely to be struck, any endeavour to make it brittle can be seen as an endeavour to make it break; and when b is not likely to be struck, an endeavour to make it brittle is unintelligible – we cannot see how a could have as a goal the making true of a conditional whose antecedent he does not expect to become true.

But the plausibility returns if we take an example involving a cluster of dispositions expressible in a long conjunction of conditionals. Suppose we are wondering whether a intends to make b afraid, or merely to make b run away. Fear, construed behaviourally, is a complex set of dispositions: not merely to run away, but to be quiet when predators are close, to leave food uneaten when there are certain smells in the air, perhaps to hide in certain circumstances, and so on. Let $(P_1 \rightarrow G_1 b), \ldots,$ $(P_n \rightarrow G_n b)$ be the conditionals which express these dispositions. Now suppose that at T a does not attach a high probability to P_1 or to ... or to P_n, but does think it highly likely that $(P_1 \lor \ldots \lor P_n)$; and suppose also that at T a does something which does in fact suffice to give b the whole set of dispositions. That is partial evidence – and the rest can be gleaned from earlier sections – that at T a intended to endow b with all those dispositions, that is, intended to make b afraid.

Now that we have the general idea of a's intending to confer a complex dispositional property on something, we can provide for his intending to produce beliefs and intentions in others.

§38. Intentions to produce beliefs

To be entitled to say that a intended to get b to believe P, we must find behaviour of a's of which we can reasonably say: a behaved like that because he thought it would get b to believe P; that is (1) he did think it would get b to believe that P, and (2) if he had not thought so he would not have acted as he did.

In §34 above I explained how a can have beliefs about b's beliefs. He can have an opinion about b's beliefs at time T, not just retrospectively through observing how b behaves at $T+d$, but also prospectively through observing b's sense-organs and environment at $T-d$. So there is no difficulty in principle about our becoming entitled to say (1) that when a did such-and-such he thought that this would get b to believe that P; for all that is needed is that a should think that his behaviour will cause the environment to be thus-and-so, which in turn will make b believe that P.

There remains the question of how we can discover (2) that if a had not thought that his behaviour would get b to believe that P, he would not have behaved as he did. Well, this counterfactual about a's behaviour may be supported by our overall theory about his goals, or his value-system, and in preceding chapters I have explained how such theories can be tested against the observed facts of a's behaviour. Now, however, we want to credit a with a rather peculiar sort of goal, namely the production of a *belief*, and I ought to say more about it.

I shall take it that a seeks to change b's beliefs only because he seeks to change his behaviour. Eventually we may be able to endow a with a different sort of interest in what b believes: for instance, we may become able to credit b with valuing true beliefs as a miser does gold, for themselves rather than for their practical value, and to credit a with an altruistic interest in helping b to augment his collection. But that would be a difficult enterprise, which I am not sure could be carried out successfully until a and b both have language; so in the meantime I shall assume that if a is to be interested in b's beliefs this must be because of an interest in b's behaviour.

Before developing this line of thought, I parenthetically note an agreeably disciplined structure which we have here. The concept of belief is a two-sided one which mediates between (i) b's epistemic intake and (ii) his behavioural output. The concept of intention also has two sides: to know that a intends to achieve G we need evidence (1) that he thinks that his behaviour is likely to produce G and (2) that the achievement of G has value for him or is among his goals. It now transpires that where there is an intention to produce a belief, these two pairs are systematically linked. If *a* intends to get *b* to believe that *P*,

(1) he must think that his behaviour will get *b* to believe that *P*, because he thinks it will (i) give *b* epistemic input for the belief that *P*;

and also

(2) he must attach value to *b*'s believing that *P*, because he attaches value to (ii) *b*'s engaging in behavioural output from the belief that *P*.

In short, belief involves intake and output, intention involves means and ends, and the two are here interlinked because the intention to produce a belief involves the provision of intake (means) so as to achieve output (end).

Now back to the main thread. If *a* is to want *b* to believe *P* because of some interest he has in *b*'s behaviour, perhaps what *a* mainly wants is that *b* shall do *x* (for some specific *x*), his desire that *b* shall believe *P* being merely ancillary to this. But not necessarily; for *a*'s desire to produce a certain belief in *b*, although based on an interest in *b*'s behaviour, need not be the result of a desire that *b* shall behave in precisely such and such a manner. That is because there is a certain slack between belief and behaviour. Even if we take *b*'s basic value-system, as expressed in the teleological laws he falls under, to be fixed, there are still two variables which can mediate between what he believes and how he behaves: given that he thinks that *P*, how he behaves may depend upon his general condition (the *R* component in the teleological laws of chapters 2 and 3) and upon his other beliefs. And either of these variables might be relevant to *a*'s intending *b* to believe *P* but not intending him to do *x* for any specific *x*.

One of them is not very plausible in this role, however. Suppose that *a* does not know whether *b* is hungry (*R*), but he wants him to believe that there are squirrels in the hollow tree so that he will catch one *if* he is hungry, or perhaps, *when next* he is hungry. That still implies that there is a specific mode of behaviour which is, for *a*, the point of getting *b* to believe that *P*; the only uncertainty concerns whether and when *b* will engage in that behaviour.

The second link between belief and behaviour – viz. other beliefs – is much more promising. It could easily happen that *a* wants *b* to believe that P, but does not intend him to perform any specific action because he does not know what all of b's other relevant beliefs are. I do not suggest that a is deferring to b's beliefs, be they true or false, out of respect for b's right to his own opinions. I have in mind the possibility that a is deferring to such *true* beliefs as b may have though a does not have them; that is, a thinks that b may have (or be going to acquire) relevant information which a lacks, and he wants b to be able to act on the basis of that extra information together with the information that P. For example, b is going on a journey during which he may learn things which could combine with P in many different ways; a cannot know in advance what true beliefs b will acquire during his journey; but he wants b to add P to them, whatever they are, because P may be relevant to how b will behave when the other information comes in.

Why does a have as a goal b's being able to act on the information that P? Perhaps he thinks that P is false, and is motivated by malice; but such cases would be hard to diagnose. We could manage better in a case like this: a thinks that P is true, so that b will be more likely to act in a manner that is satisfactory to b if he believes P; and a wants to help b to act in ways which are satisfactory to b. This desire of a's could be a matter of enlightened self-interest: a often needs b's help, and is therefore interested in his survival and also, perhaps, in his becoming or remaining party to an unspoken mutual-aid pact. So the clearest and most robust cases of a's seeking to get b to believe that P are ones where a himself believes that P and is trying to help b. This may be what underlies the common belief that language could not function unless lying were the exception rather than the rule.

5

MEANING

§39. Sufficient conditions for meaning

Before proceeding to deploy the materials which I have assembled, using them to give a behavioural base to a theory of meaning, I should say some more about what the content of the theory will be. In §4 above I offered the following Gricean sufficient conditions for meaning.[1] U (utterer) did x meaning that P if there is someone A (audience) such that U did x intending

(i)   that A should come to believe P,
(ii) that A should be aware of intention (i), and
(iii) that the awareness mentioned in (ii) should be part of A's reason for believing P.

That was for statements, i.e. utterances intended to inform or misinform. We need something parallel to this for injunctions, by which I mean utterances constituting commands, requests, advice, recommendations or the like; and in §4 I presented Grice's conditions for 'U means that A is to do X', which are the same as those above except that *doing X* is substituted for *believing P* in the first and third conditions.

Generalizing over statements and injunctions, Grice's account says that U means something by what he does or utters if he intends to produce some effect in A, and intends this to come about through what I call 'the Gricean mechanism', i.e. through A's recognizing what the primary intention is. This general account then forks downwards: on the statement branch U intends A to acquire some belief, whereas on the injunction branch he intends A to perform some action. If Grice's theory did not cover statements and injunctions in a single formula, its adherents would be committed to conceding that the term 'meaning' is ambiguous. As things are, the integrity of the concept of (non-natural) meaning is preserved, because the theory can be stated in the form '... intending to produce, through the Gricean mechanism,

[1] See Grice (1957).

some effect in an audience ...'; which has real content, and yet is abstract enough to cover both statements and injunctions. I shall return to this in §41 below.

Why bother with injunctions at all? Well, they seem to be rather fundamental: one can, I think, imagine a language consisting of them alone, and this is a kind of self-sufficiency which seems not to belong to the varieties of meaningful utterance – such as optatives, curses and poems – which I am setting aside to be dealt with when the main campaign is over. Incidentally, *questions* are set aside, although they are requests and thus injunctions (in my sense), because what they request are specifically linguistic performances.

I shall tend to concentrate on statements rather than injunctions, but the reasons for this are expository and tactical, and do not threaten the unity of the concept of meaning. I shall sometimes turn aside to expound differences between statements and injunctions – differences which turn out to be quite large but gratifyingly structured and describable.

In the above conditions for meaning, I have followed Grice's original paper and most of the subsequent literature in using the formulation: U intended to get A to believe that P (or to do X), and he *intended* that this come about through the Gricean mechanism. But we can do better than that, and it would be useful to make the repair immediately.

Consider the general notion of intending by action F to produce goal G, and intending that this come about through mechanism M. (I here use 'mechanism' to cover any 'way' in which one event can lead to another. So petitionary prayer might lead to healing through the 'mechanism' of divine intervention.) In particular, compare (1) 'He intended by doing F to produce G, and *intended that M provide* the connecting link' with (2) 'He intended by doing F to produce G, and *relied upon M to provide* the connecting link'. Very often, (1) is used to mean what (2) means, and in Gricean meaning-theory that is how (1) ought to be used. Perhaps (1) could be taken to imply that the subject prefers the connection to be made by M rather than by any other mechanism; but that implication would surely be irrelevant to whether something was a case of meaning.

I therefore drop (1) and stay with (2): U means that P, if U intends to get A to think that P and relies for the achievement of this on the Gricean mechanism; and similarly for U's meaning that A is to do X.

The notion of reliance upon a mechanism can be explained through concepts I have already introduced. Roughly, 'in seeking to achieve G, he was relying on mechanism M' means that if he had not expected his behaviour to lead through M to G he would not have expected it to lead to G at all; or, more accurately, he would not have thought$_i$ that it would lead to G, for an i high enough to get him to do F.

Strawson has shown that those conditions for meaning are not really sufficient.[2] He adduces a case like this: U intends to get A to believe that P, and relies for this on the Gricean mechanism, but expects A to think that he is relying on some quite different mechanism. This satisfies the proffered 'sufficient conditions', yet it does not look much like a case of meaning.

We can meet this difficulty by adding the condition '... and U expects A to realize that U is relying on the Gricean mechanism'; but Strawson hints, and Schiffer has shown, that this is still too weak.[3]

In fact, whatever we stipulate about what U intends or expects or relies on, there could be some element in it which U expects A to get wrong; and whenever U contrives that he and A should be at cross-purposes in that way, the case seems not to be one of meaning, properly so called. Strawson explains why: meaning is essentially an attempt to communicate; but in real communication everything is open and above-board; and so meaning cannot exploit contrived cross-purposes.

A short way along the infinity of Schiffer-type counter-examples, we meet things like this: 'U expects – but does not expect A to realize that U expects – A to realize that U expects A to realize that U expects A to realize that U intends to get A to think that P'. Perhaps this does not correspond to any humanly possible state of mind; but Schiffer is surely right in saying that we ought systematically to exclude all these counter-examples, rather than legislating against the simpler ones and then condemning the rest as psychologically impossible.[4]

The systematic treatment which I propose is really a selective borrowing from different treatments by Schiffer and Grice.[5] It requires one modest technical term, to be used just here and then discarded. Let Q be any true proposition about U. I shall say that A 'crosses' U with respect to Q if the series of propositions

(1)   A realizes that Q,

---

[2] Strawson (1964), pp. 155–8. In expounding this, I replace some of Strawson's uses of 'intend' by 'rely'.
[3] Schiffer, pp. 17–23.
[4] *Ibid.*, pp. 24–5.   [5] *Ibid.*, pp. 26, 30–9; Grice (1969), pp. 155–9.

(2) A realizes that U expects that [1],
(3) A realizes that U expects that [2],

and so on, has a member which is false because some conflicting proposition of the form 'A thinks$_i$ that S', for some fairly high i, is true. A does not count as crossing U with respect to Q just because the series are not all true; for they might fail to be true because at some level (and thereafter) A has no opinion on the matter, or even because the move down the series eventually runs us into a kind of senselessness.[6] We get a 'crossing', in my sense, only if the series contains something of the form 'A realizes that R' which is false because A is inclined to believe something which conflicts with R.

Now, the Strawson–Schiffer counter-examples are eliminated by a single strengthening of the conditions. We now say: *U intends to get A to think that P (or to do X), he relies for this upon the Gricean mechanism, and he does not expect A to cross him with respect to his reliance on that mechanism.* That could be strengthened or weakened a little – e.g. by replacing 'expect' by 'envisage' or by 'intend' – but I do not care much how strong the mixture is, so long as we have the right kinds of ingredients. (Objection: 'Your conditions allow that U expects A to cross him with respect to the fact that he does not expect A to cross him with respect to U's reliance on the Gricean mechanism.' That, if it were true, would show a defect in the conditions, for we do not want crossing in respect of *any* of U's intentions or expectations.[7] But in fact that high-level cross is implicitly ruled out by the simple condition I have laid down. Testing this claim is left as an exercise for the reader.)

This strengthening of the sufficient conditions for meaning still lets us attribute meanings on the basis of non-linguistic behaviour. It would indeed be hard to assemble non-linguistic evidence for U's expecting that A would cross him with respect to some proposition, especially one far along the series. But the conditions require only that U does *not* expect A to cross him, and that is secured by the absence of any evidence to the contrary. Similarly, we can be entitled to say that real communication occurred if the other conditions are satisfied and there is no evidence that A crossed U in any relevant way.

From now on, I shall not restrict 'communicate' to real, Strawsonian communication. I need a short way of expressing the idea of *getting*

---

[6] As is predicted by J. T. Cargile, 'A Note on "Iterated Knowings"', *Analysis*, vol. 30 (1969–70).
[7] Thus Schiffer, *op. cit.*, p. 39.

someone to believe P, and I shall use 'communicate *P*' for this purpose. In this use, '*U* communicates *P* to *A*' implies nothing about how *U* produces in *A* the belief that *P*.

§40. Weakening the conditions

The conditions which I have presented are not weak enough to be necessary for meaning, but I do not mind about that (see §7 above). Still, they may be too strong for my purposes. It may be possible to weaken them without thereby making them too complex to handle, and perhaps even making them in certain ways simpler and more manageable. In this section I shall discuss some of these possibilities.

The most important of them was actually adopted by Grice in 1968, namely the replacement of '*U* intends to get *A* to think that *P*' by '*U* intends to get *A* to think that *U thinks that P*'. On the face of it, this strengthens the conditions rather than weakening them; for, within the vast range of propositions which *U* might try to get *A* to believe, it confines him to just those which concern his own beliefs. But really it is a weakening. For in the original account of meaning, there is usually no chance of the Gricean mechanism's working, i.e. of *A*'s believing *P* because he realizes that *U* wants him to believe it, unless *A* credits *U* with believing *P* himself. So we can take it that the speaker always intends to communicate that he believes *P*, i.e. intends to get the hearer to think that the speaker believes *P*; and Grice's second version says that the speaker means that *P* just so long as he intends to communicate in the Gricean manner that he believes *P*; and the further requirement that he intend also to communicate *P* is dropped. So the change is a weakening.

Oddly, though, it does not weaken the conditions for *meaning* – only for *meaning that P*. The proposal is that if *U* intends to communicate that he believes *P*, and is relying on the Gricean mechanism, then *U* means that *P* by what he utters. Everything which counts as meaning by this standard also counts as meaning by the earlier standard, the difference merely being that some cases which the weakened conditions count as meaning *that P* are classified by the stronger ones as meaning *that the speaker believes that P*. Those will be cases where *U* seeks to communicate that he believes *P* but not to communicate *P*: he thinks that *A* already knows that *P*, but he wants *A* to realize that *he* (*U*) knows that *P* too. Perhaps we should construct some detailed examples, and see whether, when they lie clear before us, it seems right to classify them as cases of meaning that P (new, weaker conditions) or as meaning that U believes P (old, stronger conditions). But I find that when such a case does not involve the conventionally meaningful resources of a language, one has no clear intuitions as to which classification is correct. When language is involved, the results clearly favour the new, weaker conditions: If someone says 'It is going to rain', as he well might, just to inform his hearers that he thinks it is going to rain, everyone will agree that he means that *it is going to rain* and not that *he thinks that it is going to rain*. But that is inconclusive, for an adherent of the older, stronger conditions can say:

In that sort of case our intuitions are coerced by the conventional meaning of the sentence 'It is going to rain'. But that conventional meaning results from many facts about what people mean by what they say; and those facts may, for all your 'rain' case shows to the contrary, be facts about what it is that speakers intend to communicate about the world outside their own minds.

The inspection of cases, I submit, produces a stand-off. Our choice between the old, strong conditions and the newer, weak ones will have to depend upon more general theoretic advantages that we may find in one or the other.

One possible advantage is the achievement of a strongly unified theory of meaning, i.e. one which puts much into the concept of meaning and little into the difference between statements and injunctions. I shall take up that issue in my next section.

There are, however, two arguments to be dealt with first, one for and one against the weakened conditions for 'meaning that P'.

The argument against the weakened conditions is that they do not cope happily with cases like mine in §4 above, where someone makes a gesture by which she means that she is hating the opera performance. The weakened conditions will not assign that meaning unless she intends to communicate that *she believes that she hates* the performance; and there could be other cases with 'she believes she is in pain', 'he thinks he feels hungry' and the like. Even if one does not think that self-consciousness is impossible without language (§34 above), one may still be uneasy about 'she believes that she hates . . .' as what she primarily seeks to communicate. The old, stronger conditions have no trouble with this sort of case.

A proponent of the weaker conditions might meet this difficulty by yielding ground: he could revert to the old conditions for values of P such as that the speaker is in pain or feels hungry, while retaining the newer, weaker ones for everything else. That would be inelegant, though, and the weakened-conditions, theorist might do better just to stand his ground:

In the case as described, the woman did intend to communicate that she believed she was hating the performance. If 'She believed she was hating it' sounds strange, that is only because 'believe' suggests the possibility of error, and we cannot see how she could have been wrong about whether she was hating the performance. But that is only a matter of suggestion, not of meaning; and so we have no reason to deny that she believed she was hating it or, therefore, that she intended to communicate that she had that belief.

The difficulty, then, is not fatal to the weakened conditions.

Arguing in the other direction, now: the weakened conditions automatically solve a problem which makes trouble for the stronger ones, though I have so far suppressed it.[8] It is that the stronger conditions imply that, for virtually any P, if U means that P then he also means that he believes P. For if U is relying on the Gricean mechanism to get A to believe P, and if U neither is a fool nor thinks that A is one, then nearly always U must be relying on the Gricean mechanism to get A to think that U believes P. Whence we get the unattractive result that virtually always U means, in part, that he believes P.

The weakened conditions are free of this difficulty. For they say that when you have found the proposition of the form 'U believes that P' which U intends to communicate, if you peel off 'U believes that . . .' the remainder is what he means.

An adherent of the stronger conditions can respond to this in either of two ways. Like the weak-conditions theorist faced with the previous problem he can either retreat or stand his ground. He could stand his ground thus:

Usually when U means that P he *does* also mean that he believes that P. We tend to associate 'U means that he believes that P' with cases where that is all he means, and it seems strange and out of place in cases where he also means that P. Also, it is hard to notice something which is always present but is never of practical importance, like the earth's gravitational pull on one's ears; and when it is called to one's attention one may, out of sheer surprise, be inclined to deny that it is there. These failures of the human mind are natural and understandable; but they *are* failures, not serious reasons for denying that usually U means that he believes P as well as meaning that P.

This, though, seems more vulnerable than does the stubborn response

8 I am indebted to Colin McGinn for bringing this problem to my attention.

which I earlier allowed the proponent of the weakened conditions to make. Probably the strong-conditions theorist would do better to yield some ground, modifying his conditions so that they do not have the strange consequence. The best repair I can find looks as though it is tailored to achieve just this; but still it is not perfectly *ad hoc*, for soon it will do other useful work as well. To the original strong conditions (see start of this chapter) I add a further one which stipulates:

> P is not a proposition about U's state of mind, which U seeks to communicate mainly or wholly because he thinks it is a means to achieving, through the Gricean mechanism, some other effect.

This does what is needed, I think. It allows that U may mean both that P and that he believes P, if he has independent reason for wanting to communicate the latter; but it will not allow that he means that *he believes P* if this proposition enters the picture only as something which A needs to believe as part of his Gricean route to his own belief that P. Perhaps someone can devise examples which show that this repair needs repair, but I am sure that something along these lines will succeed.

Although the suggested repair of the conditions looks *ad hoc*, I am prepared to stand by it – that is, to adopt this form of the stronger conditions for meaning that P, and to reject the weakened conditions in which what U means is determined by what he intends to get A to believe that U believes.

Nothing I have said so far justifies this choice. Indeed, the balance of argument has slightly favoured the weaker conditions, since they have not been firmly pushed into the sort of complication which I have just added to the stronger ones.

My behavioural emphasis might seem to confer a tactical advantage on the stronger conditions; for it seems easier to describe behavioural evidence that U wants to communicate something about snakes or the weather, say, than evidence that he wants to communicate something about his own mind. But that is a mistake; for if U seeks to get A to believe something about snakes, relying on the Gricean mechanism, then he must also seek to get A to believe something about U's mind. I could therefore adopt the weakened conditions and still use the same examples: as I pointed out earlier, whatever counts as meaning by the weaker conditions is also meaning according to the stronger ones. Furthermore, if someone wanted behavioural evidence for U's seeking to communicate only something about his own beliefs, and not about anything else, even that could be supplied without much trouble. From a tactical point of view, therefore, there is really nothing in it.

The best reason for preferring the stronger conditions is one I shall come to in my next section.

Schiffer has proposed a different weakening in the conditions which it seems wise to accept.[9] It seems right to allow that U may mean that P even if he knows that A already believes P, e.g. where U thinks that A has forgotten P or has not noticed that P is relevant to some matter in hand. Schiffer therefore states the conditions in terms of U's intending to give A the *activated* belief that P, where this covers intending to get A to believe that P, to remind him that P, to bring his belief that P to the forefront of his mind, and so on. I want my account to be construed like that, all through; but I shall not write in 'activated' every time, and in my examples U will usually be trying to give A a belief and not merely to activate one which he already has.

A different weakening of the conditions for meaning has been proposed by Searle, who says that U's primary purpose is to be *understood*, and that he may not 'care a hang' whether A accepts either the message or U's sincerity.[10] The Gricean approach cannot give primacy to the intention to be understood, though it can accommodate the notion of understanding. If U intends to get A to believe P, he is understood if A realizes what it is that U intends to get him to believe: that separates understanding from believing, but only in a context where the primary aim is to produce belief. Gricean theory apart, there is a problem about the speaker's primarily aiming to produce understanding; for when this is combined with the intuitively plausible idea that to understand a speaker is to recognize what his primary aim is, they form a vicious circle. Searle avoids this bit of trouble by moving from understanding a speaker to understanding a *sentence*, which he equates with knowing what its conventional meaning is.[11] This is not something which my meaning-nominalist programme would let me accept as a basic account of understanding, and that is not a defect in the programme. Searle's approach strongly tends to suggest that meaning can occur only in a context of conventional meaning; I am sure that is false; and Searle has tried to dissociate himself from such a position without making clear

[9] Schiffer, p. 51.
[10] Introduction in J. R. Searle (ed.), *The Philosophy of Language* (Oxford, 1971), p. 10; see also Searle, pp. 46–7.
[11] Searle, pp. 47–50.

how he can legitimately avoid it, given that he ties meaning to the intention to be understood, and the latter to conventional meaning.[12]

Searle is now working on a different account of meaning, in which U's meaning that P need not involve his intending to have any effect on an audience. Rather, U means that P by what he utters if he intends that his utterance should *represent* reality in a certain way. Can 're-present' be elucidated adequately without basing it on convention and/or some sort of intention to communicate? The version of the work which I have seen[13] leaves the analysis of representation incomplete; the problem of completing it, in harmony with Searle's total theory, is clearly a non-trivial one; and I doubt if it can be solved. If it can, then this latest approach of Searle's might be very important indeed.

§41. Statements and injunctions

Let us return to the first weakening of the conditions for meaning P – the one according to which U means P just so long as he intends to communicate that he believes P. Armstrong has defended this on the grounds that it is theoretically beneficial.[14] Part of his case for this depends upon an analogous change in the conditions for injunction-meaning – one which replaces the clause '. . . intends to get *A to do X*' by '. . . intends to get *A to believe that U favours A's doing X*' or something to that general effect. If both revisions are accepted, the result is to strengthen the unified theory of meaning, putting more content into it and less into the two separate branches, statements and injunctions. For by the old conditions, what was common to the two was just U's intending to produce in A, through the Gricean mechanism, *some effect* (see §39 above); but under the new conditions they have in common that in each of them U intends to produce in A, through the Gricean mechanism, *some belief about U's state of mind*; and then the fork occurs, with one line running to U's belief (statements) and one running to his wishes or his favour (injunctions). This strong unification of the concept of meaning is a *prima facie* point in favour of the two revisions which generate it. (I have dropped one complexity from Armstrong's account, namely his replacement of '. . . get *A* to believe . . .' by '. . . give *A* reason to believe . . .' The reasons for this extra flourish are negligible in the context of my sufficient-conditions strategy.)

[12] For some evidence of this uncertainty in Searle's work, see Bennett (1973), pp. 164–5.
[13] An unpublished first draft, which Searle has showed me at my request.
[14] Armstrong (1971), pp. 431–3, and in personal correspondence.

In passing, I should mention Grice's own pursuit of a more strongly unified concept of meaning. This involves a doubly revised account of injunction-meaning, in which (1) U intends that A shall believe something about what U favours, and (2) the notion of A's *doing X* is replaced by that of his *intending to do X*.[15] So now U intends to get A to believe that U favours A's intending to do X. Fortunately, I need not go through the fine details of how this is supposed to produce theoretic unity, for this whole endeavour pretty clearly gets off on the wrong foot. Grice says that (2) has the result that in both sorts of meaning what U intends to achieve is 'always the generation of some propositional attitude' in A – either A's believing something or his intending something. But this misrepresents Grice's own conditions for injunction-meaning, which, because of revision (1) above, clearly imply that in injunctions as well as in statements U intends to get A to *believe* something. In the light of this, it is hardly surprising that the basic principle of the supposedly unified theory instantly falls apart: it contains an explicit, needed rider in which an extra condition is added for injunctions but not for statements.[16]

Armstrong's unified theory is not open to these objections, however, primarily because it does not replace A's doing X by his intending to do X. (That is not the entire source of Grice's trouble, but the matter is too complex to be sorted out here.) Still, the question remains of whether the unification is being bought at too high a price.

I submit that it is. The crucial objection is that the revised account of injunction-meaning obliterates the distinction between U's telling A to do X and U's *merely* informing A that U favours A's doing X. It is no defence to say that one can tell someone to do X by informing him that one wants him to do X; that is not in dispute. My point is that one can seek *just* to inform someone that one favours his doing X, not aiming to tell or advise or request or recommend him to do X; but on Armstrong's account this is impossible, for if you tell the person that you favour his doing X then you have *ipso facto* fulfilled Armstrong's conditions for telling him to do X. In short, in Armstrong's account the whole essence of injunctions, as of statements, is informative.

I seem to be open to a similar if milder charge. If U seeks to get A to do X, and is relying on the Gricean mechanism, then U must, as part of his total plan, be relying on that mechanism to get A to recognize that U favours A's doing X. Does it not follow that every injunction includes a statement, i.e. that if U means that A is to do X he must *also*

15 Grice (1968), p. 230.   16 *Ibid.*, the formula D.1 on pp. 230–1.

mean that he favours A's doing X? I could live with that result if I had to, better than with Armstrong's, but in fact I do not have to. This is an incidental benefit of the episode in §40 above, where I said that even if U is trying through the Gricean mechanism to communicate P, he does not therefore count as meaning that P if P is 'a proposition about U's state of mind, which U seeks to communicate mainly or wholly because he thinks it is a means to achieving, through the Gricean mechanism, some other effect'. Although that was introduced to solve a quite different problem it also neatly solves the present one. It blocks the inference from 'U means that A is to do X' to 'U means that he favours A's doing X'; because the proposition that U favours A's doing X is about U's mind, and U wants A to believe it just as a means to the achievement through the Gricean mechanism of some other effect, namely A's doing X. So I am not committed to allowing that every injunction includes a statement.

If U's interest in A's beliefs is ordinarily to result from his interest in A's behaviour, this threatens to absorb statements into injunctions – which would be Armstrong's result turned on its head. But the threat is easily met. For one thing, as I showed in §38 above, even if U wants A to believe P because of how this will affect A's behaviour, there need be no value of X such that U wants A to do X in particular. Also, even if U does want A to believe P so that he will do a specific X, it does not follow by my account that U is enjoining A to do X. U's utterance is an injunction to do X only if he is relying on a mechanism which includes A's recognition that U wants A to do X. If U is relying on the Gricean mechanism to get A to believe P, and on some other mechanism to get A from believing P to doing X, then he means that P and not that A is to do X. The distinction between statements and injunctions is deep and secure.

In real life someone may utter an injunction without caring whether the hearer acts on it: for instance, the clerk at the information desk dutifully advises me to change trains at Reading, but has no interest in whether I do change at Reading. But that does not support Armstrong's account against mine; for the clerk probably does not care, either, whether I think that he favours my changing at Reading. In fact, in cases like this the utterance counts as an injunction only because it involves a form of language conventionally associated with injunctions; and so they should stay out of sight until we reach the level of language or at least of conventional meaning.

It will be recalled that Armstrong's position is this: (i) Injunctions are to focus on '. . . to communicate that U favours . . .', (ii) Statements are to focus on '. . . to communicate that U believes . . .', and each is supported by the fact that together they yield (iii) a strongly unified account of meaning which gives statements and injunctions a great deal in common. I have contended that (i) is wrong; and so I reject Armstrong's version of (iii); which leads me to reject this argument for (ii). I shall now argue against (ii), using Armstrong's own general premiss that we want (iii) a strongly unified treatment of injunctions and statements.

I take my stand on Grice's original account of injunctions, in which their essence is U's reliance on the Gricean mechanism to get A to do something; and Armstrong and I agree that the essence of a statement is U's reliance on the Gricean mechanism to get A to believe something. In an injunction, then, A is to relate himself causally to some part of the world, and in a statement he is to relate himself epistemically to some part of the world. Furthermore, in the case of an injunction the relevant part of the world may be the speaker himself ('Hug me') but it may be something else ('Climb that tree'). An interest in unity and symmetry of theory inclines one to say that in the case of a statement, too, the relevant part of the world may be the speaker ('I am hungry', 'I believe that it is going to rain') and may be something else ('It is going to rain'). This view about statements, which adopts the original stronger conditions and not the weaker ones favoured by Armstrong and latterly by Grice, represents the whole difference between injunctions and statements as that between the causal and the epistemic, or between acting and believing. Whereas if we combine the original view of injunctions with the new view of statements, we get a lop-sided account in which an injunction aims at A's relating himself causally to *something*, while a statement aims at his relating himself epistemically to *the speaker*. Although a small matter, it is large enough to outweigh the tiny advantage found for the weakened conditions in §40 above. And §§52–3 below will implicitly contain a further small argument tending in the same direction.

Not that the issue is vital. The rest of this book will be based on Grice's original conditions for the meaning of a statement and for injunction-meaning; but it would not be hard to modify it to fit one or both of the revisions discussed in this section.

§42. Introducing the tribe

Having explained what I take meaning to be, I now return to the laying of behavioural foundations for it. The plan is to use the materials of earlier chapters to show how someone's non-linguistic behaviour can be good evidence that he means something by what he does or utters. I shall do this through an anthropological fiction, according to which we are observing a tribe of anthropoid mammals, and will say about them only what we can soundly base on their behaviour in relation to the nature of their environments and sense-organs. We shall gradually become entitled to credit them with having a language: either because they develop one under our very eyes, or because we learn more about them. The former option is obviously unrealistic. But so is the latter, for we would be unlikely to get our behavioural data in just the order I shall follow – getting much evidence about intentions and beliefs before getting any about meanings, then much about the meanings of whole utterances before any about the meanings of utterance-parts, and so on. But since the tribe is just an expository and heuristic device, these implausibilities do not matter. When I say 'We can now apply concept C to the tribe, but not yet concept C^*', I really mean that the application of C does not logically require the applicability of C^*. My real concern is the logical independence, not chronological order; and so it is not important that the decorative chronological garb I shall give my statements will involve a fiction about the tribe's speed in generating a language or our luck over the order in which we uncovered evidence about their abilities.

Throughout, I shall pretend that we are observing the tribe without their realizing it, so that their behaviour is not deflected by any attitude towards us, such as embarrassment or puzzlement or a desire to impress or deceive. Such deflections could be handled, for if we were affecting the tribe's behaviour, we could discover that we were doing so, and how, and adjust our account of their normal behaviour accordingly. But for simplicity's sake I shall pretend that no such problems arise.

My tribesmen are highly educable and inquisitive, their sensory organs work well, and their motor capacities are unimpaired. These stipulations are convenient, not necessary, for the programme.

We have already learned much about the tribe's intentions and beliefs. We know that they have beliefs about one anothers' intentions and beliefs, and that they sometimes try to produce intentions or beliefs in one another. For example, we know that a once thought that b intended to pull a tree down, that *c* intended to get *d* to think there were fish in the bay, that *e* thought that *f* thought that a certain noise was made by a snake, and so on. But we have never yet been in a position to apply to the tribe any concept involving language or even meaning.

So far, the only way tribesman *a* can reasonably intend to produce a belief in tribesman *b* is by revealing evidence to him. He sweeps away leaves to reveal squirrel droppings, intending to get *b* to think there are squirrels nearby; he turns *b*'s head towards the sky so that he sees the rain-clouds, intending him to think that it will rain; and so on. The evidence may concern *a* himself, as when he belches so as to get *b* to think that he has recently eaten, or lets *b* see that he is trembling so as to convince *b* that there is a predator nearby. All of these cases involve *intention-free evidence*, by which I mean items whose status as evidence does not depend at all upon why the agent revealed them.

The tribesmen are highly educable, but are not yet capable of many beliefs which are so highly theoretical, so far removed from experience, that their falsity could remain undetected for a long time. So I assume that most of their beliefs are true or nearly true. I also assume that they have, and know one another to have, some interest in producing true beliefs in one another. I could do without either assumption, but they help to simplify the exposition.

All of that background information about the tribe could be established on the basis of their non-linguistic behaviour: the foregoing chapters show how.

§43. The first case of meaning

Suppose that we have reached that stage in our understanding of the tribe, without ever having grounds for thinking that any tribesman ever means anything by what he does. Then one day we observe a tribesman, *U*, stand in full view of another, *A*, and emit a snake-like hissing sound while also making with his hand a smooth, undulating, horizontal motion which resembles the movement of a snake. Why did he do this? Countless answers are possible, but our knowledge of *U* could lead us to one in particular. I shall assemble it by layers, to make clear how behavioural evidence could support it. We could have solid evidence that *U* intended

(1)   to affect something other than himself,
(2)   to affect *A*,

(3) to affect *A* auditorially and/or visually, or in some way arising
     from the audio-visual effect,
(4) to get *A* to believe something,
(5) to get *A* to believe something about a snake,
(6) to get *A* to believe there is a snake nearby.

As regards (1), whenever *U* engages in protracted, apparently connected sequences of behaviour he intends to affect something outside
himself. Furthermore, it would be out of character for *U* to think (2)
that he was affecting anything other than *A*, or (3) that he was having
any immediate effect upon *A* other than an audio-visual one. Also, (4)
whenever *U* deliberately produces a sensory change in another tribesman, it is in order to get the latter to believe something. This, like the
backing for (1), could admit of classes of exceptions, so long as our
present situation did not belong to any of them. As for (5): this raises
the question of *what U* intended to get *A* to believe. Well, *U*'s performance gave *A* intention-free evidence that *U*'s hands were not
paralysed, and that his lungs were working; but I stipulate that we have
no evidence that *U* is interested in convincing *A* of anything like that.
And that is about as far as *U*'s performance reaches, considered as
intention-free evidence. Certainly, it cannot have been offered as
intention-free evidence of anything about a snake: there is no chance
that *U* thought that *A* might mistake his noise and hand-movement for
an actual snake. But the nature of the performance – the fact that it
naturally induces the thought of a snake – forces us to conclude that if
U is trying to make *A* believe something, it is something about a snake.
So we shall tentatively conjecture that *U* intended (5), acknowledging
that this leaves us with the problem of how *U* can have expected his
performance to convince *A* of something for which the performance
was not intention-free evidence.

   Finally, (6) could be reached on the grounds that the only belief
about snakes which *U* could want to produce in *A* on this occasion is
that there is a snake nearby. This is not based on our observation that
there *is* a snake there, but rather on a more general assessment of the
set-up: *U* has not just been bitten by a snake, there are no other tribesmen in sight, *U* is not in a position to know of a recent snake-encounter
of which *A* is ignorant, the proximity of snakes is a matter of interest to
this tribe because they fear snakes or value them, and so on.

Note that I moved from (4) to (5) on the strength of the 'iconic' aspect of U's performance, that is, its constituting a natural pointer towards the thought of a snake; and that I moved on to (6) by eliminating alternatives. These two features of my procedure seem to be inescapable.

I claim that my earlier chapters show how we could be entitled to (6) as our best account of what U intended by his performance. Fill in the behavioural details as you like.

A problem remains, though; for (6), even if we have no decent alternative to it, is hardly tenable unless we can explain how U could expect his performance to produce that result. He need not be certain of success, but he must think he has some chance. At the end of §28 above I resolved never to credit any creature with any belief, probabilistic or otherwise, which is not based on its past experience; so I may not allow intentions which are based on stabs in the dark. Well, then, what could underlie U's belief that his pantomime might lead to A's thinking there was a snake nearby?

Of many possible answers, my interest is in this one: U was relying on A's thinking that U intended to get A to believe that there was a snake nearby ('to believe P', for short); and he further expected that A would be led to believe P by his belief that U wanted him to believe P. That last move is secured if A trusts U to this limited extent: A thinks that if on this occasion U wants A to believe P, that is a reason for believing P. I shall explore trust more fully in §45 below.

But what is supposed to bring A to believe that U intends (6)? Well, A has access to all our data, and so A can come to realize that nothing but (6) will do as an account of U's intention; and U can expect A to realize this. U could then expect the following: A tentatively accepts that U intends (6), as having no tenable rivals; he is led by that plus trust in U to a tentative acceptance of P; A then reflects on the route he has followed, and conjectures that U expected him to follow it; this explains how U could expect his action to produce (6), and so A is no longer tentative in accepting that that was U's intention or, therefore, in accepting P. All that, I repeat, is what U intended to happen.

Summing all this up: When U performed his pantomime he intended to get A to believe there was a snake in A's vicinity, and he was relying on the following mechanism: A recognizes that U intends to get A to believe P, and A is led by that, plus trust in U, to believe P. U has not intended A to have any false beliefs about U's intentions or expectations, and indeed U has relied upon A's getting a pretty good grasp of what U was up to.

All of that suffices to make the case one of meaning. By performing his pantomine, *U meant that* there was a snake nearby.

I could have taken an example where *U* meant that *A* was to kill the snake. It might help there if *U*'s utterance was a pantomine not of a snake but rather of a snake-killing, but that is not essential. The essence is that *U* should be trying to get *A* to kill the snake because he thinks *U* wants him to. If *U* already knows that *A* knows that the snake is there, that would show at least that *U* is not endeavouring to inform *A* about the snake. But we could, in a virtuoso display, construct a case in which there is evidence that *U* seeks both to inform *A* about the snake and to enjoin him to kill it. As I explained in §41 above, the essence of the '. . . and to enjoin him to kill it' is that *U* should not expect that *A* will kill the snake just because he knows that it is there, but rather because he recognizes that *U* wants him to kill it.

§44. The nature of the evidence

Everything in that diagnosis could be based upon behavioural evidence. To take just one example from near the middle of the diagnosis: it is claimed that *U* expects *A* to conjecture that *U*'s intention is (6), because it cannot be anything else; and this could be one of many cases where *U* expected *A* to form negative or tentative views about *U*'s intentions. For example, on another occasion *U* and *A* are trying to extinguish a fire; *U* sees a way of smothering it by dislodging a large rock to start a landslide; he needs *A*'s help with the rock; he does not expect *A* to see how the rock could put out the fire; but he pushes at the rock anyway, expecting *A* to help because he conjectures that the assault on the rock must be intended to extinguish the fire somehow. That account of *U*'s beliefs could be challenged, but my previous chapters show how in principle such challenges can be met.

In my account of the first case of meaning, I suggested that *A* might 'reflect', going through an episodic and controlled movement from thought to thought. Could there be solid behavioural evidence that he was doing so? Probably not. Whenever I credit a tribesman with interior trains of reasoning, this is just a device for showing how the parts of my total diagnosis are inter-related. The essence of each diagnosis is the attribution of a belief which is related, through our theory about the tribesman's mind, to his epistemic input and behavioural output. Those relationships may be very complex, and it sometimes helps to clarify them if I pretend that the tribesman reaches his belief by episodically reflecting on his past experience and present goals. But those episodes have a dramatic and expository function, not a structural one, in my story; so I do not mind not having firm behavioural evidence that they are occurring. Objection: 'Perhaps the thought episodes would always be causally necessary. Perhaps no creature could have beliefs relating in those complex ways to his input and output unless he arrived at them through episodic reasonings of the sort now under discussion.' If that were true, then we could after all have evidence that a languageless creature had conducted such reasonings. For our evidence that he had beliefs which related thus and so to his input and output would itself be evidence that he had gone through inner processes of reasoning if, as we are now supposing, those processes are required for the achievement of those beliefs. It might be suggested that the reasoning, as well as being required for the achievement of the beliefs, is something of which a languageless creature would be incapable. I can see no reason for thinking that that might be true.

I do not offer to trace my 'meaning' diagnosis right back to the basic data which support it, but only to show how its various elements might resemble diagnoses which we had used in cases which did not involve meaning. I have done this for one element in the 'meaning' diagnosis, and claim that it could be done for the rest. This falls doubly short of proving that non-linguistic behaviour could make the 'meaning' diagnosis inescapable, for a proof would have to display, for *each* element in the diagnosis, a *complete* range of supporting data. The results would be unsurveyable, and I prefer to risk leaving some readers imperfectly convinced.

Were we observing an actual tribe, we would reach our first confident meaning diagnosis only through several tentative ones, rather than being able to muster conclusive evidence on our very first skirmish with meaning diagnoses. A probable route to the discovery of tribal meanings would be as follows. We observe several items of behaviour which we cannot confidently explain; each admits of a meaning diagnosis, though with some elements in it based on mere conjecture; but the unsupported elements in one diagnosis correspond to supported elements in others; and so the whole set, taken together, provide good evidence that meaning diagnoses are correct in every case.

It would also be helpful to find a case where A evidently did come to believe P although we were not sure that U intended to produce this result through the Gricean mechanism. My original snake case might be like that if the evidence about U's intention were incomplete, and one behavioural fact were added, namely that after seeing U's performance A laid about him with his machete or did something else which was best explained by the conjecture that he had just come to think there was a snake in his vicinity. This would give us evidence that U's performance had in fact led A to believe P, and thus that some mechanism was at work although we did not know what it was. That would support the conjecture that U had intended to get A to believe P, relying on that mechanism which we have so far failed to discover though we have seen its effects. ('Why is he throwing those crystals out of his plane over the parched fields?' 'Perhaps he intends to make rain fall.' 'How could he expect that action to produce that result?' 'I don't know, but here comes the rain.') This would strengthen considerably the conjecture that U intended A to recognize U's primary intention, for A might also know the thing which we did not know. We should still be obliged to explain *how* U could expect his action to get A to believe P: the mere fact that A does come to believe P does not relieve us of the responsibility for explaining U's expectation that he would do so. But that 'mere fact' could be extremely useful, smoothing the way to conjectural diagnoses which were later confirmed by further evidence.

There is another sort of help we could get. If we have incomplete evidence that U meant that P by what he did at time T, this could be immeasurably strengthened by (incomplete) evidence that on earlier occasions U had done things by which he meant that P, or Q, or R, always with the same audience as at T. For then we have an answer to the crucial challenge to our diagnosis of what U did at T, namely the question 'How can U have expected what he did to get A to believe P?' The answer is 'He can have expected A to recall relevantly similar occasions when A knows that U intended . . . etc.' This might work even if on the previous occasions communication failed; for it could happen that A did not recognize U's intention at the time, but later realized what he had been up to. For instance: while A blankly contemplates U's performance he is bitten by a snake which then undulates off into the undergrowth, hissing as it goes; and A, after recovering and brooding a little, reaches the right diagnosis of U's intention. This insight comes too late to make U's meaning a success, but it can still be helpful to A, to U, and to us on later occasions. To take the extreme case, if U again mimics the sound and motion of a snake, we shall not be puzzled if A immediately takes anti-snake action. But a helpful relevance need not be as direct as that.

These are conveniences, not necessities. I do not endorse the view that the concept of meaning requires a context of conventions or habits or general practices of meaning. On the contrary, I claim to have refuted that view by showing how we could identify an instance of meaning without suspecting that those tribesmen ever did before, or ever will again, mean anything by their actions. Taking several cases at once might ease our interpretative task, but it is not a theoretical necessity. Any way, the several cases need not constitute a convention or general meaning practice: they could be just a scatter of isolated instances of meaning, connected at most by U's relying in some of them on A's recalling earlier ones, though they could be useful to us without even that tenuous link between them.

§45. Credence

When U utters a statement, the Gricean mechanism will fail unless A thinks that on this occasion *U is unlikely to want him to believe P unless P is true*. This species of Gricean mechanism, where U's wanting A to believe P is, for A, a reason for believing P, will be called the 'credence mechanism'. Normally, it will operate only if A trusts both U's state of knowledge and his honesty, that is, both his tendency to have true beliefs and his disposition to endow A with beliefs which he himself has. P could be true because U was dishonest and ill-informed in such a way that the two cancelled out, but we can safely ignore that possibility. Indeed, I shall pretend that U's beliefs are all true and that A knows this (see the end of §42 above). Errors will occur, but they will be in a minority and can be safely ignored in the meantime.

There remains the question of A's trust in U's honesty. I shall try to sort out the issues which that raises, starting with an error I once made about it. I said: '[We cannot] discover what general propensities for scepticism a creature has by attending to its behaviour in non-linguistic contexts: the kind of scepticism in question is precisely that involved in disbelief of what is asserted.'[17] That is wrong. In the absence of meanings, and thus of language, U could still try to get A to believe things by exhibiting to him intention-free evidence, i.e. items whose status as evidence does not depend upon U's intentions in revealing it. Furthermore, A could know what was going on, including knowing what U intended each time, and he could discover that in general the beliefs U sought to give him were true (or were false), and that in general they were beliefs which U himself had (or did not have). So A could

[17] Bennett (1964), p. 62.

have a tendency to be trustful (or sceptical) with regard to U – but not to what U asserts, for he asserts nothing. If U does start asserting things, that is, relying on the credence mechanism to communicate, A's general attitude of trustfulness or scepticism will carry through to these special cases unless there is a special impediment to its doing so. In short, A's tendency to (dis)believe what U says to him is predictable in principle from his attitude to U's endeavours to get him to believe things by revealing intention-free evidence. There is no peculiarly linguistic kind of (dis)honesty: we are concerned with a kind of credence or trust which is not specifically tied to meaning.

The credence mechanism will work just so long as A thinks that on this occasion P is likely to be true if U wants A to believe P. He need not think that U is generally to be trusted, for his trust may be special to the occasion and/or to P in particular. The credence mechanism does require that A will trust U's honesty in any situation belonging to a certain class. But the class could be very narrow – e.g. that A trusts U only when he is well-fed and comfortable and the sun is shining and there is no wind blowing and U is trying to communicate something about the weather.

How much dishonesty could there be in the tribe's utterings, meaning activities, endeavours to communicate through the credence mechanism? As much as is compatible with utterers' normally expecting to be believed. That creates some pressure towards honesty. If U usually utters dishonestly, his audience will probably know this; if they do, they will probably expect further untrue utterings from him; if they have that expectation, U will probably know that they do, and so he will be unable to rely on the credence mechanism. Those probabilities are based on the axioms that the tribesmen are educable and that the relevant data are available to them. Each probability could be expressed by a fraction which is less than 1 (= certainty) by the extent of various possible kinds of good luck, bad luck, stupidity, forgetfulness, cunning and so on. When the fractions are multiplied, the product will be small enough to leave room for many dishonest utterings; but still there must be some limit to them, and this will become important in §50 below.

§46. Compliance

The general form of the Gricean mechanism is this: U has some effect on A because A recognizes that U is trying to have that effect. Injunctions involve the special case where U gets A to do X because he recognizes that U wants him to do X. I shall use the label 'the compliance mechanism' for this species of Gricean mechanism.

The compliance mechanism will fail unless A regards U's wanting him to do X as a reason for doing X. What bases can he have for this attitude? Possible answers range from 'Only one – the belief that it is in his interests to do what U wants him to do' across to 'Millions', which could be supported with hosts of detailed cases. The answer I find most helpful uses a four-part taxonomy. In what follows, every clause about A's beliefs, or A's or U's interests, may be subject to qualification: it may hold only when A is hungry, or only when U is not tired, or only when they are both foraging, or only on Tuesdays; it does not matter what the restrictions are, so long as they allow the clause to apply to the given situation where A is said to be compliant with U's wishes. I shall handle this infinitude of possible restrictions by omitting them all, and stating each basis for compliance in its unqualified form. Here they are.

(1) A thinks that U has an interest in A's welfare *per se*; so that U's wanting A to do X is evidence that it will be in A's interest to do X.

(2) A thinks that his interests tend to coincide with U's, though not because either values the interests of the other; so that whatever U wants to happen is probably something that A should also want to happen.

Each of these bases for compliance involves A's crediting U with information which A lacks; and A's belief about what U wants him to do functions as evidence about what A would have wanted to do, quite apart from U, had he been better informed.

These two bases for compliance could also be bases for credence. In both (1) and (2), A thinks that

If *U wants A to do X* then probably *doing X is good for A*,

and I invite comparison between that and credence, in which A thinks that

If *U wants A to believe P* then probably *P is true*.

The latter could be based either on U's caring for A's welfare, which is like (1) above; or on a general coincidence, not rooted in altruism, between U's interests and A's, which is like (2). The remaining two bases for compliance, however, have no analogues in credence.

(3) A thinks that if U wants A to do X, then U will make it in A's

interest to do X, by rewarding him if he does X and/or punishing him if he does not do X. If A is right about this, then his interests coincide with U's in this matter. The coincidence is produced by U's will, and not by sheer convergence as in (2); and it does not arise from U's fitting his pliable will to A's rigid interests, as in (1), but rather from U's bending A by giving him an interest which coincides with U's rigid will.

(4) U's wanting A to do X is regarded by A as a reason, just in itself, for him to do X. Here the coincidence between A's interests and U's is produced by A's will, rather than by U's as in case (3).

The reason why (3) and (4) have no analogues in credence is that in neither of them is A's belief about what U wants a mere pointer to what A would have wanted anyway if he had been better informed. On the contrary, in both (3) and (4) A's view of the situation is one in which U's wishes *affect* A's interests, rather than merely providing evidence as to what they are.

As an aid to seeing that (3) and (4) have no analogues in credence, consider the fact that a rational person cannot be brought to believe that P either (3) by threats or inducements, or (4) by his concern for the interests of someone who tells him that P.

If A's compliance is intelligible, it must have at least one of the above four bases. Facts about which basis an enjoiner is relying on are relevant to whether his injunction counts as advice, a command, a request, etc. But those differentiae would take me too far afield.

6

REGULAR MEANINGS

§47. Escaping from icons

If we could find one case where a tribesman did something thereby meaning P, then we could discover any number of them, perhaps with different values of P; and the more cases we found the securer could be our diagnosis of them all as involving Gricean intentions.

Next, we might establish certain non-vacuous generalizations of the form: Whenever any tribesman does something of kind K, he means P; where K is a physical action-kind, and 'P' stands for some sentence. It will always be a sentence whose truth-value can change according to who utters it and/or according to when or where it is uttered. For instance, one utterance-kind regularly means that it will soon rain in the place of utterance, another means that the speaker is now hungry, a third means that the place where the speaker is standing is hot, and so on. Actual human languages contain sentences which mean that P for values of P which do not change in truth-value: in English, for example, we have the sentence 'Grass is often green'. But I shall argue in §65 below that that would hardly be possible if English did not have semantic structure, that is, utterances whose meanings result from the meanings of their parts and how they are assembled; and the tribal communication system will not be endowed with structure until much later.

The human situation differs from the tribal one in another way. To explain it, I need to distinguish three ways in which U might get A to believe that P. (1) He might reveal to A some intention-free evidence for P, i.e. some item which is evidence for P independently of U's intentions in making it available to A. (2) He might employ the credence mechanism to get A to believe P, by some action containing what I call a 'natural pointer' to P, that is, something which naturally tends to induce in the observer some thought closely connected with P; for instance, a pantomime of a snake if P is about a snake. (3) He might employ the credence mechanism by means of an action which

148

did not naturally point to *P*, e.g. saying 'There is a snake near you' to warn *A* that there is a snake near him.

(2) and (3) could be described as involving, respectively, 'iconic' and 'non-iconic' vehicles of meaning. The 'natural pointer' involved in (2) need not be 'iconic' in the strict sense of involving a resemblance between the action and something to do with *P*; for the pointer could be an actual object which is involved in *P* – for example, *U* might hold up a dish meaning that he wanted *A* to give it to him. Still, 'iconic' is a handy label, and I shall use it.[1]

Iconic vehicles of meaning are poor things, which are not fit to carry most meanings. Human languages hardly use them: except for minor cases of onomatopoeia, our utterances never point naturally to our meanings; and this holds not only for semantically structured sentences but also for unstructured ones like 'Sorry!' and 'Help!', which do not suggest regret or need to anyone who doesn't know English. I want the tribal communication system to be free of iconic cramps, as human languages are, and so now I must equip the tribe with non-iconic vehicles of meaning.

In my original, primeval, Gricean example of meaning the case for saying that *U* meant that *P* – and thus thought he had some chance of communicating *P* – depended totally on the fact that *A* could be led to the thought that *P* by a route which included the utterance's iconically prompting in him the thought of a snake. Now I want the tribe to have non-iconic utterance/meaning relationships, so I must face the question: if the utterance does not relate iconically to the meaning, how can the speaker expect the audience to know or even guess what the meaning is?

The question can be nicely posed, and properly answered, in terms of some work of Schiffer's.[2] According to him, every Gricean intention requires that *U* shall believe that his utterance *S* has some feature which will lead *A* to connect *S* with *P*; and *A* can understand *S* only if it *does* have such a feature. The latter might consist in an iconic relation between utterance and meaning; but, as Schiffer points out, it might instead be the higher-level feature of *being of some kind which has been regularly associated with P*. If *S* has that feature, and the hearer knows it has, communication can succeed; and this imposes no cramps on the kinds of physical features utterances can have.

---

[1] 'Icon' was brought into the philosophy of language by Peirce; though his use of the term is even broader than mine, for what seems to be a bad reason. See C. Hartshorne and P. Weiss (eds.), *Collected Papers of Charles Sanders Peirce* (Cambridge, Mass., 1960), 2.279.   [2] Schiffer (1972), pp. 122–8.

It seems obvious that if A knows that in the past S has been regularly associated with P, this gives him a reason to expect it to be associated with P on a further occasion. But one may be sure that it gives him a reason, without being clear about *why* it does. Schiffer has good things to say about this; but I shall set the whole question aside until chapter 7, where I shall investigate certain answers to it, especially the one embodied in Lewis's theory of convention. Also, I shall in the meantime just assume that some non-iconic regularities are a going concern in the tribe, postponing until §63 below the question of how they could get started. A third important question will be dealt with right away.

§48. Learning without icons

The tribe are to be endowed with regular utterance-meaning relationships which have no sort of iconic stiffening. The question is: how can we, and how can tribal learners, discover what these relationships are? If we are to get evidence for the truth of 'Whenever any tribesman utters S, he means that P', where S is some kind of movement or noise or object with no iconic relationship with P, then we must be able to discover that on some individual occasion a speaker uttered S meaning by it that P. How could we discover that? Granted that we might have some evidence that U intended to communicate something, how can we learn, without iconic help, that it was P rather than Q or R?

Here are two sorts of help we might get. We could discover (1) that the uttering of S did lead A to believe that P, or (2) that U had good reason, just then, to want to convince A that P – perhaps U has just seen fish in the bay and knows that A has not seen them, and this makes us suspect that what U means in uttering S is that there are fish in the bay. Neither method (1) nor method (2) would let us decisively translate S by observing a single use of it, but that does not matter. Rather than restricting ourselves to a single use, we can use (1) or (2) to determine that one S-token meant something within a certain range, a second meant something within a different but overlapping range, and so on until only one P is left as common to all the cases that have been studied. (The notion of 'only one P' begs questions which I shall take up in §§77–8 below.)

That way of doing things points to a third and simpler basis upon which we, or young tribesmen, might learn that S regularly means that P. (3) By observing many occasions when S is uttered, we may notice that P seems to be the only proposition which, though often false, is nearly always true when S is uttered. For example, whenever S is uttered rain starts to fall, and we cannot find any other comparable state of affairs to be linked in this way with the uttering of S. That is evidence that S means that rain is about to fall, but it is weaker than the evidence we get by discovering that S-utterers always want their hearers to think that rain is about to fall.

Some writers, trying to elucidate language through a treatment of utterances as responses to stimuli, have sought to discover the meaning of S by observing the conditions under which a tribesman can be depended upon to utter S.[3] I agree with Ziff that we should reverse this and look rather for what is dependably the case whenever a tribesman utters S.[4] Ziff says in effect that there are no truths like 'Whenever rain impends, S is uttered', but that we may be able to determine meanings through generalizations like 'Whenever S is uttered, rain impends'. But even truths of the form 'If S is uttered, P is the case' are relevant to meanings only because they point to corresponding ones of the form 'If S is uttered, the utterer wants to communicate that P is the case'. The stimulus–response theorists to whom I have alluded banish hearers from the picture; Ziff re-admits them, but hardly gives them a noisy welcome.

Armstrong has offered the following comment on the thesis that the inferential route runs from the utterance rather than towards it:

This point of Ziff's is confirmed if we think of utterances as *signs* (in the sense that black clouds are signs). Signs probabilify the thing signified, but the thing signified only occasionally probabilifies the sign. In my view, the utterance, in normal context, of 'There is a snake behind you' is a *first-class* sign that U wants A to believe that U believes there is a snake behind A, a *rather good* sign that U believes there is a snake behind A, and a *fairly good* sign that there is a snake behind A. It is only the third of these three signified states of affairs that is a *public* happening, and no doubt successful communication depends upon a fairly good correlation between the sign and this public event. Hence, a reasonable amount of (a) sincerity, (b) reliability, is required for the actual use of language. (a) and (b) then set up good correlations between the first state of affairs signified and the second, and the second and the third, and thus a good correlation between the sign and the public happening.[5]

That seems to me perfect. It reflects – but does not require or imply – a

---

[3] For some references, see Bennett (1975).
[4] Paul Ziff, 'A Response to "Stimulus Meaning"', *Philosophical Review*, vol. 79 (1969), p. 73.
[5] From a personal communication. For more on 'signs' see Armstrong (1971), pp. 427–30.

view of Armstrong's which I disagree with, namely that 'U means that P' should be immediately tied to 'U intends to communicate that U believes P' (see §§40–1 above). The quoted passage does imply or presuppose that if S means P then someone's uttering S is a sign that P in the ordinary all-purpose sense of 'sign'. I accept this, and would express it by saying that the uttering of S is evidence for P, in the ordinary sense of 'evidence', the special feature being just that the evidence is intention-dependent.

The foregoing three ways of learning that S regularly means P are essentially for eavesdroppers. One is not available, and the others are not satisfactorily available, to the intended hearers of utterances. Here is why.

(1) Obviously, A cannot learn what S means by observing what belief he acquires upon hearing it. If it leads him to believe P, his belief must arise from his understanding, and so cannot produce it.

(2) Less obviously, A cannot ordinarily and satisfactorily be helped by discovering that U has good reason to want him to believe that P. If A does become convinced that U has reason to want him to believe P, there are two possibilities. (i) This happens in a manner which involves A's becoming convinced that P is true. But in that case, A learns that P independently of U's utterance, which is therefore rendered idle. So although A could learn in this way that S means that P, this is an essentially deviant way for him to do so, because it undercuts the very procedure which a communication-system chiefly aims to bring about. (ii) Alternatively, A gets no evidence as to P's truth, but merely learns that it would be good from U's point of view if A were to believe P. If this leads A to think that U means that P, he must be taking a dark view of U's character: he thinks that U will be apt to try to convince him that P just because it would suit U's convenience if A believed P. In that case, however, although A may understand U he will presumably distrust him, and so will not be led to believe P by his recognition that U wants him to believe it. So once again U's intention is thwarted, which implies that this too is a deviant way for A to discover what U means by uttering S.

(3) U's communicative intentions are also considerably thwarted if his intended hearer A learns what U means by S only by noting that every time U utters S it is the case that P. For that implies that U utters S many times when A does not understand it, or anyway not until much later.

I conclude that I have described three essentially eavesdropping ways of linking S with P. The first cannot be used by the intended hearer. The other two could be used by him, but any occasion when they were would be non-standard, because either the utterance would be rendered idle or some part of the speaker's intention would be thwarted.

Of those three ways of learning the standard meaning of a statement-making utterance-type, two have analogues with injunctions. If U means by S that A is to do X, we may discover this by noting (1) that when A hears S he then does X, or (2) that X is what U has most reason to want A to do just then – e.g. to throw a rope to U, who is drowning. The third lead to the meanings of statements has no analogue in the realm of injunctions. Methods (1) and (2), with injunctions as well as with statements, are not satisfactorily available to intended hearers. (1) Obviously, A cannot understand S through noting what *he* does upon hearing it. (2) If A infers that S means that A is to do X from his observation that U has a need for A to do X, then U's utterance has achieved nothing. For if A is disposed to be compliant, he will do X because he sees U's need, not because he understands S; and if he is not disposed to be compliant, he will not do X at all. Either way, S is idle.

How can intended hearers learn about meanings without help from icons? Well, one can train to be a successful intended hearer by going through an apprenticeship as an eavesdropper or as an unsuccessful intended hearer. But there are also two other sorts of help, which probably have a large part in the actual learning of human languages.

Firstly, if A understands part of S, he may come to understand the rest of it by discovering what U has reason to be saying, without S's thereby being rendered idle. For instance, U says 'Hand me a crescent wrench'; A understands 'Hand me a' but not 'crescent wrench'; but he can see just one useful tool which is beyond U's reach and he guesses it to be a crescent wrench. This could let A *complete* his understanding of the injunction without making it otiose. Similarly with statements. But this will work only with utterances having semantic structure, and so it is not yet available to my tribe.

Secondly, there is a special sort of help that non-learners can give to learners – a sort which does not need structured utterances. Recall that the problem is just to discover which proposition to associate with S, not to discover that S is uttered with a Gricean intention or the like. So the problem is solved if the child learns certain mappings of utterances onto environmental states of affairs (statements) or onto wants (injunctions); and adults can and do help by producing utterances just so as to accustom the child to the right mappings. A mother may say 'Give me the spoon' while her other behaviour shows clearly that she wants to be given the spoon: the utterance does not communicate as an injunction, but it helps the child with his mappings. Or the child's blocks tumble, and an onlooking adult says 'The blocks have fallen down' – not informing the child about the blocks, but just helping him with his mappings. This sort of help is common and helpful, but not essential. Anyone could learn the meaning-regularities in his community just by attending to utterances which are seriously intended to communicate something to him or to someone else.

Once tribesman A has somehow learned that S is regularly uttered by speakers who mean that P, he is then equipped for the role of intended hearer; for he can now connect any fresh S-token with P through his knowledge of the general link between S and P. By the same reasoning, we can now explain how U can expect A to link S with P on a new occasion, and so we can properly justify our attribution to U of the relevant Gricean intention each time he utters S.

In passing, what about the understanding of a totally unknown written language, in the absence of independent clues about the intentions of the writers or reactions of the intended readers? I have virtually implied that such understanding is impossible, and I think that it is. That is not refuted by the decipherment of Linear B, for the latter turned out to be a different way of writing a language which was already understood. Even with a language which is radically foreign, so to speak, understanding may be possible without much evidence about writers' intentions; but some such evidence is needed. Recent writers on a project for detecting radio-messages from intelligent extra-terrestrial beings comment airily on 'the problem of determining the meaning or significance' of the signals which they hope will reach us from outer space: 'There does not seem to be any great difficulty associated with the semantics problem. Compared with the acquisition problem all else is easy.'[6] But although they say that there is no shortage of clues to the meanings of the signals ('the possibilities

[6] *Project Cyclops: A Design Study of a System for Detecting Extraterrestrial Intelligent Life* (published in 1972 by N.A.S.A., Ames Research Center, Moffett Field, California), pp. 64–5.

are endless'), the only one they describe relies on the extra-terrestrials helpfully to associate linguistic signals with other signals which can be resolved into pictures.

§49. 'Novelty' in language-learning

The utterances of my tribe are unstructured: rather than having independently significant parts which severally contribute to the meaning of the whole, each one communicates all in a lump. That obliges the tribesmen to learn each utterance-type separately, rather than learning a small amount of vocabulary and syntax which would give them command of an indefinitely large number of sentences.

That is a tremendous difference between them and us, and I would not minimize it. But let us not exaggerate it either. In particular, let us avoid a certain tempting mistake about how human language-learning must differ from the young tribesman's learning of the tribal communication-system.

In a human language, there is a qualitative gap between the data of learning and the learner's resultant competence: after exposure to relatively few sentences, the young language-learner can confidently produce and comprehend more sentences than there are atoms in the visible universe. It is sometimes said that many of the latter sentences are 'new', or 'not of the same kind' as the ones which constitute one's initial learning-data, or that our use of language is 'creative' in the sense that what we are competent in outruns what we have learned. That looks like a difference between the human situation and that of my tribe, for a young tribal learner merely moves from data of the form 'Encountered instances of S have all meant that P' to the conclusion 'All instances of S mean that P', so that the only competence he gets from his encounters with S is a grasp of that very same utterance-kind, S, and nothing more.

But we should be wary of contrasting this with the human situation by saying that there is something radically 'new' about what human language-learners learn, or that the sentences in which a human gains competence are not all 'of the same kind' as those which constituted his learning-data. That whole way of talking is suspect, because we cannot use 'of the same kind' etc. in an objective way, independently of facts about what kinds of generalization someone finds natural. It was established by Wittgenstein's discussion of the continuation of number-series that the basic notion of qualitative similarity, or of 'the same kind', is this: x is of the same kind as the Fs, *for someone*, if *he* finds it natural to generalize from the Fs to x.[7] So the sentences in which humans acquire competence must be 'of the same kind' – in a certain good sense – as those which constitute the initial learning-data.

Someone who wishes to use the notion of 'creativeness', or of understanding sentences which 'go far beyond' what one has previously encountered, should explain how the trick is worked. Chomsky has advocated this explanation: the language-learner brings to his learning, as part of his innate mental endowment, something like an unconsciously held grammatical theory; and this theory gets him from the sentences which constitute his learning-data to the further, new, different sentences which are part of his resultant linguistic competence. I have no quarrel with this hypothesis, if it is properly understood. What must be grasped is that if someone moves, by virtue of a grammatical theory T, from sentences $D_1, \ldots, D_n$ to some sentence D_{n+1}, then all of the sentences $D_1, \ldots, D_{n+1}$ *are* of one kind, namely the kind 'generated by theory T'. So, instead of saying 'One acquires competence in sentences which differ in kind from those which one initially learns, making the leap with the aid of an innate theoretical endowment', we should say 'Our learning-data and the sentences in which we acquire competence do all belong to a single kind, and our innate grammatical theory defines it'.

This is not a mere quibble about 'the same kind' and its cognates, for it leads on to the crucial point that in *any* sort of 'going on' – any concluding from evidence, or re-applying of a learned skill – one proceeds *thus* rather than *so* because one has this sort of mind rather than that; and so any 'going on' owes something to one's innate mental endowments. This applies to my tribe, even at their present level. I have said that their communicative 'going on' consists only in this: when a tribesman has found tokens of type S being uttered to mean that P, he concludes that further S-tokens also mean that P. Now, the various tokens of type S will not be perfectly alike: there will be slight physical differences between them, which a successful learner will have to neglect. On the other hand, any S-token will resemble items which are not S-tokens, and the learner must neglect those similarities. In short, the tribal learner cannot properly classify utterance-tokens into types, each with its own meaning, unless he neglects all and only the

---

[7] For a lucid statement of this view, see W. V. Quine and J. S. Ullian, *The Web of Belief* (New York, 1970), pp. 55–8; see also L. Wittgenstein, *Remarks on the Foundations of Mathematics* (Oxford, 1956), Part I, §§1–23, 113–41.

negligible differences and similarities. Which ones he neglects will depend initially upon which he perceives as small or fails to notice altogether; and which those are will depend at least in part upon what sort of mind he innately has. If the whole tribe draw the negligible/non-negligible line in about the same place, that is because they have, unsurprisingly, similar innate capacities and dispositions.

It is therefore seriously wrong to announce that language-learning involves an innate endowment, as though other sorts of learning or 'going on' did not. Objection: 'You must admit that in language-learning the gap between initial data and resultant competence is, to put it neutrally, *impressive*. Isn't there something to be explained here? And couldn't the notion of an innate mental endowment help the explanation?' Yes to both questions.

Here is an explanation for the impressiveness of that gap. All our non-linguistic activities give us our predominant standards of similarity, involving size and shape and physical order etc., which determine what we find intuitively similar; and *by those standards* our initial linguistic data are unlike many sentences which we become competent to produce and understand. This is evidence for Chomsky's hypothesis that we have mental aptitudes which are used in our language-learning and in none of our other activities. This is non-trivial, for language-learning might have used only structures and skills which were also heavily involved in non-linguistic activities. It would explain why in language-learning we generalize across a gap which, when we look at it coldly, strikes us as impressively wide. In particular, it would explain why – if this is indeed the fact – language-learners do not automatically adopt the simplest grammatical rules which are consistent with their data, and why people would have much difficulty in learning certain possible grammars which nevertheless look simpler and easier than the ones which they do effortlessly learn.[8]

Do not conflate the substantive claim that there are innate language-specific skills with a nearly nonsensical one which is sometimes made. We can learn language only because of our innate endowments (trees never learn languages) and because of our experience (children exposed only to Chinese never learn French); and it is sometimes suggested that innate endowments make a larger contribution than experience does. Given that both elements are required, there can be no objective answer to 'Which contributes more?' unless one of them contributes

[8] See Noam Chomsky, 'Reply [to Max Black]', in R. Borger and F. Cioffi (eds.), *Explanation in the Behavioural Sciences* (Cambridge, 1970), pp. 469–70.

almost nothing – as would be the case if language could be learned by every organism or, at the other extreme, if one could learn every human language just by hearing sentences from one language. Some comparisons can be made without going to extremes. For example, we can say, of two people with equal competence, that the competence of one of them owes more to experience and less to mental structure than does the other's; or that the contribution which Jones's experience makes to his competence is greater (or smaller) than Smith thinks it is; but those comparisons do not put us in a position to say that Jones's language-learning owes more (or that it owes less) to his innate endowment than it does to his experience. This last kind of quantitative comparison, however, is not involved in the clear, important and possibly true claim that our language-learning involves mental skills which do not come into any of our non-linguistic activities.

This possible truth has been brought to our attention by Chomsky and sometimes he expresses it in just that way.[9] Unfortunately, though, he often mis-states it, and hardly ever gets it into sharp focus. For instance, he writes: 'It may well be that the general features of language structure reflect, not so much the course of one's experience, but rather the general character of one's capacity to acquire knowledge.'[10] This is not clear. Indeed it is barely English. Is the role of experience said to be small ('not so much'), or is it said to be non-existent ('but rather')? One way, the claim is without clear content; the other, it is manifestly false.

This failure of Chomsky's is probably linked to his repeated animadversions against 'generalization' in the theory of language-learning. I make no apology for my use of 'generalization', as a term which is handy in superficial description: to say that someone is 'generalizing', in the only sense that is relevant here, is just to say that he is confidently *going on* from premises to a conclusion, or from observed implementations of a skill to further behaviour which he takes to implement the same skill. Chomsky must mean more than this by 'generalization', when he writes that what a child comes to know about language 'goes far beyond the presented primary linguistic data and is in no sense an "inductive generalization" from these data'.[11] That it is in *no* sense an "inductive generalization" is simply false. Perhaps it is not one in Chomsky's preferred sense, but he does not explain what that is. I conjecture that he is guided by the idea that when someone finds it natural to move from the *F*s to *x*, this is an 'inductive generalization'

[9] Chomsky, *Explanation in the Behavioural Sciences* pp. 469–470; and also Chomsky (1968), pp. 75–6.   [10] Chomsky (1965), p. 59.   [11] *Ibid.*, p. 33.

only if x is of the same kind as the Fs. If that is how Chomsky's thought is moving, then his troubles with 'generalization' descend from his troubles with 'the same kind' and its logical cognates.

Chomsky is not helped by his apparent assumption that the concept of generalization is an essentially explanatory one. The idea seems to be that language-learning does not involve generalization because it cannot be *explained* through the concept of generalization: 'There [is] no known sense of "generalization" that can begin to account for [the] characteristic "creative" aspect of normal language use.'[12] That, though true, is not very informative about the creative aspect of normal language; for 'generalization' cannot begin to *account for* anything. It can be used in superficially describing many activities, language-learning among them.

§50. A problem about regular meanings

Let us return to the tribe.

I have tackled one epistemological problem, namely that of describing evidence that S is regularly associated with P rather than with Q or R. But I have slid over a second problem, namely that of describing evidence that when tribesmen utter S intending to communicate P – that is, intending to get the hearers to believe P – it is the Gricean mechanism that they are relying upon. How can we discover that regular communicating behaviour is backed by Gricean intentions? One might think: 'We know what evidence established a Gricean diagnosis in that first isolated case. All we need now is more of the same kind.' That is wrong, however, for the Gricean diagnosis of the initial case *depended upon* its being an isolated episode which had to be diagnosed without essential reference to others of the same sort. We could go on being entitled to diagnose further snake-pantomimes as meaning that there is a snake nearby, just so long as the parties to each case were not influenced by the earlier ones – e.g. had encountered none or had forgotten them. But that sort of regularity is uninteresting. Because of our concern with non-iconic utterance/meaning relationships, we must attend to regularities in which the earlier instances help to explain later ones because they are remembered by, or at least *influence*, the parties concerned. And with any regularity of that sort there is an obstacle to a Gricean diagnosis. Here is why.

12 Noam Chomsky, in J. P. B. Allen and P. van Buren (eds.), *Chomsky: Selected Readings* (London, 1971), pp. 153–4.

Take it that when any tribesman utters S he intends to communicate P, where P's truth-value changes according to some circumstance of the utterance, such as time or place or the identity of the speaker, as with 'It will rain soon' and 'Someone here has food' and 'I own a boat'. Now, what evidence can we get that a speaker who implements this procedure is relying on the Gricean mechanism to get the intended result?

We can easily discover that S-utterers intend to communicate P, perhaps by studying silences (where someone who believes P does not utter S) and lies (where someone utters S though he does not believe P). Also, we could discover that S-hearers usually come to believe P – this being required if the procedure is to survive.

Now the trouble starts. Take any single occasion when U utters S, and A thereby comes to believe P. We would like to say that A's belief came about through the Gricean credence mechanism, that is, through A's seeing what U intended; but that threatens to be undercut by a lower-level diagnosis. Suppose that A believes that *whenever S is uttered P is true* – meaning that P is true *of* that time or place or speaker etc. Using that generalization, A can get from his observation of S to his belief that P by a route which does not pass through any thought about U's intention. If the facts will accommodate that simpler diagnosis of how A came to believe P, then we should prefer it to the more complex one which says that he followed the sophisticated Gricean route. One should always prefer the lower-level or more economical of two unrefuted hypotheses about the mental causes or background of behaviour; and although it is not always obvious which of a pair of diagnoses is the lower-level one, it is clear enough here.

Furthermore, if A can reach the belief that P through a generalization which does not refer to intentions, why should not U be relying upon him to do just that? Granted that U may not be omniscient about A's mind, still we do not want a theory of regular non-iconic meaning which *requires* speaker's ignorance about what the hearer knows. So we had better allow U to be decently informed about A's state of knowledge. It seems, then, that as well as relinquishing our Gricean account of what A did, we must drop our Gricean account of what U relied on him to do, in favour of one which says that U relied upon A to get from S *is uttered* to P *is true* through the generalization that whenever S is uttered P is true. But if U's intentions involved no reliance on the Gricean mechanism, then we have no grounds left for saying that U *meant* P when he uttered S.

It looks as though the conditions for meaning which I have offered will give almost no support to the notion of regular, non-iconic meaning. That would be a dismal outcome for Gricean meaning-theory, so let us see whether it can be escaped. I here embark upon an inquiry which will not be completed until §61 below, although along the way some other matters will also be explored. I shall not say in advance what the outcome will be.

The source of the trouble is the supposition that A thinks that whenever S is uttered P is true. What justification is there for that? Obviously the argument would be boring if it were based merely on the idea that A might happen to have a wildly erroneous opinion about a general link between S-uttered and P-true. I have been assuming, rather, that there really is such a link – that my previous account of the tribe implies that it is the case that P is true whenever any tribesman utters S. Or something like that; for the argument does not really need such an extravagant premiss. If P is true *whenever* S is uttered, there is no tribal lying or error; but we can admit these phenomena without changing the basic shape of the trouble-making argument. Suppose that tribesmen sometimes utter S when P is false. There are two possibilities to be considered.

(1) There can be detected falsehood, where someone utters S when P is false, and there is some fact Q about the situation which A takes to be a good enough reason not to believe P. This could happen with error and with lying: Q might be the fact that the speaker is someone whom A never trusts, or that the speaker is blushing, or that P concerns colours and the speaker is colour-blind, or . . . and so on. In so far as A can pick out the S-utterance occasions when P is false, using independently available clues of the sort I have described, I can reconstruct my trouble-making argument by allowing A to accept generalizations of the form: *If S is uttered and Q is not the case, then P is true.* These will still enable him to get to *P is true* from *S is uttered and Q is not the case* by a non-Gricean route, i.e. without reference to the intentions of the speaker. And speakers can rely upon hearers to use such generalizations.

(2) There can be undetected falsehood: someone utters S when P is false, and A has no clues, there and then, to the falsity of P. If there are cases like this, and A knows it, my lower-level mechanism for getting him from *S is uttered* to *P is true* is somewhat weakened, for now all he can accept is that *usually* P is true when S is uttered. But the Gricean credence mechanism would be equally weakened; for if A knows that there is unpredictable falsehood floating around, that harms his infer-

ence from 'U wants me to believe P' to P. In each case, the damage to the mechanism must, if U knows about it, dim his expectation of success; and so each diagnosis of his intentions becomes less secure. Since they are weakened by the same amount, the conflict between them is unaffected.

So there is a serious problem about finding behavioural evidence that a communicative regularity, the parties to which can remember earlier instances of it, is backed by Gricean intentions rather than by something simpler. From here on I shall write as though the lower-level challenger depended, for each S–P pair, on the single generalization that whenever S is uttered P is true. But that is just short-hand for a number of generalizations, each of the form: Usually when S is uttered and Q is not the case, P is true.

Although Grice has never explicitly raised this problem, as a problem, he has written something which bears directly upon it. In this passage he clearly implies that any intentional communicating regularity must involve Gricean intentions:

Suppose that, using only the notion of simple intention, we specify U's policy as follows: 'I shall utter S if I intend A to think that P.' Now, if the particular intentions which will be involved in every implementation of this policy [are to have] some chance [of being] realized, as U well knows, A must be aware of U's policy and must suppose it to apply to the utterance of S with which U has presented him. U, then, must expect A to be in a position to think as follows: 'U's policy for S is such that he utters S now with the intention that I should think that P; in that case I take it that P'. So a formulation of U's policy for S in terms of the notion of simple intention is adequate to ensure that, by a particular utterance of S, U will *mean that P*.[13]

If that were right, it would abolish my problem at a blow, but I submit that it is wrong. If U is to implement the policy, he must indeed have reason to expect A upon hearing S to infer P; but this inference might rely not on the Gricean mechanism but just on A's having discovered that P is true whenever U utters S. It is true that Grice is working here with the version in which P has the form 'U believes Q' – that is, U seeks to convince A that U believes something (see §40 above). But that does not affect the issue, which can be rephrased thus: how is A to be led to believe that U believes Q? Through the Gricean credence mechanism, in which A recognizes U's primary intention? or through the lower-level mechanism which relies on the observed regularity

[13] Grice (1968), p. 232. The quotation omits parts of the original, and the terms 'S' and 'P' are not Grice's.

that whenever *U* utters *S* he believes *Q*?

I have challenged Gricean diagnoses with lower-level rivals which say that *U* is merely relying upon *A* to implement simple procedures of the form 'When you hear *S*, infer *P*'. If the tribe had a semantically structured language, the relevant procedures would be astronomically less simple; but that does not affect my trouble-making argument. Granted that in a structured language, the pattern of links between utterances and meanings would be so complex as to be unlearnable unless it could be derived from a few high-level principles, my point comes after that: given any specific link between an utterance and a belief, what is it *made of*? Does *A* link *S* with *P* through *U*'s intention, or only through a procedure which does not essentially involve intentions? Rewrite my argument so that it fits a structured language, and you must complicate the 'procedures' on one side of the conflict; but you must equally complicate the Gricean mechanisms on the other side. The conflict itself, therefore, stands untouched. I shall illustrate this.

I have challenged a certain Gricean diagnosis of a communicative regularity by suggesting that *A* is merely implementing a procedure which he has found to be successful, namely 'When you hear *S*, infer *P*'. If the tribal communication system had semantic structure, like a human language, *A* might have had no experience of *that* procedure at all. Still, if his linguistic competence relates to his experience as a human's does, he will have had experiences which convince him that that procedure will succeed; as someone who has discovered what to believe when he hears 'The plate [hammer, vase] is on the table', and when he hears 'The cushion [cat, newspaper] is on the chair', may be sure what to believe when he hears 'The plate is on the chair' for the first time. That example does scant justice to the breadth, by intuitive standards, of the qualitative gaps we jump in our language-learning, but that does not affect my main point. To undercut the Gricean explanation of how *U* succeeds in communicating *P* to *A* by uttering *S*, all we need is an explanation in terms of some procedure, not essentially involving *U*'s intentions, which *A* has reason to trust; and it does not matter if that trust comes from *A*'s experience not with that very procedure but rather with others which are systematically related to it.

If the gap between what *A* had experienced and what he could understand was as wide, by intuitive standards, as it is with humans, that would show something interesting about *A*'s mind. Could we not infer also that he was taking *U* to be built along the same lines as himself? No, not if that implies that he credited U with having a mind which resembled his own. All he would need is what the lowliest animal has, namely a preparedness to generalize in the way it finds natural and to impose the results upon the world; and that is all that U needs to expect A to do. So there is no basis here for a Gricean diagnosis of U's intentions in uttering things to A.

I now revert to the form of the story in which the tribe's communication system has no semantic structure. I admitted structure temporarily, just so as to show that it would give no help in establishing Gricean diagnoses of communicative regularities.

§51. Injunctions and intentions

The difficulty arises also with injunctions, but there the picture changes slightly.

Suppose that tribesmen who utter S intend to get their hearers to do X, and that they usually succeed. This requires that in general when someone hears S there is some satisfaction which he receives if he does X, for otherwise the practice of doing X on hearing S would die out.

Now, in §46 above I distinguished four possible bases which A might have for complying with what he takes to be U's wishes. That was all Gricean, of course; but the first three bases for compliance could be undercut by something non-Gricean. For they involve, respectively, A's thinking that U (1) values A's welfare, (2) has interests which happen to coincide with A's, or (3) will reward A for compliance or punish him for non-compliance. In each of these, A's reason for doing X when U utters S includes A's belief that by doing X in these circumstances he will get some benefit, that is, something which he counts as good independently of U's wishes. (In this context, getting a good may be merely avoiding a harm.) But A will hold that opinion only if he has found that in general when U *utters S there is benefit for A in doing X.* And that generalization, if A accepts it, can support a non-Gricean explanation of why A does X when U utters S, and thus also a non-Gricean account of what mechanism U is relying on when he utters S intending to get A to do X. Here again there are complexities: perhaps what A is applying is a set of generalizations of the form *Usually when U utters S and it is not the case that Q, there is benefit for A in doing X.* The extra complexities do not affect the basic fact that A can get rationally from hearing S to being motivated to do X, by a route which does not pass through any thought about the utterer's mind.

The fourth basis for compliance behaves quite differently. This is the one where A's reason for doing X when U utters S is that for A the satisfaction of U's wishes is in itself a good. In this case, A's *basic* reason for doing X is that U wants him to, and so he is moved by a Gricean mechanism which cannot be undercut by something non-Gricean. So if the tribal communication system were extensively used for making requests in reliance upon the altruism of the hearers, then we could have copious behavioural evidence that the system was backed by Gricean intentions. But altruism, though possible, is far from necessary; there could be perfectly intelligible tribes which lacked it; and so this is not a very significant or reassuring result.

Injunctions are also relevant to our problem in a different way.

A hearer of an injunction may know that there is someone who would benefit from doing X while everyone else would suffer if they did X – minimally by having the trouble of doing X without reward, but perhaps further by being punished by the speaker or 'punished' by the environment. So the hearer of an injunction may wonder whether benefit would accrue to *him* if *he* did X, and his best way of finding out may be by considering which hearer the speaker is likely to have intended to get to do X – a point I shall return to shortly.

The concept 'intended believer of a statement' works quite differently from 'intended obeyer of an injunction'. Of course U may utter S intending to get A to believe P, and hoping not to be overheard by B; but if B does hear S, and does know that whenever S is uttered P is true, B will come to believe P even if he knows that U did not intend him to. If we want to use the concept of 'benefit' here, we must say that true beliefs are automatically beneficial for anyone: they are no trouble in themselves, they may lead to benefits, and they very seldom lead to harms. Also, the benefit of a true belief is infinitely sharable, because B's believing P cannot impede A's doing likewise. But really 'benefit' is irrelevant. Acquiring a belief is not something one does voluntarily because of an inducement: one does it on evidence; and the eavesdropping B, described above, has evidence that P is true, namely the fact that U has uttered S. That he was not the 'intended believer of the statement' is unimportant.

The concept 'intended obeyer of an injunction', on the other hand, can have important work to do. If my earlier discussion of injunctions looked sadly unrealistic, that was partly because it invoked the procedure 'When you hear S, do X' rather than 'When you hear S being addressed to you, do X'; and the latter formulation is better just because it uses the concept of an intended obeyer.

Clearly, we have here the makings of something Gricean; for U might utter S, expecting to get A to do X partly through A's recognition that *he* will benefit from doing X, because U intends *him* to do X. In that case, U is relying on the Gricean mechanism. This Gricean diagnosis may not admit of being undercut by a lower-level one in which A, without any thought of what U intends, can nevertheless work out that he is the one who will benefit from doing X; for it could be that A's only clue to this consists in evidence about what U intends. Unlike the cases canvassed earlier, this one concerns A's realizing that he (not B) should do X, rather than his realizing that what he should do is X (not Y). But still a genuinely Gricean element is involved.

The power of this result should not be exaggerated. The tribe might avoid the need for this sort of Gricean mechanism in any of four ways. (1) They might refrain from injunctions. (2) They might restrict themselves to unfocussed injunctions, where the speaker does not care who performs the enjoined action so long as someone does. (3) They might use focussed injunctions but take care to be heard only by the intended obeyer; so that whoever hears an injunction will benefit from acting on it. (4) They might use focussed injunctions which could be heard by others than the intended obeyer, and adopt some physical procedure for identifying him in particular; so that it was generally understood that the hearer who would benefit from doing X was always the one the speaker touched on the shoulder, say, or the one standing closest to the speaker at the time. Then for the hearer of an injunction the crucial question need not be 'Did he intend me to do X?' but rather 'Did he touch me on the shoulder?' or 'Was I the closest to him?' This fourth possibility involves a primitive semantic structure, for it gives to injunctions two independently meaningful aspects, one expressing the thought that someone is to do X, and one indicating who the person is (cf. 'John, shut up!'). I have not properly introduced semantic structure into the tribal communication system; but still I shall do so eventually, and then the tribe will be able to use method (4) for using focussed injunctions without having to rely on anything Gricean. Given that possibility and the other three, we should not make too much of the way in which injunctions could require a Gricean element.

In all of that, the phrase 'intended obeyer of an injunction' is misleading. In those focussed cases, one does not have a complete injunction and then a question about who is to obey it. Rather, there is a kind of action and a person, and the injunction is that *that person* is to perform an action of that kind. So we really ought to re-describe the Gricean case: we should say that A has to consult U's intention not to learn whether A is 'the intended obeyer of the injunction', but rather to learn what the complete injunction *is*. The injunction has to be completed by reference to what U intends, because the only relevant meaning-regularity is insufficient to determine its whole content.

That prompts a thought: perhaps the speaker's intention might sometimes have to be consulted for other sorts of completion of the injunction – for what is to be done rather than for who is to do it. For instance: whenever U utters S, he intends to get A to massage one of U's limbs; and A must discover which limb it would be profitable for him to massage by considering what U is likely to intend. That would be Gricean, though strange.

Something like it could occur with statements too. For example, whenever U utters S he intends to communicate, with respect to some particular tribesman, that *he* is in danger from a snake; and the hearers must work out who is in danger by considering what U is likely to intend. This is not a matter of identifying an intended believer or hearer, for the statement might be intended for all possible hearers, and the endangered tribesman might even not be one of them.

Here is a more extravagant example: when U utters S he intends to communicate, with respect to some object, that it is good to eat; and his hearers have to identify the object in question by considering what U is likely to intend. Or the incompleteness could be even greater: whenever U utters S he intends to communicate, with respect to some property, that the tribal totem-pole has that property; and his hearers must consider U's intentions in order to determine what property he is referring to. That would be absurd, of course. It is on a continuum with the extreme case, the final absurdity, where the 'communicative regularity' has no propositional content at all: whenever U utters S, he intends to communicate that something is the case; and his hearers must consider U's intention in order to determine what proposition he wants to communicate. But that absurdity lies at the foot of a slope whose higher reaches contain procedures which are not ridiculous, including the intended-obeyer one which has been this section's main topic.

§52. Gricean intentions in actual languages

In human languages there are other ways in which a Gricean element may occur. I know of three, each involving ambiguity or something like it.[14]

(1) A speaker may say something ambiguous, leaving his hearers to disambiguate it by considering which meaning he is likely to have intended. Since ambiguity does not require semantic structure, my tribe could have it at their present level of development. I withhold it from them, though, because it runs contrary to the essence of language. (Contrast this with the mirror-image of ambiguity, viz. synonymy. If my tribe had many synonymous utterance-types, this would increase their learning problems, with no compensating benefits except for a little variety and, perhaps, a chance to say something digitally if one's mouth was full. So I shall not yet give the tribal communication-system any synonymies. When the tribe get a semantically structured language, they can have synonymies which impose no epistemic burdens because they are automatic consequences of the structure, and others which arise from labour-saving abbreviations. In contrast with this, ambiguity is always a defect, in prose at any rate.)

(2) A speaker may say something which can be taken as either a joke or a serious comment, either a threat or a warning, either a command or a bit of advice, either ironically or straight, and so on; and the hearer may have to decide how to take the utterance by considering what the speaker's intention is likely to be. For example, U utters something which standardly means P, intending to convey sarcastically that not-P; he gives his hearers no help through intonation-contours, leaving it to them to grasp the ironic reversal of meaning by realizing what he is likely to intend. This is not contrary to the essence of language: whereas a communication-system is harmed by having sheerly ambiguous utterance-types, it may be enriched by allowing a single utterance-type to be used for different types of speech-act. Still, I am denying those riches to my tribe by restricting them to statements and injunctions, and ignoring subdivisions of those two categories. I want to keep things simple, and also to emphasize that what I am omitting are luxuries, not necessities, in a language; which is why there is something marginal about theories of language which focus on the difference between various kinds of speech-act.

(3) There is also room for the Gricean mechanism in the understanding of utterances containing pronouns, demonstratives, or definite descriptions which do not in fact uniquely identify their referents. Very

[14] I am here indebted to suggestions from Mohan Matthen.

often a hearer can discover the referent of a use of 'he' or 'it' or 'that' or 'the man' etc. only by considering what the speaker is likely to intend; and if that is what the speaker is relying upon him to do, his intention is Gricean. (The intended-obeyer-of-an-injunction phenomenon could fit in here. When *U* says 'Pick up the hammer!' intending that *A* shall obey, it is as though he had said 'You pick up the hammer!' with *A* as the intended referent of 'you'.) Nothing like this is yet available to my tribe, for pronouns etc. involve semantic structure, which the tribal communication-system still lacks.

Suppose that the tribal language did contain (1) outright ambiguities, (2) utterance-types which could be used in various speech-acts, and (3) pronouns etc., still the tribe's communicative behaviour might not yield evidence that the Gricean mechanism was being employed and relied on. For although each of these phenomena *can* engage the Gricean mechanism, none of them must do so; the Gricean mechanism is always avoidable if the speaker provides some other way of resolving the matter in question. For instance, it might be the practice that (1) whoever uses the noun 'bank' includes some remark which is nonsensical when applied to a river's edge (or nonsensical when applied to a financial institution), so that hearers can rule out the unintended meaning by general semantic considerations, without having to think about the speaker's intentions. Obviously, also (2) there could be recognized intonation-contours to indicate jokes, sarcastic meaning-reversal etc. As for (3) the referents of pronouns and so on: we do have an abundance of non-Gricean ways of sorting those out, and a community could easily be wholly non-Gricean in this respect also.

Let 'Plain Talk' be the name of a powerful, semantically structured communication-system which some tribe use pretty much as we use language, except that they never utter injunctions in reliance on hearer's altruism (which is Gricean), and never rely on the Gricean mechanism for the completion of their messages or for disambiguation or the securing of uniqueness of reference etc. It looks as though the communicative behaviour of the Plain Talkers would offer no firm basis for Gricean diagnoses either of hearers' understandings or of speakers' intentions. (If there are some I have overlooked, I conjecture that they are as marginal and dispensable as the ones I have discussed; and so I stipulate that they too are absent from the use of Plain Talk.) And I take it that if we have no evidence that the Plain Talkers have Gricean intentions, evidence consisting of behaviour which is best explained by Gricean diagnoses, then we ought not to attribute such intentions to them. So Plain Talkers do not have Gricean intentions: when they utter intending to communicate, they do not rely for success on the operation of the Gricean mechanism in their hearers.

Must we conclude that they never mean anything by what they utter, and thus that Plain Talk is not a language? I hope not. It is boring to quibble about the precise meaning of 'language' or of any other word, and so if someone denies that Plain Talk is a language, or a vehicle of meaning, I shall not contradict him. But I shall not agree with him either. I want to use 'language' (and therefore also 'meaning') to mark some large and important distinction, and the difference between Plain Talk and human languages seems to be small and trivial.

It looks, then, as though my Gricean conditions are too strong to be satisfactory, because they do not imply that the Plain Talkers mean anything by what they utter. But since I have acknowledged from the outset that the conditions are too strong to be necessary, i.e. that some cases of meaning do not satisfy them, why does it matter that they are not satisfied by Plain Talk? It matters because Plain Talk is relevantly unlike the other cases of meaning which the conditions do not cover – I mean such things as soliloquies, reminders, the utterances of madmen, the passing on of orders by someone who is indifferent to whether they are obeyed, and the other cases which have been adduced by Grice's critics. These are all matters which a theory of meaning can legitimately set aside to begin with: some because they are peripheral and inherently unimportant (e.g. lunatic ravings), and most because they are causally or even conceptually dependent upon other kinds of meaning which are handled by the theory from the outset (e.g. soliloquies). Now, Plain Talk is not a vehicle of merely marginal and dependent kinds of meaning. On the contrary, it is behaviourally indistinguishable from much of what occurs at the very centre of ordinary human language; nor is it causally or conceptually dependent upon anything Gricean.

So *this* over-strength in the Gricean conditions for meaning should be taken more seriously than its predecessors in the literature. It also differs from them in what it calls for in the way of amendment of the Gricean conditions. Previously published examples of meaning which do not fit Grice's conditions have all invited revisions which would make the conditions still more complex and intractable; whereas I shall show that we can bring Plain Talk under the concept of meaning by revising Grice's conditions into something simpler and more manageable.

§53. The sub-Gricean conditions for meaning

I need a label for my revised conditions, and choose 'sub-Gricean'. It would be confusing to use 'Gricean', since I have tied that word to the notion of the hearer's thought about the speaker's intention, which will be absent from my revised conditions. But the material I am now embarking on is still in the area which was opened up by Grice's pathfinding work, and I count myself as revising Grice's conditions rather than supplanting them. Why so late in the book? Because the revision does not touch anything in my first five chapters, as I shall show.

Grice's 1957 paper about meaning considers a series of cases where *U* obviously does not *mean* that *P*, but where he manifestly does intend to *communicate P* – still using this in my special weak sense of 'get someone to believe *P*'. The pursuit of conditions for meaning takes the form of a search for a simple, minimal account of what is lacking from those 'rejected cases', as I shall call them. That is, Grice seeks to show that meaning is a species within the genus intending-to-communicate, and the differentia must be such that the rejected cases all fall outside the species. That is achieved by the differentia which Grice eventually fixes upon, namely the speaker's reliance on the Gricean mechanism; but no one seems to have noticed that there is a weaker differentia which also excludes the rejected cases.

In each rejected case, *U* seeks to communicate *P* by offering *intention-free* evidence that *P*, that is, by confronting *A* with something which counts as evidence for *P* independently of why *U* made it available. For example, *U* tries to convince *A* that something has occurred by showing him a photograph of it. This suggests that we might differentiate meaning from the rest of the genus of intending-to-communicate by the condition: *U intends to communicate P to A by offering him intention-dependent evidence for P.* That is the core of my sub-Gricean account of meaning.

If it is to be weaker than Grice's account, then it must not say that what *U* offers *is* intention-dependent evidence for *P*; for Grice's conditions do not say how or whether *U*'s utterance could get *A* to believe *P*, but only how *U* expects it to do so.[15] So my sub-Gricean condition must say that *U* thinks he is offering intention-dependent evidence. Or perhaps, even more weakly, that *U* thinks he is offering

---

[15] This was pointed out to me by David Lewis.

evidence and does not think that it is intention-free: he does not see himself as merely exploiting an independently existing evidential link (like that between a photograph and the event it portrays), though he may not have the positive thought that what he is offering is intention-dependent evidence. That possible further weakening will become relevant in §60 below; but in the meantime I shall silently assume that U knows what is going on, so that I can contrast the Gricean and sub-Gricean accounts in terms of what U is doing, rather than of what he thinks he is doing. Nothing of theoretical importance hangs on this – it is just for ease of exposition.

Gricean and sub-Gricean conditions part company when applied to a case where U utters S intending to communicate P, this being an implementation of Plain Talk (see §52 above). In such a case, as I have shown, the Gricean conditions are not satisfied, because A has a route from 'S is uttered' to 'P is true' which by-passes the lemma 'U intends to communicate P'. Yet the sub-Gricean conditions are satisfied, because the only evidential link between S and P is an intention-dependent one. When A moves from 'S is uttered' to 'P is true' on the strength of some generalization approximating to 'Whenever S is uttered P is true', he follows a route which does not include any thought about U's intention; but the route nevertheless depends on U's intention, because if U had not intended to communicate P when he uttered S, it would have been inappropriate to bring his uttering S under the generalization that whenever S is uttered P is true. The crucial background fact is that the generalization is true only because of the intentions of past S-utterers: the general link between S-uttered and P-true owes its existence to one link between S-uttered and intention-to-communicate-P, and a second link between intention-to-communicate-P and P-true. So if someone uttered S without intending to communicate P, it would be a sheer coincidence if on that occasion P were true. Therefore, if U utters S without intending to communicate P, and A infers from this that P is true because in his experience whenever S is uttered P is true, the inference is not unreasonable but it is nevertheless vitiated by error. And that gives the content to my claim that A's route from 'S is uttered' to 'P is true' is, whether or not he realizes it, an intention-dependent one, or that the uttering of S is intention-dependent evidence that P is true.

A simple analogue. Whenever the Illecillewaet Glacier is unusually noisy during the spring, the river below it is unusually full during the following summer. Someone who knows this, and who hears the glacier creak and rumble this spring, can reasonably infer that the river will be high this summer; and his inference need involve no thought about the weather. But in fact the noisiness of the glacier is weather-dependent evidence that the river will be high, for the link between noise and subsequent water results from one link between noise and warm weather (the noise is made by shifting, melting ice) and a second link between warm weather and the river's being high (from unusually copious meltwater from the glacier). So if one spring the glacier happened to be noisy for some reason other than warm weather, someone who was ignorant of the relevance of weather might infer that the river would be high that summer; this inference would not be unreasonable, but it would be wrong. The noise in the glacier is weather-dependent evidence for what the state of the river will be, even though one can reasonably move from one to the other without thought of the weather.

I repeat that when someone utters S, intending to communicate P, and employing the communication-system I call Plain Talk, whose users never need to rely on the Gricean mechanism, he is offering intention-dependent evidence that P is true. He therefore counts as meaning that P by my sub-Gricean conditions though not by the original Gricean ones or any of their descendants in the literature to date. In offering the sub-Gricean conditions as sufficient for meaning, I run no risk from Grice's rejected cases; for, as I indicated earlier, they all involve intention-free evidence that P, and so they no more satisfy my weak conditions than they do Grice's stronger ones.

So much for statements. Now for the sub-Gricean conditions for injunction-meaning. Remember that in an injunction, according to the original Gricean conditions, U utters S in an endeavour to get A to do X; and this is unintelligible unless U thinks that his utterance gives A evidence that he would benefit from doing X, using 'benefit' to cover everything to which A attaches positive value. The rest of the story was the characteristically Gricean part about how U expected A to get from 'S is uttered' to 'A would benefit from doing X' – namely through the lemma 'U wants A to do X', which connects with benefits to A in the four ways discussed in §46 above. The sub-Gricean conditions do not mention U's wants or intentions, of course; but they still say that U views his uttering of S as giving A evidence that he would benefit from doing X, to which they add only that U thinks it is intention-dependent evidence (or, perhaps, does not think it is intention-free evidence.) Anything satisfying these conditions must also satisfy the Gricean ones, but the converse fails: the injunctions of the Plain Talkers are all sub-Gricean, and none of them are Gricean. There is one species of injunction, however, which must be Gricean, namely the sort where A's benefit is just the satisfaction of complying with U's wishes. Such injunctions, which rely on the hearer's altruism, had to be excluded from Plain Talk in order to make it non-Gricean throughout.

There is a unified sub-Gricean account of statements and injunctions: when U utters S he means something by it if he utters S intending (i) to produce some change in A by (ii) inducing in A a belief for which (iii) the uttering of S constitutes intention-dependent evidence. In an injunction, U intends (i) to get A to do X, by (ii) inducing him to believe that he will benefit from doing X, for which (iii) U's uttering of S constitutes intention-dependent evidence. In a statement, U intends (i) to get A to believe P [by (ii) getting A to believe P], for which (iii) U's uttering of S constitutes intention-dependent evidence. Notice that in an injunction (i) and (ii) are distinct, whereas in a statement they are identical. This reflects a real difference between statements and injunctions, and not a mere product of wrong theory like the asymmetry which threatened us near the end of §41 above. Its source is the fact that in both statements and injunctions U tries (i) to achieve an end by (ii) applying an epistemic lever to A; but only in statements is the end itself also epistemic, for in injunctions it is rather physical or practical. So in an injunction the (epistemic) lever must be distinct from the (non-epistemic) end, whereas in a statement there is nothing to prevent the (epistemic) lever from being the (epistemic) end which is aimed at. Of course in each case there is a lever for the lever: the belief (ii) is produced by giving A (iii) evidence for it; but there symmetry is restored.

If there is no behavioural regularity to the effect that whenever S is uttered P is true (or the injunction analogue of this), the sub-Gricean conditions cannot be satisfied unless the fully Gricean ones are satisfied. For if there is no S-uttered/P-true generalization, the route from S to P cannot depend upon U's intention except in a way which takes it through a lemma about U's intention; and that is Gricean.

That could explain why we did not notice that Grice's conditions were too strong. We followed Grice in considering the isolated, individual case, with no thought of regularities governing types of utterance; and in that context – the home ground of meaning-nominalsm – the Gricean conditions are equivalent to the sub-Gricean ones. To see how the sub-Gricean conditions can be satisfied in non-Gricean ways, we must enlarge our view to include *systems* of communication.

I cannot prove that the sub-Gricean conditions suffice for meaning, but I can rebut one possible attempt to disprove this. The 'glacier' example points up the fact that any sub-Gricean case which is not Gricean is one where A is – or is expected by U to be – unthorough, superficial. He employs an intention-dependent generalization, but does not dig deep enough to discover what it rests on. That might be thought to disqualify such cases from counting as meaning; but it cannot do so, for some degree of unthoroughness – some failure to get to the bottom of the situation – is always present, even in the very Gricean transactions of human linguistic life. When you utter S, I infer that you intend to communicate P, from which I infer P; and this latter inference is based on my finding that what you want me to believe is generally true. But I do not – and you do not expect me to – dig down to discover *why* you are in general to be trusted, identifying the classes of situation where it would be wrong to trust you; and yet your utterings clearly involve meaning. I conclude that unthoroughness or superficiality as such is not disqualifying. If sub-Gricean conditions which are not Gricean do not suffice for meaning, the reason must concern the particular kind of unthoroughness which they involve.

The argument cannot be left there, however. One wants to know more about the unthoroughness which is involved in a sub-Gricean, non-Gricean case. Are we to suppose that A has no opinion about why S-uttered is a sign of P-true. Does he just accept it blankly, as one might the generalization that whenever the glacier groans the river becomes full? That seems unlikely; for A, though not himself a glacier, is himself sometimes an S-utterer. Clearly this matter needs exploring, and in my next chapter I shall come at it through Lewis's theory of convention. The latter is interesting and important in its own right, as well as being variously relevant to my concerns.

7

CONVENTION

§54. Lewis on convention

Back in §47, before the sub-Gricean trouble started, I wrote: 'It seems obvious that if A knows that in the past S has been regularly associated with P, this gives him a reason to expect it to be associated with P on a further occasion. But one may be sure that it gives him a reason, without being clear *why* it does so.' I have obliquely hinted at one explanation, namely that A gets from past S–P associations to future ones by simple, incurious induction. But now I shall face the problem openly, starting with the explanation which is provided by Lewis's theory of convention. The core of this is as follows.

Two or more agents have a coordination problem if they are in a situation where their interests do not conflict but where what it is best for each to do depends upon what the others *do* do. If they wish to meet, it is best for each to go where the others go. If they wish to re-establish a broken telephone connection, it is best for one to dial if and only if the other hangs up and waits. Now, suppose that a group have a recurring kind of coordination problem, and that for some reason (or for none) they achieve coordination on several occasions by adopting procedure C. There might be many different features which are common to what the group did on those occasions, but 'C' stands for the description which picks out the 'salient' common feature, i.e. the one which is most conspicuous to the group. Suppose that it is *mutually known* to all the members of the group that they have handled this sort of problem by adopting procedure C; that is, each knows that this is what they have done, knows that the others all know this, knows that everyone knows that everyone else knows, and so on; or, if you wish, replace 'knows' by 'believes' throughout. In that case, each member of the group has good reason to follow C yet again when that problem next arises; for, almost certainly, each has reason to think that C is the only procedure he can expect everybody to expect everybody to follow, and so it is the only procedure he can expect everybody to follow, and so it is the procedure it is best for him to follow.

For example: you and I are talking on the telephone, our connection is broken, and we need to re-establish contact quickly. Thinking over past troubles of this sort, I realize that we have always, somehow, achieved coordination. I notice that on even-numbered days you re-dialled while on odd-numbered days I did; but that does not help, because I doubt that you would notice that (or I doubt that you would credit me with noticing it, or the like). Then I realize that the one who initiated the call has always been the one who re-dialled, and I think that you too will probably find that the most salient single feature of our past solutions of this kind of problem, and will probably think that I shall probably do likewise, etc. Since I initiated this telephone call, I re-dial; and you, having gone through just this same train of thought, hang up and wait. So coordination is achieved through our mutual knowledge of a behavioural regularity which achieved coordination in the past. A *convention* has been born.

A convention, then, is a behavioural regularity which a community maintain because they mutually know that they have maintained it in the past and that it has solved for them a recurring kind of coordination problem. This makes the maintenance of a convention something more than a mere regularity in behaviour; yet it does not base a convention upon explicit agreement, nor does it explain 'convention' with the aid of metaphors or of 'tacit agreement' or 'behaving as if they had agreed' or the like. It also shows how the departure from a conventional regularity may be criticizable, either as involving an inefficient pursuit of one's ends, or as disappointing the known expectations of others, or both. I emphasize that my brief exposition does nothing like justice to the subtlety and power of Lewis's own treatment.

§55. How to coordinate speakers with hearers

If Lewis's theory of convention is to be applied to communication, a problem must be overcome. In communication, what is being co-ordinated with what? Lewis speaks only of coordinating actions with actions, but in communication there may be no action, properly so-called, which is expected of the hearer. With injunctions the speaker's utterance has to be coordinated with the hearer's subsequent action; but what about statements?

In his book, Lewis applies his concept of convention to speaker-hearer relations only for a special class of communications which are, in effect, cases of injunction: in each of them the hearer is expected to act in some determinate fashion. Lewis acknowledges that a general theory of linguistic conventions could not be based upon anything so restricted.[1] He therefore brings his theory to bear upon language in a different way, dropping speaker–hearer in favour of speaker–speaker coordination: he takes conventions to coordinate my speech with your speech, not my speech with your understanding.

This, I submit, is also too narrow to support a theory of linguistic conventions. In practice, no doubt, you can understand me only if you can speak as I do, but still the notion of understanding is more basic and should be treated in its own right. Just because language is essentially a transaction between speaker and hearer, we can imagine a language with many hearers and only one speaker; such a one-speaker language could still have what would ordinarily be called conventions, and could be helped by them, e.g. to escape from the need for iconic utterance/meaning relationships. There is something wrong with a theory of convention which is silent about a language like that.

I have propounded, and Lewis has accepted, a solution to this difficulty.[2] The problem arose because he tied convention to action, whereas the statement-hearer's essential role is one of belief-acquisition, which 'is normally not a voluntary action and hence not an action in conformity to convention'.[3] I propose that we broaden Lewis's account by systematically replacing 'actions' by *'doings'* – the latter term standing for a larger class which contains actions and belief-acquisitions and other items as well. I italicize 'do', when using it in this way, as a reminder that it is a term of art.

When I say that someone *does* something at time T, I mean that at T he ψs, for a value of ψ such that *one's beliefs can be a partial reason for one's ψing*. Actions are all *doings*, therefore. So also are belief-acquisitions: the reasons for one's coming to believe that P can include other beliefs that one has. In deliberating about what to believe (and whether to believe that P), as in deliberating about what action to perform (and whether to perform X), one weighs reasons which include beliefs.

This class of *doings* is a conceptual natural kind, not the mere product of a pun. Of course there are differences within it. Notably, reasons for actions include not just beliefs but also wants and approvals and aversions, whereas reasons for belief-acquisitions do not. (I am con-

[1] Lewis, pp. 160 ff.

[2] Bennett (1973), pp. 152–5; David K. Lewis, 'Language and Languages', in K. Gunderson (ed.), *Language, Mind, and Knowledge* (Minnesota Studies in the Philosophy of Science, vol. VII, 1975).

[3] Lewis, p. 180.

cerned only with reasons which tend to confirm P's truth, not ones which imply that one would enjoy being a P-believer.) Yet reasons for action and reasons for believing have enough in common for my purposes. Crucially: what someone will come to believe, just like what actions he will perform, can be predicted through what beliefs he now has.

That common feature enables Lewis's theory to survive the replacement of 'action' by '*doing*' throughout. The resulting broader theory covers all Lewis's cases and also ones like the following.

In a two-member community, U wants to communicate to A that P, using the Gricean mechanism; and when U utters something, A wants to know what he means by it. In this situation, 'coincidence of interest predominates',[4] and coordination is achieved if U utters something intending to communicate P, and A does think that what U means is P. Less long-windedly, understanding is a special case of coordination. Now, if U and A mutually believe that in the past whenever U has uttered S he has meant that P, and A has taken him to mean that P, then this mutual belief *both* gives U a reason for again uttering S if he wants to communicate P *and* gives A evidence that when U next utters S he means P. In this way a certain coordination in their *doings* is achieved: their mutual knowledge of a past regularity has led them to maintain it in further instances because it is their best chance of continuing to achieve that coordination in which A takes out of an utterance what U put into it. The vital point is that the relevant *doings* in this situation are all under the control of beliefs in such a way that they can be explained as arising from a certain mutual belief and can be predicted accordingly.

So we can smoothly combine Grice with Lewis: conventional meaning involves the use of Lewis-conventions to coordinate the Gricean intentions of speakers with the belief-acquisitions of hearers.

A curious result now emerges, namely that a statement of the form 'In uttering S, U conforms to regularity R as a convention' may entail that U has a Gricean intention, even if R in itself does not involve Gricean intentions. Let R be the following regularity:

S-utterers always intend to get their hearers to believe P, and S-hearers always come to believe P.

Any full, two-sided implementation of R solves a coordination problem,

4 Lewis, p. 14.

namely that of getting the hearer to extract from an S-uttering the proposition which the speaker put into it; so R is the sort of regularity which could be maintained as a convention. R is not itself Gricean: all that is stipulated is that S-utterers intend *somehow* to get their hearers to believe P, not necessarily through the Gricean mechanism. However, if R is maintained as a convention, each instance of it will be Gricean. The crucial ingredient which is missing from R itself, namely the utterer's reliance on the hearer's recognizing why S is uttered, is added by the concept of convention.

In showing how, I must use the notion of R's being a convention *for someone*: conventionality is a matter of reasons for conforming to a regularity, and one person's reasons may differ from another's. What I shall show, then, is that if the above-described regularity R is a convention for utterer U, then his S-utterings are Gricean; that is, he utters S intending thereby to get his audience A to believe P, and relies for the achievement of this upon the Gricean mechanism.

We start with the premiss that U utters S on some occasion, that he thereby conforms to R, and that R is for him a convention. That implies that he conforms to R because he expects A to conform to it, and that he expects *that* because he thinks that A will expect him to conform to it. But that means that U utters S intending to communicate P, and expecting to succeed only because he thinks that A will think that he utters S with that intention; which means that he is relying upon A's recognizing what his intention is, which means that he is relying on the Gricean mechanism. So a non-Gricean communicative regularity becomes Gricean if it is maintained as a convention.

That discovery is not mine, but Lewis's, and he proves it rigorously.[5] My proof is simpler, because it cuts some corners, but also because it is helped by my broadening of Lewis's analysis.

If the Gricean mechanism, properly so called, must be free of the sorts of contrived cross-purposes discussed in §39 above, then the implementation of R is not fully Gricean unless it satisfies an infinity of further conditions such as that U does not expect A to think that U does not rely on A to recognize U's primary intention in uttering S. Those are all automatically implied by 'R is a convention for U', because they are embodied in that notion of mutual knowledge (or 'common knowledge', as he calls it) which Lewis uses in analysing the concept of convention.

[5] Lewis, pp. 154–6.

Something else should be noticed. In a coordination problem with *n* people, a procedure which assigns roles to *n*-1 of them automatically dictates how the *n*th should behave if the problem is to be solved. In a two-person problem, therefore, the parties have their solution if they mutually know how *one* of them will behave; and so we can lop off half of the description of any regularity which has solved a recurring two-person coordination problem. In the telephone connection case, for example, we need only say that such problems have always been solved because *the one who initiated the call has always re-dialled*. If that has always solved the problem, it follows that *the one who did not initiate the call has always hung up*, and so the latter clause can be dropped from our description of the regularity.

Now, speaker–hearer coordination problems are essentially two-party ones: there may be many hearers, but there is only one hearer's *role*. So if a community mutually know that speaker–hearer coordination has generally been achieved for them by *S*-utterers' intending to communicate *P*, they can infer that *S*-hearers have always come to believe *P*; and if they know that coordination has resulted from *S*-hearers' coming to believe *P*, they can infer that *S*-utterers have always intended to communicate *P*. We need state only one half of the regularity, and it does not matter which.

We can now doubly simplify our account of the behavioural regularities which give the content of meaning-conventions: for we can omit any reference to Gricean intentions, and we can also drop one half of each regularity. So our tribe have a meaning-convention, in the full Gricean sense of 'meaning', just so long as they maintain *as a convention* a regularity of the form 'Whoever utters *S* intends thereby to communicate *P*'. In that formulation, and from here until late in §60 below, I ignore injunctions. It would be a tiresome, routine matter to modify the discussion to fit them as well.

§56. Direct evidence for conventionality

We are now well placed to re-open the question which dominated §§50–2 above. I there looked for cases where a speaker who utters *S* intending to communicate *P* must rely on the Gricean mechanism. It turned out that there is usually no need to rely on that, for the hearer can connect *S* with *P* just through knowing that *S* has been regularly associated with *P* in the past. This non-Gricean link between *S* and *P* seemed to be the only one which need ever be used by the Plain

Talkers – that community whom I introduced in §52, who never utter injunctions relying on the altruism of the hearers, and who never need the Gricean mechanism to complete messages, resolve ambiguities or the like. That in turn cast doubt on the importance of Gricean intentions in the daily life of actual languages, for Plain Talk captures a high proportion of what actually goes on at the linguistic centre.

Let us re-open the question, this time from the perspective of Lewis's theory of convention in its recently-broadened form. Let us consider a community who utter *S* only when they want to communicate *P*, and who when they hear *S* generally acquire the belief that *P*. That description of their regular *doings* contains no Gricean elements, and so in itself it does not conflict with any of my sceptical manoeuvres in §§50–2. Now, can we get evidence that those regularities are maintained *as a convention*? If we can, then we shall after all have found something Gricean in the communicative behaviour of the community.

I will start with the perfectly general question: how can one have behavioural evidence that a regularity is a conventional in Lewis's sense? Then I shall tackle the special case of communicative regularities.

If a community do conform to a behavioural regularity which solves a recurring type of coordination problem, this might be a matter not of convention but rather of unthinking habit. What shall we require for it to count as conventional? It would be too much to demand that every time anyone conforms to the regularity he consciously argues: 'They expect me to expect them to do ψ, so they expect me to do ψ, so they will do ψ, so I shall do ψ'. On the other hand, we ought to demand more than merely that the behaviour in question *could* be justified by such inferences. The statement 'For *x* the regularity is a convention' concerns the reason *x* *has* for conforming to the regularity, not merely reasons which, if *x* had them, would justify his conforming to the regularity. Now, any claim about reasons which the community actually have must imply some conditionals about how they would behave if . . . If John does ψ because he thinks that Henry expects him to, then it follows – except in special circumstances – that if John lacked that belief about Henry he would not do ψ. So we must identify some of the relevant conditionals, and consider how we might get evidence that they are true.

We might get indirect evidence, like discovering that something is soluble without dissolving it. First, though, let us look for direct evidence of conventionality, provided by the very behaviour whose conventional status is in question. That is, let us look for cases where the antecedents of the directly relevant conditionals are actually instantiated – cases where we can learn that someone's believing Q is a reason for his doing ψ because we find that he doesn't do ψ when he doesn't believe Q.

Suppose that a community maintains a regularity of this form: whenever n of them are in a φ situation, they implement procedure ψ – where ψ is an assignment of actions to each of them individually, and a situation's being φ is the *problem-setting fact* that they have a coordination problem which would be solved by carrying out ψ. Is this regularity a convention from the point of view of community-member x? If it is, then x's reasons for conforming to it must include what I call a *looped thought*, which is a thought about someone else's thought about x's own thought. If the regularity is not a convention for him, on the other hand, his reasons for conforming to it may be based on the simpler, unlooped thought that in the past he has found it profitable to do (his bit towards) ψ in φ situations.

Lewis's account of convention requires an infinity of further 'loops' – from x's thought to y's to x's to y's and so on – but they can be left to take care of themselves (see the end of §39 above). All I want is direct evidence for that very first loop: I want behaviour which can best be explained on the hypothesis that x thinks that y thinks that x thinks that P, for some P.

There are just three sorts of proposition that P can be, if x's looped thought involving it is to show that for him the regularity is a convention. If there is a regular practice of doing ψ in every φ situation, how x behaves can depend upon his opinion regarding (1) whether the regular practice is as just described, or (2) whether he is in a φ situation, or (3) what would count as his doing ψ at this time. (1) concerns the content of the accepted regularity, (2) concerns the problem-setting fact, and (3) concerns the *role-assigning facts*, which I shall illustrate though the familiar telephone example. Whether x re-dials may depend upon whether he thinks (1) that usually the person who initiated the call re-dials after the connection has been broken, (2) that his telephone connection has just been broken, and (3) that he initiated the call. What gives (3) a place in some regularity-maintaining behaviour is the fact that ψ is an assignment of actions to the people involved in the problem: it may have the form 'If you are F, do A; if you are G, do B; if . . . etc.', which x cannot act on without having an opinion about whether he is F or G or . . . etc. Of course, in cases where everyone is to behave in the same way (3) is vacuous, and behaviour guided by the regularity will then be based on beliefs about (1) and (2) only.

That was all addressed to the lowest-level case, where x acts on the strength of what he thinks about (1), (2) and (3). At a more sophisticated level his behaviour will depend rather on what he thinks that others think under those three headings. For example, x's 'phone link with y has just been broken; x thinks that the usual procedure is for the wealthier party to re-dial, but he thinks that y thinks that it is usual for the one who initiated the call to re-dial; and so x, who did not initiate the original call, hangs up and waits for y to re-dial. There is an endless hierarchy of ever higher levels of sophistication and complexity, and we are mainly interested in the very next one up, where x's behaviour depends upon what he thinks that others think that he thinks under headings (1), (2) and (3). For instance, x re-dials because he thinks that y thinks that x thinks that x initiated the original call.

However far up the hierarchy we go, the relevant beliefs of x will all be ones which *terminate in* beliefs about (1) the content of the regularity, (2) the problem-setting fact, and (3) the role-assigning facts.

The following seems also to be true. Any 'looped' belief of x's which is evidence that for him the regularity is a convention must be a belief which credits someone else with what x thinks to be a mistake: either the mistake of believing that P (when really $\sim P$), or of believing that x thinks that P (when really he doesn't), or . . . and so on. To see why this is so, suppose that x's belief does not accuse anyone of error: x thinks that y sees the situation exactly as x does, with regard to the problem-setting fact, the nature of the regularity, and the role-assigning facts. In that case, why say that x is guided by his (looped) belief that y believes that x believes that P, rather than merely by his belief that P? Whenever the connection is broken, x re-dials if it was he who initiated the call: because that practice has worked out well, he continues with it; and his re-dialling can always be explained through his thinking that that is the practice, that the connection is broken, and that he initiated the call. We need not say that he thinks that y thinks that he thinks that he initiated the call.

Given those principles governing what could give direct evidence for conventionality, it is easy to construct cases. My examples may look peculiar, and may feel atypical; but their main features are apparently essential to any direct behavioural evidence of conventionality.

(1) Here is an example where P concerns the content of the regularity. A community have a procedure whereby two sailing boats, passing

close to one another and going in opposite directions, always pass port-to-port. On a given occasion x is sailing through the fog, he barely discerns y's boat dead ahead, and he swings his boat to port, as though to pass y's boat starboard-to-starboard. This could be because x thinks that that is what the convention demands, or because he thinks that that is what y thinks; but neither of those beliefs has a full 'loop' from x's thought to y's and back to x's thought again – and so neither is direct evidence for conventionality. But we might discover that although x knows the procedure and thinks that y knows it, he also thinks that y thinks that x does not know it. Fill in the details to suit yourself. Perhaps x has evidence that y thinks that when a boat is flying a red flag (as x's is) it is being sailed by a novice, . . . etc. What matters is that facts about looped beliefs are accessible to behavioural investigation in the manner described in §34 above; and so we could discover that x's behaviour was explicable by a 'looped' belief and not in any lower-level way. That would be evidence that for x the regularity was a convention rather than something more simply motivated.

What is at issue in that example is not merely x's knowledge of the right procedure, but his possible adherence to a wrong one. Had x merely thought that y thought that x was ignorant of the port-to-port custom, that might have caused him to dither, but it would hardly give him reason to swing to port. I conjecture that if any case like this is to provide firm evidence of x's having a looped thought, there must be some question of someone's being positively in error, and not merely ignorant, about what the content of the established regularity is.

(2) For an example where P concerns the problem-setting fact, we could stay with the sailing-boats: x thinks that y thinks that x thinks that the two boats are facing the same way. Here is a different example. Smith and Jones meet for lunch at the Quarry House every weekday noon, except on public holidays when they meet at Vong's Kitchen instead. On a certain non-holiday Smith goes to Vong's Kitchen at noon: he does not think it is a holiday, nor does he think that Jones thinks so, but he thinks that Jones thinks that he (Smith) thinks it is a holiday. We could get independent evidence that Smith has that looped belief, and could be entitled to reject every lower-level diagnosis of his behaviour.

(3) I have already sketched an example where x acts on a looped belief terminating in one about a role-assigning fact. When the 'phone connection is broken, x hangs up and waits for y to re-dial; because he suspects (from something y said) that y thinks that x is under the

misapprehension that y initiated the original call, though really it was x who initiated it – as he and y both know full well. It would be easy to construct examples which, unlike this one, did not involve language.

§57. Conventionality in communication

Now let us apply these principles to a regularity of the form: Whenever S is uttered, the utterer intends to communicate P and the hearer acquires the belief that P. How can we get direct evidence that this is, for some individual, a convention? In exploring this question, I shall be further elucidating the notion of a communicative convention, showing in more detail how to apply to communicative regularities the broadened version of Lewis's theory of convention. This may be of interest apart from the pursuit of behavioural evidence for Gricean intentions.

(1) If our evidence for conventionality is to concern a belief about what the procedure is, I have conjectured, there must be a question of someone's being wrong about the procedure, not merely ignorant of it. That seems clearly right where communication is concerned. If I want to get you to believe P, but I think that you take me to be ignorant of the S–P link, I might still utter S in the hope that this would convince you *both* that I do after all know the S–P link *and* that P is true. And even if I were deterred from uttering S, my mere silence would be poor evidence of my having a looped thought. But suppose that I think that you think that I wrongly think that S^* is regularly used to communicate that P: I could manifest that looped thought by uttering S^* at a time when the evidence shows that I want to communicate P, and that I do not think there is an S^*–P link and do not think that you think so either.

Although such things could happen, they seldom do. I doubt if I have ever been present when a speaker did something like shouting 'Water!' as a warning of fire, knowing what 'Water!' means and knowing that his hearers also knew, but thinking that they would expect him to give to 'Water!' the normal meaning of 'Fire!' So we must look further for plentiful evidence that actual human linguistic behaviour is conventional.

(2) When we come to looped thoughts terminating in beliefs about the problem-setting fact (Are the boats facing one another? Is this a public holiday?), the picture is even darker. In communication, there is no single problem-setting fact. There is a coordination problem,

[handwritten marginal note, left side:] But a real example might be drawn from an interchange between a race-traitor & a negro whom he presumes ignorant of all but pidgen.

because what the hearer draws from the utterance is to be coordinated with what the speaker puts into it; but there is no pre-existing fact, accessible to both, to which each must accommodate himself. The speaker's wish to communicate *P* sets his problem, but not the hearer's; while the speaker's utterance sets the hearer's problem, but not of course the speaker's. In theory the speaker could provide behavioural evidence that he had a looped thought terminating in a belief about the nature of his utterance, i.e. a belief about the hearer's problem-setting fact. Here is the simplest way this could happen:

> *S* is regularly uttered to communicate *P*, and *S** is not. *U* wants to communicate *P* to *A*, but he thinks that if he utters *S*, *A* will not credit him with thinking that he has uttered *S* (perhaps he thinks that *A* thinks there are defects in *U*'s hearing); but *U* also thinks that if he utters *S* A* will think that *U* takes himself to have uttered *S*. So *U* utters *S**, intending to communicate to *A* that *P*.

Probably nothing like this has ever occurred on our planet. As for describing a relevant looped thought terminating in a belief about the speaker's problem-setting fact (his wish to communicate *P*): that seems to be harder still, though the reasons are obscure.

(3) We can get nowhere with role-assigning facts: there could not be a case where someone handled a communicative transaction in a peculiar way because of some mistake about whether he was the speaker or the hearer. This connects with the previous point that in communication there are different problem-setting facts associated with the different roles: until you have your role straight, you have no coordination problem.

I conclude that little if anything in the basic outlines of our actual linguistic behaviour shows it to be conventional. It *is* conventional, if certain conditionals about our behaviour are true; but even if they are, since their antecedents are seldom instantiated their truth can make little visible difference. On this showing, our having conventional and not merely regular linguistic procedures is like having courage in a perfectly safe world. If there is a case for saying that language must be conventional, and thus perhaps that meaning must be Gricean, it needs a better foundation than the counterfactual conditionals explored in these two sections.

§58. Indirect evidence for conventionality

One can sometimes get evidence for a conditional without instantiating its antecedent. Let us see what indirect evidence we might have that a regularity was a convention for x, and then see whether our results are helpful with communicative regularities in particular.

A certain tribe maintain a regularity R – when in a φ situation they do ψ – which solves a recurring kind of coordination problem. We can get plenty of behavioural evidence that

(1)   Each tribesman maintains R because he thinks it solves problems,

that is, when he is in a φ situation he does ψ because he thinks that this is the best he can do in the circumstances. If the tribe are intelligent and observant, it will also be true that

(2)   Each tribesman thinks that R solves problems only because everybody maintains it,

that is, he thinks that doing ψ in φ situations gives him good results only because everybody else there does ψ also. If we found that in general a tribesman in a φ situation would not do ψ if he could see that the others were not going to do ψ, that would be evidence for (2), and for (1) and for

(3)   Each tribesman maintains R because he expects everybody else to maintain it.

If (1) and (2) are true of the tribe, then (3) will also be true just so long as the tribe have what I call *transitive reasons*. By that, I mean that they realize that if P's truth is a reason for doing X, and that Q's truth is a reason for P's truth, then Q's truth is a (deeper) reason for doing X.

I believe that strong evidence for (1) and for (2) would automatically include evidence for (3). Look at it contrapositively: if we had good evidence for (1) and against (3), that would count against (2); and evidence for (2) and against (3) would count against (1). That suggests that the having of transitive reasons is just the thorough having of reasons: to the extent that we had evidence that (3) was downright false of the tribe, our case for (1) and (2) would be attenuated. We might still be entitled to say (1′) that R-maintaining behaviour was based on some belief about the success of R, and (2′) that the tribe connected R's success with some facts about others' behaviour; but (1) and (2) themselves, as I have expressed them, would have to be counted as overstatements. But whether or not that is right, the possession of transitive reasons does manifest intellectual capacity, and can be exhibited in behaviour.

We might have evidence for (3) based on what tribesmen do in φ situations where they can see that the others are not going to do ψ. But we could also get less localized evidence, by discovering that in general *the tribe's reasons tend to be transitive*. And (1) and (2) as well as (3) could be supported by evidence, not drawn from φ situations, that the tribe are generally able to form true conditional beliefs about their environment, including beliefs about why their successful procedures do succeed (see §30 above). I shall now take it that we have established (1), (2) and (3) as sound conjectures about the tribe's R-maintaining behaviour.

From now on I shall simplify the wording by considering one tribesman, x, in a particular φ situation in which doing ψ would coordinate his *doings* with those of one other tribesman, y. So I move from (3) to a single instance of it:

(3′)   x does ψ because he expects y to do ψ.

And we shall carry on from there.

Now *we* expect y to do ψ in a φ situation, and furthermore we have evidence that he does so because he expects x to do ψ likewise – this being included in the evidence for (3). Since this evidence is equally available to x, and since I am supposing that x is intellectually equipped to handle evidence properly, we have general and admittedly inconclusive grounds for saying that

(4)   x thinks that y will do ψ because y expects x to do ψ.

Given that, and the general thesis that x's reasons are transitive, we get

(5)   x does ψ because he thinks that y expects him to do ψ.

In theory, we could get direct evidence for (4) and (5) together, by observing an occasion when x doesn't do ψ in a φ situation, this being explained by his not expecting y to do ψ because he doesn't think that y expects x to do ψ. But our chances of encountering and soundly diagnosing such episodes is so low that I prefer to base (4) on facts about x's general intellectual abilities and about what evidence is available to him, and to base (5) on the transitivity of x's reasons.

Now we have x engaging in R-maintaining behaviour because of what he thinks y believes about x's *behaviour*. This does not yet attribute to x a looped thought – a thought about y's thought about x's *thought*. That requires

(6) x thinks that y will do ψ because y thinks that x expects y to do ψ;

from which, with a further application of reason-transitivity, we can get

(7) x does ψ because he thinks that y thinks that x expects y to do ψ.

At last we are crediting x with doing something because of a looped belief.

Our evidence for (6) will probably consist only in evidence that y's reason for doing ψ *is* indeed of that sort, combined with the fact that this evidence has been available to x and that he is intellectually equipped to process it. It is theoretically possible to get direct evidence for (6) and (7) together, by observing a case where x does not do ψ in a φ situation and where the simplest explanation is that he does not think that y thinks that x expects y to do ψ; but we are not likely to encounter and understand such cases.

The foregoing is the best case I can make for saying that for x R is a convention rather than something less sophisticated. Conspicuously, it credits x with beliefs whose evidential support becomes ever frailer as we move towards (7); and if we carry on beyond (7) to the further 'loops' which are involved in the fully fledged concept of conventionality, the evidence becomes fainter still, so that one must doubt whether x would notice or make anything of it. Lewis speaks of the ever stronger 'assumptions of [x's] rationality' which we need as we proceed through the infinitely ascending hierarchy of explanations of x's doing ψ in φ situations.[6] It seems to follow that genuine conventions cannot occur except in tribes of archangels.

My reply to this is an adaptation of Lewis's, and runs parallel to my treatment of certain difficulties in Gricean meaning-theory (§39 above). It is that R is a convention for x just so long as (7) is true and nothing above it in the hierarchy is false because x has some conflicting opinion on the matter in question. By that standard, R is not a convention for x if this member of the hierarchy

(8) x thinks that y will do ψ because y thinks that x thinks that y expects x to do ψ

is downright false because x has a rival opinion about why y will do ψ. But so long as everything to level (7) is true, and the likes of (8) are not

[6] Lewis, p. 59.

ruled out through x's having rival beliefs, R is a convention for x. And we can reasonably assume that x has none of those rival beliefs, unless there is unignorable evidence that he does. That would be unlikely to happen once we get as far up the hierarchy as (7): from there on up, there will be virtually no evidence for or against any rival; but the possible rivals are beliefs of a sort which it would be mad to hold except on overwhelming evidence. So unless x is perversely peculiar, we can take it that if (7) is true then R is a convention for him – that is, he has none of the wilful and unsupported beliefs which would conflict with the remaining conditions for conventionality.

It is presumably clear that if we assert (7) on the strength of the evidence I have adduced, we do not imply that when x does ψ in a φ situation he consciously has the thought: 'I am doing ψ because y thinks that I expect him to do ψ'. But then I do not think that any attribution of reasons to x implies he consciously presents the reasons to himself: such attributions are safe as long as the relevant behavioural conditionals are true. Now, however, even the counterfactuals may be in jeopardy. Our basis for (7) is so indirect and thin that it would be risky for us to conclude that if x were in a φ situation where he did not think that y thought that x expected y to do ψ, he wouldn't do ψ in that situation. We have asserted (7) on the grounds that (5) is true, and that the move from (5) to (7) requires only some information which x has and perhaps some (transitivity-of-reasons) reasoning which is within his compass. But *that* doesn't settle what he would do in the peculiar situation just mentioned: for all we know, he would panic, or be overcome by bewilderment at the oddity of the situation, or let the moment for doing ψ slip by while he mused about what to do.

Perhaps we can construe (7) as reporting a reason which x could become aware of, and even act upon in appropriate circumstances, if he had enough time, calmness of mind, and so on. But that is as far as (7) can safely go; and it is further than we can take (9) – or, if x is *very* clever, further than we can take (11) or (13). Still, each of these has content: it says something about x's total epistemic state in relation to his lowest-level reason for doing ψ. Each of them says that x's mind contains all the materials for a certain reason for doing ψ, which it would not do if, for instance, the whole hierarchy from (4) upwards was false because x thought y was an unthinking automaton.

The fact that (7) does not imply the standardly associated counterfactual conditional connects with the fact that although (7) says that x

does ψ because he believes . . . etc., it does not imply that if x lacked that belief he would have no reason to do ψ. On the contrary, (5) gives him a solid reason for doing ψ, and (7) merely adds a certain kind of depth to it; just as (5) deepens (3′) which deepens (1). So if (7) were false, the upshot might be only that x's reason for doing ψ had lost depth.

Objection: 'If the standardly associated conditional is not true of x, then (7) is just false. The thin construal you are suggesting is an abuse of the words.' That is not unreasonable. But someone who takes that line must continue it the whole way up the hierarchy: so he must deny that there are any conventions, because there cannot be a community of whom the whole hierarchy is true, if each member of it entails a fresh counterfactual conditional. The only alternative would be to drop Lewis's account of what a convention is; but then what other account is there? I prefer to retain Lewis's theory, and also to allow that some regularities are conventions, and simply accept the implication that (7) and (9) can legitimately be construed as thinly as I have in this section.

§59. Communicative conventions again

That abstract discussion applies to every sort of coordinating regularity, including communicative ones. Let R be a communicative regularity: being in a φ situation is wishing to communicate P (speaker) or hearing S uttered (hearer); and doing ψ is uttering S (speaker) or believing P (hearer). Then take a more detailed statement of the now familiar proposition (7), namely:

In a φ situation, x does ψ because he thinks that y's being in a φ situation will lead y to think that x expects y to do ψ.

Perform the above substitutions in this, and the result is

When x wishes to communicate P, he utters S because he thinks that y's hearing S will lead y to think that x expects y to believe P.

In other words, when x wants to communicate P he utters S in reliance on the Gricean mechanism. So the journey down to (7) corresponds to one which concludes that the parties to a communicative regularity have Gricean reasons for what they are doing.

That calls into question my treatment of the system I call Plain Talk (§§52–3). Plain Talkers never need to rely on the Gricean mechanism to be understood, e.g. for the completion of meanings or the removal of ambiguities; and this led me to claim that Plain Talk is not Gricean. But the results of §58 suggest that there may be something Gricean in Plain Talk after all.

Let us re-examine a Plain Talk episode in the spirit of my §58 discussion. U utters S intending to communicate P; the uttering of S is intention-dependent evidence for P, and U knows this; and so the sub-Gricean conditions for meaning are satisfied. The Gricean conditions seemed not be satisfied, because instead of relying on the Gricean mechanism U could rely instead on A's moving from 'S is uttered' to 'P is true' through his knowledge that

(i) Whenever S is uttered, P is true.

I left it at that, pretending that A had no views about why (i) is true. But if A is alert and intelligent he will know more. For one thing, he will know that

(ii) Whoever utters S intends to communicate P.

Apart from knowing his own performances as an S-utterer, A can know that (ii) is true of the others. S is uttered on only some of the occasions when P is true, and A can discover that what is special about those occasions is that they are the ones where someone wants to communicate P.

Also, A could know that the uttering of S is intention-dependent evidence for P. That is, he could know that

(iii) (i) is true because (ii) is true.

Discovering (iii) to be true would be automatically involved in a thorough job of establishing (ii). A proper study of the conditions of S-utterings would show that whether S is uttered depends partly on whether P is true, and would uncover no dependence in the other direction except one which proceeds through the intentions of the utterer.

If A accepts (iii), then he does not see the simple generalization (i) as standing on its own feet. When he hears U utter S, he does not merely employ (i) in the inference

U has uttered S, so P is true;

but rather employs (iii) in the inference

U has uttered S; so U intends to communicate P; so P is true.

If that is his route from 'S is uttered' to 'P is true', then his belief that P is after all reached through the Gricean mechanism. Furthermore, if U thinks that A accepts (iii), then U must expect A to acquire the belief that P in that manner; and so U is after all relying upon the Gricean mechanism.

This result should be treated circumspectly. If U really *relies* upon the Gricean mechanism, he must think that if that mechanism does not operate he will fail to communicate P. But that might be wrong. Even if A thinks that this time U does not intend to communicate P, A may nevertheless go ahead and infer P's truth on the strength of the generalization (i) that whenever S is uttered P is true – being too careless or slow-witted to inhibit this inference. Even if in some thin sense A does have (iii) within his epistemic grasp, it cannot be depended upon to affect his practice in the proper way. Given time to reflect, he will no doubt realize that he ought not to infer P's truth unless he thinks that U intended to communicate P; but in the heat of the communicative moment A might blunder, and fall back on (i) as though it were basic, thus inferring P's truth in a non-Gricean manner.

A defender of Gricean conditions for meaning might respond by weakening slightly what he means by 'relying on the Gricean mechanism'. He could deem U to be relying upon the Gricean mechanism if he is strictly relying upon some mechanism which (in U's opinion) A knows to have a Gricean basis, even if that knowledge of A's is too dim, too much a matter of remote, background theory, to affect his behaviour in the heat of the moment. That weakening is defensible; and it has the incidental merit of helping the Gricean conditions to describe more realistically much of what goes on in human language-use.

It still leaves the Gricean conditions in trouble, however. I have argued that U thinks that A accepts (iii), from the premiss that U and A have a certain degree of alertness and intelligence. But U and A could *mean*, even if they were not bright enough for that modest premiss to be true; and even if it were true, my conclusion does not really follow. My next section demonstrates these two claims.

§60. Dullards and Condescenders

Consider first a community I call the Dullards. They employ a form of Plain Talk, and hence never directly rely on the Gricean mechanism to be understood. They utter with the intention of communicating, and when any Dullard utters S, he thinks he is offering evidence for P, and he does not think it is intention-free evidence; so the Dullards meet the sub-Gricean conditions. But when a Dullard hears S, he infers P purely through the generalization that when S is uttered P is true; he cannot resolve this inference into two steps with a lemma about the speaker's intention in the middle, and the speaker does not expect him to. The intentions of the Dullards therefore fail to meet the Gricean conditions, even when these are construed as weakly as they were at the end of §59.

Any given Dullard, A, is aware that when *he* utters S he intends to communicate P. He also has some inkling that the same holds for U, so that A sometimes knows in advance that U will utter S, and is not surprised on some occasions when P is true and U does not utter S. Furthermore, A does not think that any S-utterer – A or U – is offering intention-free evidence for P. But he intellectually cannot get hold of the thought that U's uttering S is purely intention-dependent evidence for P, so that if U does not intend to communicate P the inference to P should be inhibited.

The Dullards have concepts of *truth* and *falsity*. On rare occasions A hears someone utter S, and P turns out to be false; these episodes disappoint him, and slightly weaken his trust in the S-uttered/P-true generalization. He also has the concept of personal *reliability* and *unreliability*: he can learn which Dullards are more reliable on which topics, and which (if any) are unreliable on all topics. What he cannot do is to explain unreliability or false utterance as a product of *error* or *insincerity* on the speaker's part. These two concepts are used to give two different explanations of a break in the link between intention-to-communicate-P and P-true. But A knows only that there has been a break in the chain between S-uttered and P-true, and he cannot decompose this into one link between S-uttered and intention-to-communicate-P, and another between that and P-true. He therefore cannot raise the question of why the second link has been broken on a given occasion.

What does A think is happening when *he* utters S insincerely? Must he not realize that when he breaks the connection between S-uttered and P-true, this is because he has disconnected intention-to-com-municate-P from P-true? No, he need not and does not realize that. He is very good at Plain Talk – his employment of it, as a speaker, is competent and effective – but he cannot theorize about this skill of his. That is why I said that he thinks he is offering evidence for P, and does not think it is intention-free: to credit A with thinking that it is intention-dependent would be to exaggerate his level of theoretical self-awareness. The question of whether in his own case the S-uttered/P-true chain depends on the S-uttered/intention-to-communicate-P link is altogether beyond A's reach.

He sometimes tells lies, for the intelligible purpose of communicating something which he thinks is false. But he cannot theorize about his own lying: it is something he intelligently and purposefully does, but he cannot stand back and draw general conclusions about it.

Since A is an absolutely typical Dullard, his disabilities are U's also. *A fortiori*, U will never expect from A performances which are above him, and so U will never rely on A to get from 'S is uttered' to 'P is true' by anything more sophisticated than the generalization that usually when S is uttered P is true.

Even the Dullards have room for the idea that linguistic regularities have a normative force. If a Dullard misapplies one of the going regularities, his performance may be criticized, if not by other Dullards then by himself, either as inefficient or as unkind; that is, either as unlikely to achieve what he aims at, or as likely to induce a false belief in the hearers or at least to withhold from them a true belief which they could be given. Admittedly, the notion of irregular behaviour's being not merely unusual but wrong is weaker here than in a genuinely conventional system; but it has some grip wherever speakers intend to affect hearers.

I see no convincing reason for denying that Dullards mean things by what they utter, Their communicative behaviour will in fact closely resemble much actual linguistic behaviour among humans. (It could well have semantic structure – see §49 above.) I therefore offer the possibility of the Dullards' use of Plain Talk as a reason for thinking that the sub-Gricean conditions are sufficient for meaning and that they cover a region of logical space not covered by any Gricean conditions.

Now, suppose we are confronted by a Plain Talking community who are much too bright to be Dullards. They are, in short, a community who honour the basic assumptions I was making in the argument I presented in §§58–9. That argument said, in effect: 'The raw materials for a Gricean diagnosis are all there; and one cannot see how to form a coherent overall picture except by postulating that there is something Gricean going on quietly in the background.' That Gricean diagnosis is a stab into the non-behavioural dark, and I now oppose it with a different one. This rival probably could not be supported by any impressive evidence: it is a large hypothesis which has no support except that it could help to make sense of what we observe; but that puts it on a par with the hypothesis that the community's intentions are invisibly Gricean.

My hypothesis is that the community are Condescenders. Each of them is sure that any uttering of *S* – his own or another's – is intention-dependent evidence for P; so when he hears *S* uttered he infers P in the Gricean manner. He thinks it would be appropriate for his fellows to do likewise when they hear *S* uttered, but he does not think that their performances as hearers are Gricean: he believes that they are intellectually incapable of getting from *S*-uttered to P-true by anything but the simple route through the generalization that whenever *S* is uttered P is true. Each Condescender, then, thinks that he alone can operate the Gricean mechanism. Thus, the communicative intentions of the Condescenders are sub-Gricean and not Gricean; and yet their behaviour could appear so like the employment of actual languages that we ought to agree that they mean things by what they utter.

Here, as with the Dullards, I must avoid crediting the entire community with false opinions which fly in the face of available evidence, for a system which was based upon avoidable falsity would be too fragile and vulnerable to be interesting. Furthermore, the Condescenders are *ex hypothesi* highly intelligent, and positively good at handling evidence. That is all right, though. We can easily suppose that the Condescenders employ the Gricean mechanism only in a subdued, background manner: it has few upshots in behaviour, being little more than a silent theoretical underpinning for their inference of P from the uttering of *S*. *U*'s opinion that his fellows have no theoretical underpinning for that move, though mistaken, does not risk a collision with any significant amount of behavioural evidence.

Still, what positive basis does *U* have for his condescending view of how his abilities relate to those of his fellows? He must not have a scintilla of evidence for the view: we are not interested in the case where *U is* brighter than everyone else, for we are considering a community every member of which thinks his mind to be at least one level more complex than anyone else's. Nor are we interested in the possibility that the community are all mad. But there is another possibility.

A typical Condescender, *U*, thinks he is intellectually one up on his fellows in a certain way, but this is not a matter of contingent opinion – his answer to a question he has raised – but rather the direct result of a fundamental, unexamined, philosophical cast of mind. *U* is dominated by the thought that 'The world is my world', by the idea that he is the centre of his universe and that everything else is real to him only in so far as it impinges upon his senses. He is inclined towards solipsism, phenomenalism, behaviourism – not just as philosophical doctrines but also as sources of his fundamental everyday *Weltanschauung* – and it does not enter his head that he might be just one among others, or be part of someone else's 'world'. He is respectful towards behavioural evidence. If he acquired evidence that his fellows can follow the Gricean inference, he would accept this; though he would continue to place himself 'one up', for he would assume that they were capable of the Gricean mechanism but not of the thought that they were capable of it.

U need not be embarrassed by the discovery that in some contexts his fellows exhibit more speed, sureness and accuracy than he does. What is at issue is not overall intellectual capacity, but just degree of reflectiveness. In his opinion, his fellows cannot handle the Gricean inference not because it is logically too complicated for them (as though they would be defeated by anything so tricky as a two-step argument), but rather because it involves the thought '*He* wants *me* to think that *he* intends . . .', and *U* does not believe that he is part of any-one else's world in the way that they are parts of his. As for their cleverness: I can easily imagine crediting a computer with intellectual skills far above mine, while still believing that I could think about it as it could not think about me or about itself.

If this sort of philosophically based condescension is so easily main-tainable, why does it not occur among humans? Not, I think, because, we are free of the underlying quasi-solipsism, nor because of our natural humility. What prevents each of us from adopting a downsloping attitude to his fellows is a fact about our language. Our ability to say things of the form 'I think that you think that I think that *P*', and the like, presents us with abundant evidence about one another's beliefs; so that if someone suspects that he can have thoughts which are more encompassing than anyone else is capable of, he can express this con-jecture in language and risk being brought up short by the dissent of his hearers. Perhaps our language also works at a deeper level still to prevent philosophical condescension. Any belief I can have can be expressed in a sentence, and obviously my whole repertoire of sentences is also available to you; so I *cannot* escape the thought that I may be just one among others. I may resist it from time to time, as when thinking about the problem of other minds; but the mere form of our language destroys our chances of indulging in the kind of axiomatic, unexamined philosophical condescension which I have been describing.

I entertain the Condescenders only because I think they mean things by what they utter. It might be objected that they are disqualified because they are guilty of the sort of contrived cross-purposes about which Strawson and Schiffer have theorized (see §39 above). I do not agree. For one thing, in the Strawson–Schiffer examples the speaker seeks to exploit his hearer in a special way on a particular occasion, whereas what the Condescenders do is systematic and tribe-wide. Also, when a Condescender utters something, he is not hoping that his intentions will be misunderstood: he is merely expecting that they will not be thought about.

Like the Dullards, the Condescenders have concepts of truth and falsity, and of personal reliability and unreliability. Unlike the Dullards, they also have fully developed concepts of insincerity and of honest error.

It is time for the notion of *understanding* to receive a place in this chapter. Can we use this notion in connection with the Dullards and the Condescenders? A satisfactory answer must allow that speakers typically want to be understood by their hearers, though this is not their primary aim (see §40 above); and that understanding what is said is a part but not all of believing what is said.

We shall have to say that for a Dullard to understand S is for him to bring it under the generalization 'Whenever S is uttered P is true' rather than '. . . Q is true' or '. . .R is true' and so on. Every utterance-type in Plain Talk is systematically linked with just one proposition, and a Dullard understands an utterance if he associates it with the right proposition.

On that account, Dullard speakers do aim to produce understanding, as a means to producing belief. Furthermore, understanding could occur in the absence of belief. Suppose A has imperfect confidence in the generalization linking S with P, and on one occasion he hears S while having other evidence that P is false; he therefore does not infer from the utterance that P is true, but still he understands the utterance because he knows that P is the proposition it points to.

The understanding which Condescenders actually achieve, and which each of them knows that he achieves, is Gricean. When U utters S, A understands if he knows that P is what U intends to communicate; and A knows that this is what his understanding consists in. But U does not credit A with a capacity for Gricean understanding, and so does not aim at producing it in A. He aims only at A's having the Dullards' kind of understanding, that is, at A's linking S through a simple generalization with P rather than with Q or R; and in U's view that is required for the achievement of his principal aim, which is to get A to believe P.

It is easy to see how the Dullards and the Condescenders would handle injunctions. A Dullard will utter S intending to get his hearers to do X, and his uttering S will be intention-dependent evidence that they would benefit from doing X. But a Dullard who hears S, and infers that he will benefit from doing X, is merely applying his general knowledge that when he hears S it is good for him to do X; there is no thought of the utterer's intention. The 'benefit' which he expects, therefore, cannot include sheer compliance with the utterer's wishes: the Dullards are too stupid for altruism.

The Condescenders can be moved by altruism, but they would never credit one another with this ability, and hence they are not in a position to utter injunctions in reliance upon the hearers' altruism. A general account of their injunctions can be derived from the account for the Dullards.

§61. Evaluating the Gricean conditions

That the intentions of human speakers are largely Gricean is beyond question. Our linguistic resources let us directly express looped thoughts,[7] and let us say that something is uttered in reliance upon others to have looped thoughts about it.[8] Furthermore, we have familiar kinds of communicative transaction – involving ambiguity etc. as discussed in §52 above – which cannot be understood except in Gricean terms. But the concept of meaning, and even that of language, should extend to systems which lack the apparatus of 'I think that he thinks . . .' and its like, and which avoid the ambiguities etc. treated in §52. The question arises, then, of whether the Gricean conditions are too strong; and I have posed a related but more useful question – are my sub-Gricean conditions strong enough to be sufficient for meaning?

---

[7] 'I believe, dear John, that you believe that I believe that we have as much money as we require.' Charles Dickens, *Our Mutual Friend*, Bk. IV, ch. 5.

[8] 'The Americans are signaling us that Lewinter is real *in the expectation that we will discover they are signaling us that he is real and conclude he is a fraud*. Ergo, they want us to believe he is a fraud. Ergo, he must be real.' Robert Littell, *The Defection of A. J. Lewinter* (New York, 1973), ch. 17.

These, I noted, were as well supported as the Gricean conditions by the materials adduced in Grice's 1957 article (see §53 above). I now briefly recapitulate what the preceding five sections have done with the question of whether the sub-Gricean conditions are strong enough.

In §56 I looked for direct evidence that a behavioural regularity is a convention, and in §57 I applied those findings to the special case where the regularity is a communicative one; the point being that if a communicative regularity is a convention, that automatically makes it Gricean. It turned out that we should be extremely unlikely to get any direct evidence that a communicative regularity was a convention, and that if we did it would be so strange and unappetizing that one would hesitate to build on it. So this source would not yield any powerful reasons for saying that language must be conventional or, therefore, that meaning must be Gricean.

In §58 I showed how one might get more ordinary and copious evidence that a coordinating regularity is a convention. This required (i) an assumption that the community are fairly intelligent and observant etc., (ii) somewhat relaxed standards of evidential adequacy, and (iii) some loss of content from statements of the form 'x does ψ because . . .' and thus some weakening in the concept of conventionality. Re-applying this line of thought to a communicative regularity, in §59, I showed how we might base a somewhat attenuated Gricean diagnosis of speakers' intentions on some postulates about their overall level of alertness, acuity and so on.

One aim of §60 was to show that those postulates are too strong. A community (the Dullards) might be too stupid for §59 to be applied to them, and yet not too stupid to count as meaning things by what they utter. I further contended in §60 that the argument of §59 fails anyway; it would sometimes require the assumption that each member of the community sees himself as just one among others, and this could, as with the Condescenders, be false.

The Dullards and the Condescenders, I submit, present possible cases of meaning which are sub-Gricean but not Gricean. If I am right about that, the sub-Gricean conditions are weaker than the Gricean ones and yet still sufficient for meaning; which would be a fairly important result. Even if I am wrong, however, I think that my inquiry – I mean the central thread which runs through §§50–3, 56–60 – will have achieved several things.

(1) If I were wrong because really the sub-Gricean conditions are not weaker than the Gricean ones, then the sub-Gricean conditions should

take over, as doing the same work more simply. I imagine, though, that anyone who thinks I am wrong will attack the other flank, claiming that the sub-Gricean conditions are too weak to be sufficient for meaning. Suppose they are: I can still salvage something.

(2) If the Dullards and Condescenders do not mean anything by what they utter, it follows that the case for saying that *we* mean things depends partly upon our not being Dullards or Condescenders. If the applicability of the concept of meaning to our communicative activities depended on our being as bright as we are, and on our tending to take a level rather than a downsloping view of one another, that would be an interesting result which had been brought to the surface by the foregoing inquiry.

(3) It is clear beyond any possibility of dispute that the concept of meaning can rightly be applied to some versions of Plain Talk, and thus to communicative systems whose use does not ever involve a direct *reliance* on the Gricean mechanism for understanding to be achieved. So the Gricean conditions must be construed rather weakly if they are to be satisfied by every communication-system which involves meaning, properly so called. That is, even if I am wrong about the Dullards and the Condescenders, and must concede that every meaningful system has something Gricean about it, this Gricean element may be much feebler than was evident when we looked only at isolated cases which did not instantiate known regularities.

(4) The sub-Gricean conditions are at least a stepping-stone between meaning, properly so-called, and certain phenomena which are commonly though wrongly thought to involve meaning, namely the systematic communicative activities of non-human animals in the wild. In my next section I shall look at these in the light of the sub-Gricean conditions. The discussion will assume that those conditions are sufficient for meaning, but it would not be substantially altered if I had to retreat to the claim that they merely express an important ingredient in the concept of meaning.

§62. Animal communication

Non-human animals on our planet have communication-systems which are sometimes called languages. I favour restricting 'language' to systems with a kind and degree of semantic structure which is probably not to be found among non-human animals in the wild. But there is also a question about motivation: if languages, properly so-called, must fit my sub-Gricean conditions, then probably no non-human terrestrial species has a language; because probably the systematic communicative behaviour of animals in the wild is not intentional.

An animal which has intentions and which communicates may nevertheless not intend to communicate. Dolphins have intentions, and they communicate, but yet:

Two bottle-nosed dolphins, a male and a female, were separated in two adjacent enclosures with no visual access between them. The male was required to press one of two paddles in order for either to receive food, but the visual signal which indicated which paddle was appropriate on a given trial was presented only to the female. The female had to transmit this information acoustically to the male so that he could press the correct paddle. They succeeded in thousands of trials at this task. Furthermore, the female had been given the opportunity to know that her visual signal did not occur in the male's enclosure. This looks like an instance of signaling actions determined by the intention to transmit information. But there is no evidence of the female's understanding of the relation of her emissions to the male's action and quite a bit indicating her complete innocence. For example, when the visual barrier between the animals was withdrawn, and even when the male was removed from his enclosure, she continued to emit the signals as long as they resulted in her getting food.[9]

The writers suggest, surely rightly, that the female had learned 'to emit signals differentially in the presence of different visual signals', and the male had separately learned 'to press his paddles differentially with respect to these acoustical signals'. The moral is clear. If the female in uttering her acoustic signals intended anything, it was to get fish, not to communicate with the male.

Also, there may be animals which sometimes intend to communicate but never in their natural systems of communicative behaviour. The best evidence for the intention to communicate in non-human animals seems to come from anecdotes about domestic pets;[10] and the crucial point may not be that pets are thoroughly observed, or that pet-owners, unlike academic ethologists, are not shy about anecdotal material, but rather that domestic pets have humans to communicate with. That captive chimpanzees sometimes exhibit individual intentions to communicate seems to be beyond doubt; but it is not clear that

[9] W. E. Evans and J. Bastian, 'Marine Mammal Communication: Social and Ecological Factors', in H. T. Andersen (ed.), *The Biology of Marine Mammals* (New York, 1968), pp. 432–3. The passage has been modified slightly in the interests of brevity and clarity.
[10] W. H. Thorpe, 'Animal Vocalization and Communication', in F. L. Darley (ed.), *Brain Mechanisms Underlying Speech and Language* (New York and London, 1967), p. 3.

their 'displays' – their systematic communicative behaviour in the wild – involve any such intentions.

Although it would be foolish to dogmatize about this, I shall henceforth assume that the intention to communicate is not exhibited in the displays of animals in the wild. For this does *seem* to be so; yet many people confidently speak of the 'languages' of non-human animals; and I want to explain why.

In a language, properly so-called, the utterance of *S* is evidence for *P* because of the utterer's intention. In animal displays, the utterance of *S* is evidence for *P*, and may produce the belief that *P*; but its being evidence for *P* is not due to any intention to communicate *P*, but rather due to the existence in that species of certain inflexible, wired-in behaviour-patterns whose instances do not exhibit intentionalness of any sort. Given that enormous difference – on the one hand an intention to communicate, on the other no intention at all – what is the similarity which many people feel so strongly?

It cannot be merely that the 'displays' are in fact informative; for virtually all behaviour is informative in the sense that information could be gleaned from it.[11] Nor can it be merely that the displays do inform; for some animal behaviour which regularly informs other animals still does not strike anyone as linguistic. When a trapped fly thrashes around in the web, it conveys 'information' to the waiting spider, yet this behaviour on the fly's part does not seem like language even to those who freely credit honey-bees with language.

The linguistic feel of some animal behaviour is explained by the fact that it, like linguistic behaviour, is 'for' communication in some sense; and the relevant senses are closely connected. A linguistic utterance is for communication in the sense that it is performed with the individual intention of getting a hearer to believe something. In infra-human displays, the 'utterance' does not manifest an individual intention, and sometimes not even an individual goal of a lower kind; what it does manifest is a species-wide analogue of intention – namely a rigid behavioural disposition whose biological *function* is to transmit information. I here use that concept of function which I discussed in §23 above. A behaviour-pattern has the function of achieving *F* if it does regularly achieve *F* and that fact explains its becoming part of the genetic heritage of the species. I believe that the relevant explanation is always evolutionary rather than theological or something else; but,

---

[11] See J. Bastian, 'Psychological Perspectives', in Thomas A. Sebeok (ed.), *Animal Communication* (Bloomington, Indiana, 1968), especially pp. 575–80.

since the evolution of behaviour is hard to study directly, we must be able to discover the functions of various behaviour-patterns without having independent evidence about their origins. This can be done, though. One can base a well-founded guess about the function of a given behaviour-pattern on one's observations of how it serves the present life of the species.

I take it, then, that a behaviour-pattern has communication for its function if and only if the species evolved it because of the survival-value to them of the information-transfers which it makes possible. The movements of the trapped fly do not have communication as their function: they do communicate something to the spider, but this item occurs in the flies' genetic repertoire for a different reason, namely that flies which thrash around sometimes break free.[12] That explains why the fly's behaviour does not feel linguistic, even to those to whom display behaviour does feel linguistic.

That explanation presupposes that the two senses of 'for communication' are closely related, that is, that individual intention is significantly like biological function. So it is, despite the fact that a behaviour-pattern which has a biological function may admit of a single mechanistic explanation, and thus not admit of legitimate teleological explanation (see §21 above). The likeness is as follows.

Consider a species whose members do not have individual intentions: they are, then, highly inflexible or unadaptable in their behaviour. If some of them have a behaviour-pattern which proves unsuitable to their environments, they cannot modify it; but they are likely to serve their species by dying before they mature, and so those unsuitable behaviour-patterns will tend to drop out of the species' genetic repertoire. Thus, natural selection serves a species as intelligent adaptability serves an individual. There is also a similarity which does not depend upon a specifically evolutionary view of biological function. It is that intentional and functional explanations of items of behaviour, although in many ways very different, both give an explanatory role to the behaviour's being apt to produce such-and-such a result.

I prefer to reserve the terms 'meaning' and 'language' to communication-systems which manifest individual intentions to communicate. Intentional behaviour is attuned to the particular circumstances as wired-in displays frequently fail to be: displays often occur in the absence of observers, or the absence of suitable observers, or more

12 See J. C. Marshall, 'The Biology of Communication in Man and Animals', in J. Lyons (ed.), *New Horizons in Linguistics* (Penguin Books, 1970), at p. 233.

often than they are needed, and so on. The relatively blind and mechanical look of most display behaviour puts a great behavioural gulf between it and the employment of a communication-system which reflects individuals' intentions to communicate. But the common desire to stretch the concept of language further is explicable. If we leave semantic structure out of the story, the stretch is achieved simply by replacing 'intention-dependent evidence' by something like 'display-dependent evidence' – that is, something whose force as evidence for P depends upon its being a display, which is a manifestation of a behaviour-pattern whose function is to communicate. In essence, then, the shift is just from *intention* to *function*, and they have enough in common to make the shift inviting.

§63. How language might begin

It might be thought that something Gricean must be involved at least in the beginnings of any intentional communication-system. I shall show that that is not so.

I can find two coherently describable ways in which a tribe could acquire a communication-system through which they utter S as intention-dependent evidence for P, where S contains no iconic pointer towards P. There are doubtless others which cannot be captured in the concepts I have chosen to work with.

The first manageable possibility is this. The tribesmen sometimes seek to communicate, with Gricean intentions, and sometimes succeed. In these communications, as in my snake-warning one in §43 above, the utterance relates iconically to the meaning. After a few such occasions, all with the same 'icon' and the same tribesmen, the icon is allowed to decay, its force being taken over by memories of earlier communications. For example: the second time that U wanted to warn A of a snake, his snake-depiction was cruder than the first one; A might have failed to think of a snake if he hadn't recalled the earlier warning – this being what U intended. The third time, the depiction was even less realistic without being a less effective warning. This process could gradually establish a regularity in which S means that P although it does not relate iconically to P.

The process might take generations. There could be a period when the S–P link depended both upon an iconic relationship between utterance and meaning and upon the memories of the tribesmen: the icons were not explicit enough to point to the meaning without help from memories of earlier occasions, and the memories were too dim to succeed without constant iconic prompting. The tribe could lose their need for iconic help only through developing better memories, whether through evolution or through training.

That account of language-beginning needs Gricean mechanisms at the start. There is another possibility, however, where the origins are wholly non-Gricean: for an intentionally used, non-iconic system of communication could develop out of something which was not intentional at all.

Suppose that some species have a wired-in, non-intentional display system of the sort discussed in §62 above. They could evolve greater complexity and flexibility of cerebral function, giving them richer and more powerful intentions, and this could lead to the system's becoming intentional. For instance: there could be a gradual shift from (a) anyone who sees a snake utters cry S, to (b) anyone who sees a snake, and sees one of his fellows shortly thereafter, utters S, and from that to (c) anyone who sees a snake, and then sees one of his fellows in an unalarmed state, utters S, . . . and so on. Also, more importantly, the flexibility of communicative behaviour could increase: individuals would be increasingly disposed to modify behaviour-patterns which proved unsuitable to their wants. This would be a matter of individual initiative, but it would be made possible by a growth of intelligence resulting from evolution through thousands of generations.

The process need not be the evolving of a higher all-round level of intelligence; for creatures who had intentions in some behavioural areas might evolve a capacity for that same flexibility, educability, in respect of further types of behaviour. Humans are flexible about many things, but not about the dilation of the pupils of their eyes in the dark. One can imagine a series of mutations through which our species gradually became flexible in that area too, so that the dilating of one's pupils became something that a person did whenever he thought it appropriate, rather than something which happened to him whenever the light decreased.

Those are two possibilities, then: one intentional and Gricean, the other not intentional at all. We really need more options than this, especially if we are thinking about the origins of semantically structured languages such as humans have. I have no idea how semantic structure, or any other aspect of languages, did originate; but I want to discuss possibilities.

There could be structure before any of the communicative behaviour became intentional. A rigid communication-system might consist of eight utterance-types with the following properties: the four which warn of different kind of danger (bears, lions, fires and floods) have feature *D*, the four which advise of the availability of different kinds of food (birds, squirrels, corn and fruit) have feature *F*, and the four which have to do with animals (bears, lions, birds, squirrels) have feature *A*. Thus, an utterance's having *D* and *A* would warn of danger from an animal, one having *D* and not *A* would warn of danger from something other than an animal, one having *F* and *A* would advise about animal food, and one having *F* and not *A* would advise about plant food. That would be the beginning of semantic structure, and a display system could have it from the outset.

Actual infra-human display systems have little of this sort. Apparently none of them involves even as much structure as the one just described. The dances of honey-bees may be an exception; but there is now controversy over whether bees do communicate to one another through their dances.[13] Even if they do, this biological anomaly is too remote on the evolutionary tree to throw light on how our languages might have developed.

Furthermore, what little significant structure there is in animal display systems is mostly 'analogue' rather than 'digital'. That is, it correlates matters of degree in the utterance with matters of degree in the message – e.g. *how loud* the cry is correlates with *how alarmed* the animal is.[14] Virtually all the semantic structure of human languages depends not upon the degree to which utterances have various features, but just on whether the features are present or absent. For example, if I say 'Bring me a . . .' and then utter a sound half-way between 'seat' and 'sheet', no one will bring me an object which is intermediate in character between a seat and a sheet – say a pillow.

Still, there is no conceptual difficulty in the idea of a non-intentional communication-system which had an elaborate structure of the digital kind. But it is presumably not necessary that all the semantic structure of actual languages was present in them before their users were capable of intending to communicate. Languages do develop, structurally and in other ways, while being used intentionally; and I should like a picture of how this might happen.

Structure is introduced through the birth of new meaning-regulari-

[13] See P. H. Wells and A. M. Wenner, 'Do Honey Bees Have a Language?', *Nature* (1973).
[14] This point is emphatically remarked upon in Chomsky (1967), p. 74.

ties (and perhaps the death of old ones, but I shall ignore that). For instance: if the tribe regularly use S to mean that the fish are biting in the bay, their system might inch its way towards structure if they came to use S' to mean that the speaker has caught some fish, where S' shares with S some (non-iconic) physical feature which none of their other utterance-types have. The addition of S', with that meaning, would be a tiny move towards a situation where that utterance-feature means *fish*. There is vastly more to semantic structure than this, but it can all be built up out of such additions to (and deletions from) the communication-system.

If there is truth in Chomsky's conjecture that we have innate mental capacities which are exercised only in grasping linguistic structures (see §49 above), then the origins of human language must have involved cerebral evolution. But that does not imply that only non-intentional, wired-in patterns of behaviour were involved; for facts about cerebral evolution could well explain changes in a species' patterns of intentional behaviour.

How could it happen, then? How could the tribe acquire the regular practice of using S' to mean P? Such a regularity might be launched by an innovative and determined individual: the possible details of what he might be up to – how he might expect his invention to be adopted by the tribe – can be worked out by the reader without help from me. One aspect of the innovator's motivations should be mentioned, however, namely that he need not be trying to increase structure in the tribal communication-system. The situation might instead be as follows. A tribesman wants to make some utterance-type mean that he has caught some fish; he selects S' for the purpose, this being similar to S which already means that the fish are biting; but his choice of S' is explained by a low-level mechanism of association of ideas, or perhaps by recondite facts about his mind such as those postulated in Chomsky's conjecture, but *not* by a desire to augment structure. He acts intentionally, and it is no accident that his action augments structure; but he does not intend to augment structure.

Still, the individual-initiative account is implausible in all of its versions. The only other kind of account I can find, other than ones where structure precedes communicative intentions, is as follows. The tribe occasionally drift or stumble into certain communicative behaviour-patterns, for reasons other than that anyone intends them to do so; and only the most serviceable patterns are retained. This would be analogous to biological evolution: from a large pool of behavioural possibilities, the most advantageous ones are selected; and they, I am suggesting, might be ones which jointly endowed the system with structure. It would not be an instance of biological evolution, however; for the advantageous patterns would be selected because the tribe *realized* that they were advantageous, and the others dropped because the tribe had *reason* to drop them – not because those who are wired to follow them tend to die young.

That account needs to be supplemented by something analogous to chance mutation in the theory of evolution, something explaining how the tribe might initially 'drift or stumble' into the behavioural innovations from which only the most useful ones are retained. If there is anything in this whole approach, communicative regularities presumably grew out of behaviour-patterns which were not communicative at all. For example, the tribe might reach a stage where their thinking was helped by the use of outer models, and this could lead to their engaging in behaviour in which types of sound or gesture were systematically modelled onto propositions, with no communicative intent or function. These could then be exploited for communicative purposes, in the way I have described. Language *is* used to aid thought, as well as to communicate, and it could have originated in something of that kind. That is not to concede that language is primarily or centrally or essentially an aid to thought; and I stand by my opinion that it is illuminating to view language rather as being essentially an instrument of communication.

Still pursuing the idea of language as growing by selection from a pool of behavioural regularities which were not originally communicative at all: one possibility, suggested to me by Michael Beebe, is that the original regularities began in *play* – taking this to cover anything a species does just because they enjoy it. There is nothing biologically unusual about play. It may seem unlikely that any species would enjoy purposeless behaviour falling into patterns of the form 'Sounds of kind K are emitted only when P is the case'; there is little of that sort in the animal kingdom as we know it. But an improbable hypothesis may be tolerated in explaining such an improbable fact as human language.

All I have offered in this section are some highly abstract descriptions of ways in which languages could have begun. My aim has been to show that various hypotheses about this are open to me – that I have not committed myself to denying that languages could begin – and to show that difficulties about the origins of language are not significantly lessened by the postulation of Gricean mechanisms and intentions.

8

A LANGUAGE

§64. Introducing structure

The foregoing chapters have concerned the whole meanings of whole utterances, ignoring all the ways in which the meaning of a whole utterance can result from the meanings of its parts. I have shown how we could learn that some tribe use S to mean that P, but only by observing how they use S in particular (see §48 above), and not, as one can in actual languages, by deriving the meaning of S from the meanings of other utterance-types through certain general principles. It is now time to take that further step. I think it is the step from 'communication-system' to 'language', but I shall not insist upon that.

We are now confronted by a tribal communication-system regarding which we have learned many facts of the form 'S means that P'. Each of these is based upon what tribesmen mean by uttering S, and these claims about what they mean satisfy my weak, sub-Gricean conditions for meaning (§53 above) – and also stronger Gricean conditions, if you like. I have shown how we could learn all this by studying the tribe's behaviour; and I shall now push the inquiry into behavioural evidence further, trying to show how we might discover facts about semantic structures in the tribal communication-system. That will be the task of the present chapter, during which my tribe will gradually be credited with a quite richly structured language, on the evidence of their linguistic behaviour.

The language I call Tribal has a less rich structure than any actual human language has, and it is not offered as throwing any light upon the structures of any actual natural language. The basic structure of Tribal will in fact be that of the formal language of quantification, enriched in certain ways which will let it stand on its own feet in a manner that a purely quantificational language possibly cannot.[1] I choose an invented, formal language as a model because such a language, being a human invention, has a simple, known structure, whereas the structures of

[1] See P. F. Strawson, 'Singular Terms, Ontology and Identity', *Mind*, vol. 65, (1956).

natural languages appear to be highly complex and are largely un-known.

If this chapter will not increase our understanding of the structure of natural language (to which it will not be addressed), or of the language of quantification (which is perfectly understood already), what is the point of it? Its purpose is to throw light, from my chosen behavioural angle, onto the concept of *structure in language*, by showing how one might find that a communication-system has semantic structure and thus come to be able to understand sentences one had never encountered before.

With the exception of Ziff (see §82 below), philosophers who have begun with whole utterances have not been expansive about the move to utterance-parts. Grice in his 1957 paper stayed entirely with whole utterances, as does Armstrong. Searle and Lewis both move from un-structured to structured utterances by an epistemic jump, addressing themselves to utterances which are known to have semantic structure without discussing how one might come to know this. That is per-fectly acceptable, but it leaves open an epistemological question. Quine (1960) acknowledges the question, but his answer to it hardly goes beyond saying that one moves from the meanings of utterances to the meanings of their parts by formulating and testing 'analytical hypo-theses' about the communication-system.

Schiffer's final section, brief as it is, says much of what needs saying; but I plan to say more still, showing how one might, gradually, cautiously establish that a given communication-system had a complex structure. It must be obvious that there can be behavioural evidence about semantic structure; but it may not be obvious that such evidence could be assembled, and related to the structural conclusions, in disci-plined and controlled ways. Even someone who accepts my rational reconstruction of the epistemic story up to here might say that from here on – as structure is discovered – one can only plunge into the midst of the tribal chatter, flailing around with one hypothesis after another until eventually a few things begin to look right. That, though plausible, is false; and my refutation of it should illuminate some aspects of the concept of linguistic structure. As for the possible objection that my procedure will work with Tribal, but not with the more complex structures of actual human languages: I cannot disprove that, but I do not believe it either.

Many other theoretical issues will be urgently raised by my intro-duction of semantic structure into Tribal. Rather than letting them break the thread, however, I shall postpone them until the final chapter.

§65. The sentence-dictionary

I shall use the form 'S means P' as a shorthand for 'There is a non-coincidental regularity such that whenever a tribesman utters a token of type S he means by it that P'. In practice these regularities would be imperfect, but I shall ignore the scattered exceptions. I am also implicitly banning ambiguity from Tribal. Grice wishes to accommodate it from the outset, and so he replaces the form 'Whenever U utters S he intends to communicate P' by 'U has in his repertoire the procedure: to communicate P, utter S', which allows his repertoire also to contain the procedure: to communicate Q, utter S.[2] I prefer the simpler form, and do not mind ignoring ambiguity (see the opening of §52 above).

I stipulate that S is always a type of sound. I thus restrict Tribal to the auditory mode, and within that I classify in terms of sounds (product) rather than noise-makings (action). If noise-makings can have features which are not reflected in the noise that is made, they will not – I hereby stipulate – be relevant to the definition of any meaningful utterance-type. That excludes little; see the opening of §5 above.

(If the utterings were object-makings, it would make a big difference whether we classified by features of the action or features of the product. I should in fact opt for features of the products – the inscriptions, smoke-signals, piles of stones, etc. Communicating through object-making is laborious, and the only justification for the labour is that an object may be perceived at more times or places than can the making of it: an inscription lingers after the writing of it is over, and a smoke-signal can be seen from further away than can a blanket-waving. That advantage would be lost if utterances were classified wholly or even partly through features of their makings.)

The tribe's communication-system is describable in a lengthy list of statements of the form

S_1 means P_1
S_2 means P_2

and so on. The whole list constitutes what I call the tribe's *sentence-*

[2] Grice (1968), pp. 233–4.

dictionary. If 'sentence' really ought to be restricted to items with semantic structure, my use of the word is premature; but never mind.

Each sentence, each S_i, is a physically recognizable kind of sound. We need not specify in advance what sound-features will enter into the S_i classifications: we shall simply use whatever features we need in order to generalize truly about the tribe's communicative behaviour. However, I do make two stipulations about how we shall classify tribal utterances. Each stipulation brings Tribal closer to human languages, and each gives work to the concept of a *phoneme*. When that concept is applied to actual, natural languages it involves complexities which are not present here.[3] So my concept of a phoneme is a simplified relative of the one that linguists wrestle with, but it does contain the latter's solid core.

(1) The tribe often treat two slightly dissimilar sounds as instances of a single sentence, regarding the differences between them as mere differences in pronunciation. They are principled, not random or arbitrary, about what they count as differences of pronunciation of a single sentence; and in discovering what principles guide them in these judgments, we shall discover what the phonemes of Tribal are. A phoneme is a *kind* of sound, or of inscription etc., so defined that two sounds may belong to it if their differences are ones the tribe regard as mere differences in pronunciation, but they cannot belong to it if they differ in ways which the tribe regard as making a difference in what they – or the sentences containing them – mean. So a grouping of sounds into phonemes might be right for one language yet wrong for another.

(2) Each Tribal sentence consists of a string of phonemes, each of which also occurs in many other Tribal sentences. This permits streamlining, for each sentence can be described as consisting of such and such phonemes (perhaps in a specified order), the basic number of phonemes being vastly smaller than the number of sentences.

For illustration, consider a communication-system which looks just like semaphore, with each separate semaphore-signal counting as a sentence which means that P for some particular P. The phonemes in this system would be the eight positions which a flag can occupy; and each of the thirty-six sentences would be specified by saying which one or two of the eight positions contain a flag. That is advantage (2) in the concept of a phoneme. Advantage (1) is that in this system the

[3] For help with this and other matters in this chapter and the next, I am indebted to Terrance Tomkow.

flag-positions could vary a little without change of sentence: there could be general principles governing which sorts of approximation would be tolerated as mere matters of pronunciation, as it were.

So much for the sentences. Now for their meanings; and first the question of what it is for one S-token to mean the same as does another S-token.

I do not raise this question because I am postulating meanings or propositions as 'entities', and therefore want identity-criteria for them. My entitlement to 'meaning' and 'proposition', I contend, comes not from postulation but from hard work: I have introduced 'register that P', 'believe that P' and 'mean that P'; and from these it is sometimes convenient, for expository purposes, to peel off the 'that P' and call it a 'meaning' or a 'proposition'. I doubt that this puts meanings into my ontology, as entities, though I confess to some unclarity – and much indifference – about such ontological matters. Anyway, my present question is not motivated by ontological concerns. The point is just that each sentence in the dictionary is to be assigned a meaning; that involves saying, where s and s' are tokens of a single sentence, that s means the same as what s' means; and there is an issue about how strictly 'the same' is to be construed here – an issue which need have nothing to do with meanings as entities.

By the strictest standard of identity, we should have to associate each sentence with a saturated proposition – one which is completely determinate in every way, and has a single truth-value for all times and places and speakers. But if the sentences had that sort of meaning, it would be hard to construct the sentence-dictionary in the first place. Ziff insists that the meanings of the sentences must not be fully determinate;[4] and he is clearly right, given that he wants to establish them through generalizations of the form 'When S is uttered, P is true'; for if P is either always true or always false, that generalization either fits every utterance or fits none. If meanings are to be learned in the way I favour, by establishing things of the form 'When S is uttered, the speaker wants to communicate P', the situation looks better: even if P has one truth-value always and everywhere, the wish to communicate P might come and go; and someone might discover that it is present whenever anyone utters S. But although this is possible, it is hard to make plausible.

So I shall avoid it, as I said I would back in §47 above. I shall take it that when someone utters a sentence which occurs in the initial sentence-

[4] Ziff, pp. 126–9.

dictionary, whether he has said something true depends not merely on which sentence he has uttered but also on one or more of these: who he is, where he utters, when he utters. These three features of an utterance – the speaker, the place, and the time – are ones which it must have and which a hearer can hardly escape knowing; and so it is efficient to let them carry part of the meaning of the utterance.

Notice that we have just helped ourselves to something analogous to semantic structure: certain aspects of sentence-tokens are systematically correlated with aspects of their total meanings – for example, S_1 can be uttered by different people, each meaning that *he* is ill; S_2 can be uttered in different places, each time meaning that *that place* is fertile; and so on. This is not semantic structure: to describe an utterance's speaker, time and place as aspects of its 'structure' would be to misuse that word. But the systematic dependence on who/when/where resembles semantic structure, and indeed either could be used to achieve the very same results. Consider these two procedures: – (i) To communicate that a given place is F, a tribesman will point to it while uttering S; to communicate that a place is F' he will point to it while uttering S', and so on. (ii) To communicate that a given place is F, a tribesman will stand in it while uttering S; to communicate that a place is F' he will stand in it while uttering S', and so on. The former of these clearly involves structure: each total utterance has one part which designates a place, and one which indicates the predicate which is being affirmed of the place; and that is semantic structure, if anything is. The second procedure, on the other hand, does not exploit structure, because *where* something is uttered is not a fact about its 'structure' in any reasonable sense. Still, the two procedures – saying that a place is F by pointing to it while uttering S, or by standing in it while uttering S – are two comparable means to the same end.

The same line of thought can be applied with regard to the speaker, and to the time of utterance; though each of those has special features which create problems. I shall pursue the matter no further.

In my rational reconstruction of a possible course of language-learning, our early encounters with Tribal will expose us to a few hundred sentences each of which is frequently uttered so that we can discover its meaning without help from its structure. How such discoveries are made is explained in §48 above. The means of discovery will be called *independent inquiries*, for short.

Having by independent inquiries established a sentence-dictionary, we will have a basis for some conjectures about the significance of certain aspects of some of the sentences. These will help us to guess the meanings of more sentences, checking our conjectures by further independent inquiries. With the help of our enlarged stock of understood sentences, and what we already know about structure, we can then formulate and test still further structural hypotheses; and so on. Although I shall here base structural claims about Tribal simply on facts about regular meanings, those facts are rooted in something deeper, and would not be relevant to structure if they were not. That, however, can wait until §80 below.

Although each structural hypothesis must be tested by 'independent inquiries', we may come to understand some sentences which we could not have understood through independent inquiries alone. Suppose that S is such a sentence, and that we are helped to translate it by our knowledge that a certain part of it is a conditional operator. This knowledge is impossible unless we can test, by independent inquiries, the conjecture that the part in question has a conditional force. But those inquiries might concern sentences other than S, which can be understood through independent inquiries alone. And even S itself could play a part, for procedures which could not establish what S means might still refute some conjectures about its meaning.

I shall pretend that Tribal sentences come to our attention in a maximally convenient order: first, ones which can be understood through independent inquiries, then ones which need only independent inquiries and a little structural theory, and so on. This is quite unrealistic. In practice, one's early encounters with a language would involve many sentences which were unintelligible until vast amounts of structure had been understood. But this implausibility in my account derives from its expository garb, not its substance. The implausible chronology is just a device for keeping clear about conceptual dependences.

§66. Names and predicates

Our sentence-dictionary pairs sentences with meanings. There will be similarities amongst sentences, and amongst meanings; and our first move towards structure occurs when we find that certain sentence-features are associated, through the dictionary pairings, with certain meaning-features. Specifically, we discover facts of the following form: *All the sentences with feature F have meanings with feature G; where F* is a physical feature and G a semantic one. For example, all the sentences which start with a whistling sound mean something about fish.

A sentence-feature which is thus associated with a feature of meanings presumably has meaning or significance in Tribal. If that whistling sound occurs only when something about fish is meant, we can reasonably guess that the sound means something like *fish*.

If we are to assign meanings to something other than sentences, to what should we assign them? I have just conjectured a meaning for a sound, which is a *part* of a sentence, but strictly speaking the meanings belong to sentence-*features*, since these are the basis for the whole structural theory. However, it could happen that all the relevant features had the form 'containing W [in such and such a position]' – for instance, 'starting with a whistling sound' – and it is convenient to abbreviate 'the meaning of S's containing W' to 'the meaning of W'. It is important, though, that when I speak of the meanings of parts of sentences this is just a brief way of speaking of the meanings of certain of their features. In natural languages, indeed, some aspects of an utterance's meaning depend upon features of it which do not concern what parts it contains or their order – these are 'suprasegmental' features such as intonation-contour. For simplicity's sake, however, I shall keep those out of Tribal.

(Could there be a powerful language whose meaningful sentence-features were all suprasegmental, so that it provided no work for the notion of a meaningful part? No; for the following very abstract reason. We shall see that in a richly structured language there must be significance not only in items other than sentences, *but also in relations amongst those items*: for example, there is a significant difference between 'The man bit the dog' and 'The dog bit the man'. If the related items are spatial or temporal *parts* of utterances, the relations between them can be spatial or temporal; and they can be as complex as we wish, without threatening the individual integrity of the parts which are related. For example, (1) a whistling sound, (2) a grunt, and (3) a gasp can be recognized as such, whatever order they occur in. Suppose, however, that the items to be related are sentence-*features* which are in no way tied to parts. For instance, let us suppose that we have to attach significance to (1′) the sentence's spreading over a certain volume-range, (2′) its spreading over a certain pitch-range, and (3′) its having the timbre of a flute. There may be relationships amongst these three: for instance, if we can somehow commensurate pitch and volume, we can relate (1′) to (2′) by saying that the volume-spread *is greater than* the pitch-spread. But this relation, like every other I can find between features, logically follows from what the features are. There could not be two sentences, S and S', which contained all three features, and differed only in that the features were inter-related in one way in S and in another way in S'. If that holds for features generally, then a system which gave significance to features but not to parts could not give *extra* significance to relationships amongst them, for all the relationships would be determined by the features themselves. That loss of relations as a source of extra meaning would, as the ensuing sections will show, drastically reduce the system's expressive power.)

Strictly speaking, since a sentence is a *kind* of sound it is not the sort of item that can have parts. But I am harmlessly using 'S contains E as a part' to abbreviate 'Every token of S contains a token of E as a part'. Thus the items I call 'parts of sentences' are also kinds of sound (e.g. phonemes are kinds of sound). Any meaningful part of a Tribal sentence will be called an *expression*.

I shall refer to Tribal expressions by naming them – that is, using my names for them – not by quoting or instantiating them. For example, I shall introduce a Tribal conjunction operator, 'And'. In giving it the name 'And', I say nothing about how, if at all, the tribe name it, still less do I say what it sounds like. Analogously, if I give someone the name 'Charlie', that does not tell you how if at all his own friends name him, still less does it tell you his height or the colour of his eyes. I shall at no stage give the least hint about how Tribal sounds.

We are to associate sentence-features with meaning-features. Of the various sorts of meaning-features that we might pick on, I start with two: a proposition may be about a certain individual, and it may involve a certain universal. We could make discoveries under each of those headings.

(1) We might find that expression C occurs in all and only the sentences which mean something about the chief of the tribe. That would support the conjecture that C *names* the chief. Similarly, we might tentatively translate many other expressions as names of particular people, animals, places and so on.

(2) We could discover that certain expressions were correlated with universals – that is, with properties, relations, states, kinds of process and so on. For example, we might find that H occurs in all and only the sentences which mean something of the form '... is hot ...', B in all and only those meaning '... bites ...', T in all and only those

meaning '. . . is between . . . and . . .', and so on. We could then reasonably guess that these expressions were *predicates*; and with each predicate we can identify the universal which it connotes (as I shall say). Thus, *H* connotes heat, *B* connotes biting, *T* connotes betweenness.

Our understanding of names and predicates is based upon feature-correlations: we find that a certain physicalistically defined class of sentences is matched through the sentence-dictionary with a semantically defined class of meanings – e.g. the sentences containing *C* are paired off with the meanings which are about the chief of the tribe. As our knowledge of Tribal progresses, we shall find that those correlations do not hold throughout the language: there will be ways of talking about the chief without using *C*, and uses for *H* other than to say that something is hot; and so the biconditionals through which our names and predicates are launched will eventually have to give way to conditionals in only one direction for names, and in only the other direction for predicates. (I do not fully understand why it works out like that.) But it does no harm, and sharpens the exposition, if we pretend that our early encounters with Tribal luckily bring us into contact only with sentences for which the biconditionals are true. That is, sentences which refer to the chief without using *C*, or which use *H* but do not mean '. . . is hot . . .', and so on, happen to escape our notice until through the biconditionals we have firmly established that *C* names the chief and *H* connotes heat.

That is one way of idealizing the account of how we come to understand Tribal. In another way, however, I can now modify the extreme idealization with which I started. I took it that we first establish a sentence-dictionary, on the basis of several hundred sentences each of which we hear uttered many times, and that then we move on to establish feature-correlations which help us to identify some names and predicates. But now we can switch to a more realistic account. In this, we do not hear the very same sentence very often, but we do have a rich experience of partial recurrences: we hear many utterances which instantiate different sentences which have meaningful expressions in common. So we generate the sentence-dictionary simultaneously with the feature-correlations. Rather than fully translating many sentences containing *H* and then proceeding to associate that expression with heat, we hear *H* used in different sentences and conjecturally associate it with heat through conjecturally translating these sentences – the two sorts of conjecture progressively confirming one another.

That is still an idealized picture of a procedure which, in the real world, would inevitably be jumbled and hard to describe. Still, this latest version is nearer reality than the original one was. Similar remarks could be made, and similar moves taken towards realism, at various stages throughout this chapter; but I hope that the general point is now clear enough not to need further illustration.

Here and throughout, 'translate' means 'come to know the meaning of', and nothing else. To 'translate' *S*, in my sense, is to *come to know that S means that it is raining*; it is not to *translate S by the English sentence 'It is raining'*.[5]

§67. Translation through structure

The identification of names and predicates through feature-correlations will be the cornerstone of a series of further discoveries about the semantics of Tribal – discoveries which will enable us to translate Tribal sentences without subjecting them to independent inquiries. But although almost all such translations depend upon what we get through feature-correlations (the only exception comes in §72 below), the correlations do not in themselves enable us to translate any sentences at all. I shall illustrate this in the present section, in which we shall take our first small steps towards the ultimate goal of translating every Tribal sentence.

For convenience, I shall suppose that we discover that Tribal predicates always precede all the names with which they are associated in a sentence – as though we were to say 'Is-burning the-forest' and 'Hits James John' and 'Is-between Baltimore Boston Washington' and so on. This feature of Tribal is taken from the usual notation for the predicate calculus.

It might be thought that that suffices to let us translate some sentences without independent inquiries. If we encounter a sentence consisting of just a monadic predicate followed by a name, mustn't it mean that the bearer of that name instantiates the universal connoted by that predicate? If the sentence consists of *H* followed by *C*, is it not bound to mean that the chief is hot? No, for even that modest translation has to assume that every Tribal sentence is present-tense, affirmative and indicative, unless there is some indication to the contrary. I now stipulate that that assumption is correct, but it is not necessary. In the language Tribal* all sentences are injunctions unless they contain a statement operator; in Tribal** they are all about the recent past unless they

[5] The difference between these is given importance by Davidson (1973), pp. 316–18.

contain a present- or future-tense indicator; and so on. However, let us suppose that our independent inquiries provide early evidence that our assumption about Tribal is right; and that we do not later get any evidence that it is wrong.

So we can now translate any sentence consisting of a monadic predicate followed by a name, and any consisting of a *symmetrical* dyadic predicate followed by two names. For example, a sentence consisting of a predicate which connotes having-the-same-weight-as, followed by the names of the chief and of his dog, means that the chief has the same weight as his dog; and it does not matter in which order the names occur, because their relation is symmetrical. Non-symmetrical predicates will be treated in my next section.

This first tiny result is something we *find* to be true of every sentence in the sentence-dictionary, and *conjecture* to be true for every sentence of Tribal. That will be the procedure throughout: to establish a result as holding within the small set of sentences already translated, and to conjecture that it holds throughout the language. This heuristic may look ploddingly inductive; but it is equivalent to the procedure, apparently more dashing, of confronting a maze of data and boldly and creatively bringing them under hypotheses which are then subjected to test.

In what follows, I shall need some shorthand. I shall use the form '$[x]$' as an abbreviation for 'the individual (or universal) which is named (or connoted) in Tribal by x' – where 'x' may be replaced by the name of a name, or the name of a predicate, or a variable ranging over names or predicates. When brackets are placed around the name of an actual name or predicate, the result is an expression which names an individual or a universal, by reference to how that individual or universal is named or connoted in Tribal. Thus '$[C]$' refers to *the chief*, by referring to him as *the individual who is named in Tribal by C*. Analogously, the phrase 'the species which is least well represented in the San Diego Zoo' refers to an animal species, by reference to its relationship to a certain zoo.

When the [ ] notation is used in connection with actual names and predicates, therefore, it is always dispensable. Instead of writing '$[C]$' we can write 'the chief', instead of writing '$[H]$' we can write 'being-hot', and so on. (Similarly, instead of writing 'the species which is least well represented in the San Diego Zoo' we can write 'the Oryx' or whatever.) In these contexts, we can dispense not only with the [ ] notation itself, but also with the concepts of naming and connoting which it involves.

Where we really need the notions of naming and connoting, and thus have real work for the [ ] notation to do, is in contexts where the brackets enclose variables, thus making further variables. Here, for example, is the rule I introduced above, which let us translate certain elementary sentences (in all descriptions of sentences in Tribal, '-' means 'immediately followed by'):

For any Tribal sentence *s*, and any predicate *p* and name *n*, if *s* consists of *p-n* then *s* means that [*n*] instantiates [*p*].

The consequent of this, namely '*s* means that [*n*] instantiates [*p*]', unpacks into '*s* means that the individual named by *n* instantiates the universal connoted by *p*'. We cannot express this without using the concepts of naming and connoting – either explicitly or through the [ ] notation which embodies them. We cannot replace '[*n*]' or 'the individual named by *n*' by an expression which refers to that same individual without using the concept of naming; for there is no such individual. Because '*n*' is a variable, so is 'the individual named by *n*' and also the shorthand '[*n*]'. So neither of these expressions, as it stands, refers to anything; although each of them can contribute, when its variable is bound by a quantifier, to the meaning of a rule.

Analogously, the instruction 'Hunt for the species least well represented in the San Diego Zoo' might be replaced by 'Hunt for the Oryx'. The more general instruction 'When employed by any zoo, hunt for the species which is least well represented in that zoo' cannot be freed of its use of the concept of zoo-representation. We cannot replace 'the species which is least well represented in that zoo' by the biological name of the species in question, for there is no species in question. The phrase 'that zoo' works like a variable, and so the phrase 'the species which is least well represented in that zoo' does likewise.

It follows that our simple rule, to the effect that *p-n* means that [*n*] instantiates [*p*], is not a mere matter of feature-associations. There can be no question of picking out the class of sentences which consist of *p-n*, and the class of propositions which mean that [*n*] instantiates [*p*], and discovering that the two are paired off in the sentence-dictionary. There is no such thing as 'the class of sentences which consist of *p-n*' or 'the class of propositions which mean that [*n*] instantiates [*p*]', any more than there is the class of shirts which can be bought at Harrods for *n* pounds sterling, or the class of days when the Vancouver temperature falls below *n* degrees.

There is something we can say about class-correlations: members of

(a) the class of sentences consisting of a monadic predicate followed by a name, all mean members of (b) the class of propositions in which a monadic universal is attributed to an individual. But this says vastly less than does our rule, with its variables; and anyway (a) is not purely physicalistically defined as are the classes involved in feature-correlations.

It is easy to extend all this to cover symmetrical predicates. For any Tribal sentence s, and any symmetrical predicate p and names n and m, if s consists of p-n-m then s means that $[n]$ and $[m]$ jointly instantiate $[p]$.

An important caveat, which applies to the whole of this chapter: Everything I say using the [ ] notation should be construed so as not to imply that the tribesmen have the concepts of naming and denoting. If they have semantic concepts, this is a special fact about them, not an automatic consequence of our having a theory about their language. So the statement 'If s consists of n-p, anyone who utters s means that $[n]$ instantiates $[p]$' is to be understood as entailing only things like this:

Anyone who utters A-C means that the chief is angry,

Anyone who utters H-V means that the volcano is hot,

and so on. These do not credit the tribe with wishing to communicate any beliefs about naming or connoting. The latter are concepts which we use in theorizing about the meanings of particular Tribal sentences.

I could have reworded my meaning-formulae so as to make that caveat unnecessary. If I had replaced 'that' by 'something which is true if and only if' in my formulae, the result would have been things like: 'If s consists of n-p, anyone who utters s means *something which is true if and only if* $[n]$ instantiates $[p]$.' That clearly does not imply that the tribe ever use semantic concepts, because obviously one need not employ such concepts in order to mean something which is true if and only if $[C]$ instantiates $[A]$, say. It would do no harm if all my meaning-formulae in this chapter were thus expanded, so that 'something which is true if and only if' acts as a buffer, so to speak, between the tribesmen and the semantic concepts which are embodied in the [ ] notation.[6] Alternatively, the formulae can be taken as they are, subject to the caution given in the preceding paragraph.

§68. Non-symmetrical predicates

Sentences consisting of nothing but a monadic predicate and a name

[6] This is a variant on something proposed by Brian Loar; see Schiffer, pp. 162–3. It raises an issue which will be discussed in §79 below.

were easy; so were ones consisting of a dyadic predicate and two names, just so long as the predicate was symmetrical. With non-symmetrical predicates the situation is more complex. I shall go into it carefully, because it involves important general principles.

Given that C names the chief, D names his dog, and B connotes biting, we want to translate the sentence B-C-D; but we cannot yet tell whether it means that the chief is biting the dog or that the dog is biting the chief.

We could discover by independent inquiries that B-C-D means that the chief is biting his dog, whereas B-D-C means that the chief's dog is biting the chief. That would be a very limited result, however, for it yields translations for only those two sentences.

We might learn more, still at the level of the sentence-dictionary and the feature-correlations. With a little luck in the kinds of sentences that came to our notice, we might find that sentences consisting of B-D-(item) mean something of the form 'The chief's dog bites . . .', while ones consisting of B-(item)-D mean something of the form '. . . bites the chief's dog'. And analogously for B-C-(item) and B-(item)-C. From this, the more limited result of the preceding paragraph would automatically follow.

Still we do not know much. Given the above result, and the datum that P names the chief's pig and X names his horse, we still cannot translate B-P-X and B-X-P. It is natural to suppose that the same rule applies. Very well, let it apply; but what rule is it? We have a strong intuitive sense that these matters can and should be handled in the same way; but I have not yet said explicitly what this way is. Here it is:

For any Tribal sentence s, and any names n and m, if s consists of B-n-m then s means that [n] bites [m].

That secures that in sentences which report a biting, the name of the biter always precedes that of the bitten; which entails the results of the two preceding paragraphs, and also yields translations of hosts of other sentences which report bitings, many of them not involving the chief or his livestock.

We test the above principle for B by examining some of its instances. An instance will involve a sentence containing B followed by two names, say N and N'; the feature-correlations determine what these are names of; we see in which order they occur in the sentence; and independent inquiries establish whether the sentence means that [N] bites [N'] or vice versa.

We have moved from a result about a mere two sentences using B and C and D to one about many sentences using B and either C or D, and from that to one about many sentences using B and any pair of names. Can we now derive that from a still more general result about all non-symmetrical predicates in Tribal? Not quite.

We could discover something which applies to all such predicates, namely that each obeys a rule like the one for B. That is, we could establish a general non-symmetry principle which says, roughly, that for any non-symmetrical predicate p and name n, the sentences with p-n have meanings which relate $[n]$ to $[p]$ in one way, and those with p-(item)-n have meanings which relate $[n]$ to $[p]$ in the other way.

But that, even if it were made precise, would not generate any translations at all. Suppose we have that general non-symmetry principle, and the data that K connotes kicking and that C and D name the chief and his dog respectively. This let us infer, with regard to the the sentences K-C-D and K-D-C, that one means that the chief kicks his dog and the other means that the dog kicks the chief; but we have no way, yet, of determining which sentence carries which meaning. To say that K connotes kicking is just to say that sentences containing K mean *something about kicking*; but that is equivalent to meaning *something about being kicked*; and so 'K connotes kicking' does not associate K with 'kicks' rather than with 'is kicked by'. For each separate non-symmetrical predicate we need an extra fact about which way the predicate slopes, so to speak. That could be ascertained by independently translating just one sentence containing the predicate; for from that, and the general non-symmetry principle, all the rest would follow. That one must always examine at least one sentence containing the particular predicate which is in question is hardly surprising, for one could not expect to discover that K means 'kicks' rather than 'is kicked by' without attending to how K is used.

The question of how a given predicate slopes, e.g. whether it means 'kicks' or 'is kicked by', is the question of how to apply to it the general non-symmetry principle. It would be a mistake to think that we could discover that some Tribal predicate means 'kicks' rather than 'is kicked by' before learning the rules which determine the difference in Tribal between 'x kicks y' and 'y kicks x'. That would, in fact, be an instance of the general mistake of thinking that the meaning of a word can be determined independently of the facts about how the word is used in sentences.

A similar treatment can be given to predicates which are triadic, tetradic and so on upwards. There is presumably no need to drudge through the details.

§69. Complex designators

So far, an individual item can be designated in Tribal only through its proper name, that is an expression whose whole function is to designate that individual. But the tribe may sometimes want to communicate propositions about clouds and bowls of food and rabbits and events and other items which they cannot conveniently have proper names for. I shall now endow them with other resources for designating individuals.

Suppose we know that E connotes edibility in Tribal, and that we encounter a repeatedly used sentence E-Dem, where 'Dem' is an expression about which we know nothing. Independent inquiries show that on one occasion this means that a certain piece of pork is edible, on another that a certain leaf is edible, and so on. The topic varies, but what ought to be the topic-fixing part remains the same.

This could be because our theory of monadic predicates is wrong. But we might – and in my story we do – find a happier explanation. It turns out that there is a physical relation R such that whenever someone utters E-Dem, intending to communicate of some thing x that it is edible, he has R to x. I shall call R 'pointing towards', but it could as well be looking-towards, or touching, or the like.

It would be a routine matter to discover that Dem works in the same way in combination with all predicates, including polyadic ones. For example, if any sentence consisting of G-n-m-o means that $[n]$ gives $[m]$ to $[o]$, then whenever a tribesman utters G-n-Dem-o he means that $[n]$ gives to $[o]$ the item the speaker points to at the time of utterance. This would be like pointing to a book and saying 'John gave this to Mary'.

So Dem is a demonstrative, comparable with the English 'this' and 'that', and with some uses of 'you' and 'he' and 'she'. I simplify Tribal by giving it just one expression in place of all these, and by supplying just one physical auxiliary, here called 'pointing', whereas we have many.

Dem, as so far described, requires that the speaker point to only one thing. I could endow it with a plural use as well, so that a speaker could designate several things by using Dem and pointing to all of them; but that lets in complications which I prefer to avoid. However, I shall stretch the use of Dem in a different way. As our observations of its uses continue, I now announce, we note that sometimes a speaker utters a sentence containing Dem-*p*, where *p* is a monadic predicate, while pointing to several objects; but only one of the objects instantiates [*p*], and independent inquiries show that that object is the one concerning which the speaker is trying to communicate some proposition.

That lets Dem function not just like an unadorned 'this', but also as a component in designating phrases which work like 'this trombone' and 'that weasel'. That comparison needs caution, however. In each of those two phrases a demonstrative is followed by a general noun, but Tribal has no category of general nouns. All it has are *predicates*, which are sentences with one or more designators removed. We may translate the monadic ones by such English expressions as 'is green', 'is a house', 'owns a house', 'is under a house', 'explodes', and so on; but the apparatus of copulas, adjectives, nouns, verbs, prepositions and so on has no counterpart in Tribal. A Tribal predicate meaning 'is a house' must be thought of as an indivisible predicative atom, is-a-house, and not as having internal semantic structure corresponding to 'is' and 'a' and 'house'. It is best to think of Dem, in the context Dem-*p*, as meaning 'that item which', for then we get tolerable English if we add any monadic predicate such as 'is green', 'is under a house', 'is a house', 'explodes' and so on.

We now discover Dem to have another use as well. Sometimes a tribesman utters a sentence containing Dem-*p* while not pointing at all; but there is only one object anywhere which instantiates [*p*], and independent inquiries show that that is the object about which the speaker seeks to communicate. This use of Dem, aided by a predicate and no pointing, is like the English use of 'the' – or, more accurately, 'the item which'.

Tribal now has something natural and efficient which English lacks: a single expression, Dem, which is used to designate an object with the aid of pointing, or a monadic predicate, or both together. Also, of course, a speaker using Dem may partly rely on the hearers' realizing something about which object he is likely to intend to designate. This Gricean element (see §52 above) could supplement pointing or a predicate or both.

If the form Dem-*p* is ever to succeed without help from pointing or anything Gricean, there must be Tribal predicates which are applicable to only one thing. That seems unlikely; and if there were such a predicate, how could it have a busy enough linguistic life for us to learn its meaning? In my next section I shall answer this, by endowing Tribal with predicates which can be understood through something other than feature-correlations in the sentence-dictionary. Some of these could be applicable to only one thing, or indeed to nothing, in the entire universe.

Tribal also has a designator called Self, meaning what 'I' means in English. It is obvious enough how we could discover that this is so.

So now the understood portion of Tribal extends to every sentence consisting of an n-adic predicate followed by n designators – the latter including proper names, demonstratives (aided by pointing and/or predicates), definite descriptions, and an expression for self-reference,

From now on, the [ ] notation will be applied not just to names but to designators generally. Thus '[Dem-p]' means 'the object which is designated by Dem-p', that is, it refers to the object which instantiates $[p]$.

§70. Complex predicates

If any Tribal sentence means that *That brown dog is fierce*, the language needs one predicate for being-fierce and another for being-a-brown-dog. That a language should be able to express *That brown dog is fierce* is no great thing, yet it seems too much to expect it to have, among the predicates which recur often enough to be translatable through feature-correlations, a predicate which connotes being-a-brown-dog. The difficulty would not be solved by sentence-conjunction, if Tribal had it; for 'That brown dog is fierce' does not mean 'That brown item is fierce and that dog is fierce'.

Clearly, Tribal needs some way, given predicates which connote being-brown and being-a-dog, of constructing one for being-a-brown-dog. I shall present such a procedure in this section. It is borrowed from quantificational logic, but also has a counterpart in English.

Really, it is a way of forming predicates from sentences. An n-adic predicate *is* just a sentence with n designators removed from it: the monadic predicate '. . . is tall' is derived from 'John is tall' by removing 'John'. The dyadic '. . . loves . . .' can be derived from 'John loves Mary' by deleting both names, and so on upwards. We could also follow Peirce one step downwards, and describe a complete sentence as a 'medadic' or no-place predicate.[7]

---

[7] See C. Hartshorne and P. Weiss (eds.), *Collected Papers of Charles Sanders Peirce* (Cambridge, Mass., 1960), 3.465.

This approach yields an abundance of predicates. For a start, the deletion of one designator from any sentence produces a monadic predicate; so '. . . loves Mary' is a monadic predicate, which groups individuals into those that love Mary and those that do not, just as '. . . is square' groups them into those that are square and those that are not. Similarly, the expression '. . . regularly uses a Porsche to transport elderly ladies to stock-car racing meets', though not likely to occur among the primitive descriptive resources of a language, is an honest monadic predicate which divides the universe of individuals into those which do and those which do not regularly use a Porsche in that way.

Dyadic predicates group pairs. A symmetrical predicate like '. . . has the same size as . . .' partitions the world of pairs into those whose members are equal in size and those whose members are not. A non-symmetrical predicate like '. . . loves . . .' groups *ordered* pairs according to whether their first member loves the second. Here again there are extravagant predicates, such as 'The B.B.C. will mention . . . on a day when . . . is crowned King of England', which probably applies to {Queen Elizabeth II; Prince Charles}, probably does not apply to {Idi Amin; Prince Charles}, and certainly does not apply to {Prince Charles; Idi Amin}.

How can we give Tribal the benefit of these facts? We might try: 'Any expression in Tribal is an *n*-adic predicate if the addition of *n* designators would turn it into a sentence'; but that would generate incurable ambiguities. Suppose that *L* connotes loving, and that the lover's designator always precedes the beloved's. The suggested proposal would imply that *L-D*, where *D* is a designator, is a monadic predicate, because a sentence results if we add another designator to it. But we do not know which predicate it is, i.e. whether it connotes loving-[*D*] or being-loved-by-[*D*]. Other cases would be even worse.

If a predicate is to be derived from a sentence by removing designators, there must be some indication of where in the sentence the deletions have occurred. I now stipulate that Tribal contains an expression, called Blank, which marks the designator-positions which have been vacated in order to turn the sentence into a predicate. Thus, *L-Blank-D* connotes loving-[*D*], *L-D-Blank* connotes being-loved-by-[*D*], and *L-Blank-Blank* connotes loving-oneself.

If an expression contains one or more Blanks, and would become a sentence if some one designator were substituted for each Blank, I shall call it a 'clause'. On this definition, clauses are all monadic.

Although a clause may have several Blanks, they are to be thought of as replaceable by several occurrences of a single designator. For instance, Dem-*B*-Blank-Blank designates the item which is biting itself.

In saying these things about Tribal, I am supposing that we have discovered the following. Any expression consisting of Dem immediately followed by a clause designates the individual *x* such that: if in the clause each Blank were replaced by a designator of *x*, the clause would become a true sentence. (That is for the case where Dem is supported only by the clause; it is easily extendable to cases where pointing and/or something Gricean is also at work.) Suppose that *B* connotes biting, with the biter's designator always preceding that of the bitten, that *C* names the chief, and that *F* connotes fierceness. Then *F*-Dem-*B*-Blank-*C* means that the item which is biting the chief is fierce; and *F*-Dem-*B*-*C*-Blank means that the item which the chief is biting is fierce. Such facts as these could be discovered in the first instance by independent inquiries.

The foregoing rule about clauses governs only their use as auxiliaries to Dem. That is because we have no other use for them, though we shall get one more use when quantifiers are introduced in §73 below. If a clause were to be used in a sentence in any role other than as an adjunct to Dem or a quantifier, it could only be by having its Blanks replaced by a designator. But that would abolish it as a clause, by merely reversing the process whereby the clause was formed from a sentence in the first place. The concept of 'clause' is just idle here. It is like saying that 'John loves Mary' results from substituting 'John' for the dots in the clause '. . . loves Mary', where the latter is explained as what results from putting dots in place of the first name in a sentence such as 'John loves Mary'. That would clearly be a uselessly long-winded account of a sentence which is better described as one in which a dyadic predicate is suitably combined with two names. But there is real work for the concept of a clause to do when the clause occurs within the scope of a demonstrative or a quantifier – as in 'the person who loves Mary' or 'There is someone who loves Mary', each of which contains 'loves Mary' in a context where it is not simply preceded by a name or other designator.[8]

§71. Nested clauses

The above treatment allows for clauses which contain clauses. For

[8] In this paragraph I follow Dummett (1973), pp. 30–1.

example, if *B*-Blank-*C* means '. . . is biting the chief' (so that Dem-*B*-Blank-*C* designates the thing which is biting the chief), and if *L* connotes loving and *D* is some designator, then *L*-*D*-Dem-*B*-Blank-*C* is a sentence which means that [*D*] loves the thing that is biting the chief. From this we can form a clause by replacing *D* by Blank; and if we prefix this clause by a Dem we get Dem-*L*-Blank-Dem-*B*-Blank-*C*, which designates the thing which loves the thing which is biting the chief. It is a routine matter to describe Tribal expressions which designate the thing which is loved by the thing which is biting the chief, the thing which loves the thing which the chief is biting, and so on.

We can nest clauses as deeply as we like, e.g. constructing a Tribal designator which means 'the thing which loves the thing which is biting the thing that is being buried by the thing which is married to the chief'. That sounds un-English, but only for superficial reasons. One is that English has the personal 'who' as well as the impersonal 'which', a trivial luxury which I deny to Tribal. The other is that we use 'the dog which' and 'the boy who' and 'the mountain which' etc., more than the abstract 'the thing which'. But Tribal will be able to follow suit, when it acquires sentence-conjunction in §72 below; for then it can express 'the thing which is a dog and which . . .', which is tantamount to 'the dog which . . .'

Now a difficulty arises. It connects with Tribal's need for polyadic as well as monadic clauses, but I shall not pursue that account of it. The following is clearer, I think.

I built a clause containing a Blank into a clause containing one more Blank, then built the result into a further clause containing one further Blank, and so on. Everything went smoothly, the Dems alternating regularly with Blanks, so that each Dem was linked with the very next Blank and no other. Now consider these:

(1) the thing which is biting the thing which it loves
(2) the thing which is biting the thing which loves it
(3) the thing which is biting the thing which loves itself.

These have different meanings, yet my rules provide only a single Tribal rendering for all of them, namely

Dem-*B*-Blank-Dem-*L*-Blank-Blank.

This does not express any of (1) to (3), because it gives no indication of how the Blanks should be grouped. Intuitively, (1) puts the first two

Blanks together, (2) puts the first together with the third, and (3) groups the second and third. The following elaboration of Tribal enables it to make such groupings explicit.

Firstly, I replace Blank by a set of expressions having the same function as Blank. They are called $Blank_1$, $Blank_2$, ... etc. – or, collectively, 'the Blanks' – and they are so inter-related that once a tribesman has encountered $Blank_1$ and learned a certain general principle, he can produce and recognize any of the Blanks.

Secondly, I replace Dem by a set of expressions having the same function as Dem. These are distinguished by the same physical features as distinguish the Blanks from one another, so that the Dems can be paired off with the Blanks, one for one, on the basis of their physical features. A given Dem is thus paired with a given Blank if and only if my names for them have the same numerical subscript; but there may be nothing numerical about the Dems and Blanks themselves.

With these additions to its resources, Tribal can make the needed distinctions. The three English expressions displayed above are expressed, respectively, by:

(1′) Dem_1-B-$Blank_1$-Dem_2-L-$Blank_1$-$Blank_2$
(2′) Dem_1-B-$Blank_1$-Dem_2-L-$Blank_2$-$Blank_1$
(3′) Dem_1-B-$Blank_1$-Dem_2-L-$Blank_2$-$Blank_2$.

Each of these contains the fragment B-$Blank_1$-Dem_2, which ensures that $Blank_1$ always marks the biter and $Blank_2$ the bitten. Also, each of them ends with something of the form L-x-y, which ensures that the penultimate Blank marks the lover and the final Blank the beloved. These facts jointly imply that in (1′) the biter is the lover, and the bitten is the beloved; that in (2′) the biter is the beloved, and the bitten is the lover; in (3′) the bitten is the lover who is also the beloved, and that the biter may be someone else. All of this perfectly expresses the English (1), (2) and (3).

That example gives the general idea, I trust. But we need a rule governing the meaning of the Dem–Blank terminology. Here it is:

Let D be a Tribal expression consisting of Dem_1 followed by a clause containining Dem_2, ..., Dem_k. If there is a unique set of items I_1, ..., I_k such that the clause would become a true sentence if $Blank_1$ were replaced throughout by a designator of I_1, $Blank_2$ by a designator of I_2, ..., and $Blank_k$ by a designator of I_k, then D designates I_1.

We can add that if no set of items satisfies the stated condition, E does not designate anything; just as 'the thing which is biting the thing which loves the chief' does not designate anything if nothing loves the chief. If more than one set of items satisfies the condition, then E alone does not designate anything; but if it is accompanied by pointing and/or by something Gricean, it may help to designate something, and what is then designated can be worked out from what I have said already.

The discovery-procedures for that rule raise no difficulties in principle. We might first grasp the use of Dem–Blank where there are no nested clauses, by encountering such sentences and conducting independent inquiries into their meanings. We could tackle sentences with a single nesting, aided by renewed inquiries into communicative intentions and by what we had learned about un-nested clauses. At that stage we might tentatively adopt the general rule for nested clauses: this would over-step our data, but so does any interesting generalization. Alternatively, we might bring un-nested and single-nested cases under a rule which fits just them; then encounter double-nested cases – e.g. ones meaning something like 'the thing which is biting the thing which loves the thing which is cooking the dinner' – and *then* adopt the general rule. Or . . . and so on. The general rule, incidentally, implies that there is no limit to how long a Tribal expression can be, and thus no limit to how many sentences Tribal contains. I shall return to that point in §81 below.

§72. Propositional operators

The next development is the discovery of propositional operators in Tribal. This could have occurred right after the sentence-dictionary: these operators do not need the feature-correlations through which I launched names and predicates.

From now on, I shall extend the [ ] notation to sentences. Just as $[D]$ is the individual designated by D, and $[E]$ the universal connoted by E, so $[S]$ is the proposition which is meant or expressed in Tribal by S. And if 's' is a variable ranging over sentences, '$[s]$' is a variable ranging over propositions.

Suppose we observe that some sentences occur within longer sentences, and independent inquiries reveal that these sentence-inclusions are associated with meaning-inclusions. We find, for example, that S means that there are fish in the bay, and that Not-S

means that there are no fish in the bay. (Remember that 'Not' is my name – chosen for obvious reasons – for a certain Tribal expression. The expression need not sound like the word 'Not' any more than in music a perfect fifth sounds like the phrase 'perfect fifth'. It is vital to remember this throughout: the Tribal expression 'And' need not resemble the English 'And', nor is the Tribal 'If' like my name for it, and so on.) I now stipulate that we discover that for any Tribal sentence s, Not-s means the contradictory of $[s]$. So 'Not' is a propositional operator meaning 'It is not the case that . . .'

Similarly, we could learn that for any sentences s_1 and s_2, the sentence And-s_1-s_2 means the conjunction of $[s_1]$ and $[s_2]$, while If-s_1-s_2 means that if $[s_1]$ is the case then $[s_2]$ is the case; and so on through the other truth-functional operators. Incidentally, Tribal operators always precede the sentences on which they operate: that enables ambiguities of scope to be avoided without the use of anything like parentheses.

Other propositional operators can be detected in similar ways. The expressive powers of Tribal would be greatly increased, for example, if it had expressions Past and Future such that, for any s, Past-s means that $[s]$ was the case and Future-s means that $[s]$ will be the case. It is clear enough how we could translate these tense-operators on the basis of facts established by independent inquiries and embodied in the sentence-dictionary.

Our discoveries about operators are not mere matters of feature-correlation. What we have learned is not merely that sentences starting with Not mean something negative, ones starting with Past mean something about the past, and so on. Rather than merely indicating that the meaning is negative, 'Not' *negates* the proposition meant by the rest of the sentence; and analogously for the other operators as well.

Obviously, therefore, feature-correlations could at best yield much weaker results than we actually have. Less obviously, they might sometimes be entirely impotent. It might be unclear whether someone has a belief which is negative (conditional, etc.) in itself, independently of how he would express it in language; and so we might not be able to extract from the right-hand side of the sentence-dictionary the class of negative propositions, the class of conditional ones, and so on. But we do not need such classes in order to establish that Not-s always means that $[s]$ is not the case, that If-s_1-s_2 always means that if $[s_1]$ is the case then $[s_2]$ is the case, and so on.

Consider also the attribution of beliefs about the past. I have shown how several bits of behaviour might admit of a unitary explanation only if the creature was credited with a belief about the past (§33 above). A special case would be someone who regularly utters S intending to communicate something about the past. He utters S only after exposure to a dead seal, or a dying seal, or a smug young tribesman with blood on his knife, or . . . etc.; in each of these situations *a seal has been attacked*, and the speaker has reason to communicate this fact; and so we conjecture that by S he means that a seal has been attacked. Still, we might be wrong. Perhaps those situations share some present feature, undetectable by us, which the speaker has reason to report to his fellows; in which case he may mean by S that that feature is present. But this possibility is ruled out if we find that S consists of a past-tense operator followed by something which means that a seal is being attacked. To identify something as a past-tense operator, we need independent evidence that sentences containing it mean something about the past. Such evidence is available: independent inquiries can support the guess that a certain sentence means that a seal was recently attacked. My point is just that as various tentative translations of this sort lead to the identification of a past-tense operator, that can reflect back on the translations and immeasurably confirm them.

For that reason, my present programme does not force me to renounce the view I once adopted that a languageless creature cannot rightly be credited with belief about the past (see §§31–3 above). Even if such attributions were always wrong, we could still get feeble *prima facie* evidence that someone intended to communicate something about the past; that might be enough to let us tentatively identify a past-tense operator in his language; and then the attribution to him of beliefs about the past could become perfectly secure. After quantifiers are introduced, analogous remarks will hold for the attribution of general beliefs.

It is easy to see how we could learn that a given Tribal expression means 'I fear that . . .', that another means 'I believe that . . .', and so on. For example, independent inquiries could show that whenever anyone utters Fear-*s* he means that he fears that [*s*] is the case. But I want Tribal speakers to report one another's propositional attitudes, as well as their own. So I endow Tribal with the following rule for Fear:

For any sentences *s* and *s'* and any designator *d*, if *s* consists of Fear-*d*-*s'* then *s* means that [*d*] fears that [*s'*] is the case;

236

and similarly with other operators for believing, hoping, wondering, and so on. I shall call these expressions *attitude operators*. To discover what they mean, we need independent evidence that tribesmen sometimes intend to communicate information about one another's thoughts. There is no difficulty of principle about that, however (see §38 above). In practice, such attributions would have to be extremely tentative; but once we had enough of them to support translations of attitude operators, the latter could strengthen tremendously the belief- and intention-attributions on which they rested.

That whole matter could have been handled differently: one might have treated sentences as *designating* propositions, and thus treated attitude operators as a special sort of dyadic predicate. I prefer my own treatment, but not for any deep reason; and I mention the issue just to illustrate a kind of question which could arise in theorizing about anything. (1) Someone might prefer one theoretic treatment because it permits a simpler and smoother theory. That is important, indeed; but since Tribal's structure is simple by any standards, I need not strain for the utter maximum of theoretic efficiency, especially if that would make the theory harder to grasp intuitively. (2) A preference might reflect a concern about the ontological commitments of one's theory: e.g. someone might deny that sentences designate propositions on the grounds that 'Only individuals can be designated, individuals are the basic items the world is made up of, and propositions are not among those basic items'. I decline to be influenced by such considerations in this chapter. (3) Someone might prefer one theoretic treatment of the facts because it could best be expressed in some favoured language, such as that of quantificational logic. This might be a basic desideratum for him, or it might reflect an underlying concern with ontological commitments – e.g. because he thinks that to be is to be the value of a variable. Either way, I am not now interested.

Now that we understand Tribal clauses, and propositional and attitude operators, there is a sudden jump in the complexity and subtlety of Tribal sentences that we can translate. For one thing, clauses may contain operators, so that objects may be designated by clauses with meanings like 'which is believed by John to be sacred'. Also, we can now fully deal with 'that brown dog'; for the conjunction operator gives us the form 'x is brown and x is a dog', from which the Dem-clause apparatus lets us construct a designator which means 'that item such that it is brown and it is a dog', which is not significantly different from 'that brown dog'. Examples can be multiplied at will.

One further operator should be introduced: the present chapter has so far treated only of statements, and it is time to let injunctions back in. Of various possible devices, I opt for the strongest and simplest. I stipulate that Tribal contains an expression 'Imp' whose meaning is governed by the following rule:

> For any sentences s and s', if s consists of Imp-s' then s is an injunction which means that [s'] is to become the case.

For example, if S means that John has prepared the supper, then Imp-S means that John is to prepare the supper. If S means that the supper has been prepared, then Imp-S means that the supper is to be prepared. If the part of the injunction which follows Imp does not indicate who the intended obeyer is, this may be indicated in one of the non-semantic ways discussed in §51 above. And there could be a further rule to the effect that if d is a designator and s is a sentence, then d-Imp-s means that [d] is to bring it about that [s] is the case. This resembles a common form of injunction in English – 'John, prepare the supper'. The use of Imp could be elaborated further still, but I shall leave it at that.

My rule for Imp allows the formation in Tribal of injunctions which could not be complied with. For instance, if S means that the chief died, then Imp-Not-S enjoins the achieving of a state of affairs in which the chief did not die. Still, we can express temporally futile injunctions in English, too, though slightly less smoothly.

§73. Quantifiers

My penultimate addition to Tribal is an existential quantifier, that is, a device for saying things of the form 'There is a . . .' To start with, I shall suppose that this expression, 'Ex', obeys the rule:

> For any sentence s and any monadic predicate p, if s consists of Ex-p then s means that at least one item instantiates [p].

We might be led to this rule by cases like the following. A tribesman utters Ex followed by a predicate which connotes being-on-fire; we have evidence that he can smell smoke but does not know what is burning, and that if he thought something was burning he would want to communicate this, e.g. so that his hearers would search for the fire and extinguish it. That would give us some evidence that his utterance meant that something was burning, and thus that Ex obeyed the above rule; and, as such evidence piled up, the case could become over-whelming.

The use of Ex can easily be extended so that Ex operates not only on predicates but also on monadic clauses. Thus Ex-*B*-Blank-*C* means that something is biting the chief, and Ex-*L*-*C*-Blank means that the chief loves something, and so on. The chief may even love some*one*, but Tribal lacks specially personal quantifiers such as English has.

As well as Ex, Tribal also contains a universal quantifier 'Un'. Its work could be handled through Ex and Not, but I prefer to introduce it separately. If p is a monadic predicate then Un-p means that every-thing instantiates $[p]$; and a sentence consisting of Un immediately followed by a clause means that everything instantiates that clause. For instance, Un-*L*-Blank-*C* means that everything loves the chief.

The Tribal quantifiers cannot yet deal with nesting. For example, the above account does not enable Tribal to distinguish

(1)   Everything bites something

from

(2)   Everything is bitten by something;

because I have provided only a single rendering for both, namely

Un-Ex-*B*-Blank-Blank.

This resembles a problem we had with Dem, because a demonstrative is like a quantifier in that each operates on clauses – one to form designators and the other to form sentences. To see this, prefix '... loves Mary' first with 'the thing which' and then with 'Something' or 'Everything'.

Exploiting this overlap, I equip Tribal with a range of existential quantifiers $Ex_1, Ex_2, \ldots$ and of universal quantifiers $Un_1, Un_2, \ldots$ which are systematically paired with the Blanks which I introduced to help with the Dems. This apparatus works like the collaboration of quantifiers with variables in the language of quantificational logic. For example, of the above two sentences, (1) is expressed in Tribal by

(1′) Un_1-Ex_2-*B*-Blank$_1$-Blank$_2$,

and (2) is expressed by

(2′) Un_1-Ex_2-*B*-Blank$_2$-Blank$_1$.

Intuitively, the idea is that (1′) associates Un with the biter, and (2′)

associates it with the bitten, which is what (1) and (2) respectively require.

As well as an intuitive guide, we need explicit rules. They will be helped if we add to our semantic vocabulary the notion of a clause's being *true of* an item. I mean this in its natural, ordinary sense, but here is a definition: Clause c is true of item x if the result of replacing every free Blank in c by a designator of x would be to turn c into a true sentence. A 'free Blank in c' is a Blank which is not paired with any Dem or quantifier occurring in c. Now, Ex is governed by the rule:

> For any sentence s and clause c, if s consists of Ex_i-c then s means that c is true of some item.

The rule for Un says that a sentence consisting of Un_i-c means that c is true of every item. Remember that we are not crediting the tribesmen with having any semantic concepts such as 'true of'. The force of the above rule for Ex lies purely in the set of all its instances; an instance of it might be expressed in the form

> ... means that B-$Blank_1$-C is true of some item;

but we must construe it as not involving semantic concepts at all, by taking it in the form:

> ... means that something is biting the chief.

This merely repeats the caution which I offered late in §67 above.

To see how the rules for Ex and Un work out in practice, let us apply them to this Tribal sentence, where [B] is still biting and [L] loving:

> (1) Ex_1-Un_2-And-B-$Blank_1$-$Blank_2$-L-$Blank_2$-$Blank_1$.

It is intuitively evident that (1) means that there is something which bites everything and is loved by everything; but we have to see how that translation of (1) is yielded by the rules. According to the rule for Ex, (1) means that the clause following Ex_1 is true of some item. That is, there is an item such that if it were designated by D then

> (2) Un_2-And-B-D-$Blank_2$-L-$Blank_2$-D

would be a true sentence. We can see intuitively that (2) means that everything is bitten by [D] and loves [D], but let us again apply the rules. According to the rule for Un, (2) means that everything is such that if it were designated by D' then

> (3)   And-B-D-D'-L-D'-D

would be a true sentence. And we know from earlier sections that (3) means that [D] bites [D'] and is loved by [D']. What (1) says is that there is something which can take the role of [D] in this, with anything at all taking the role of [D'], the result being true.

Or, in more familiar terms: (1) means that there is at least one thing x such that for any thing y it is the case both that x bites y and that y loves x. It is no accident that variables help me to express (1)'s meaning in a manner which clearly reflects the rules for Ex and Un.

The rules for Ex and Un, through their use of 'true of', speak of what would result if Blanks were replaced by designators in certain ways. They do not require that the designators actually exist in Tribal.

It seems clear how we could discover that Ex and Un obey the rules I have given. Independent inquiries could, in the way I have sketched, show that sentences of the form of Ex-p mean that something instantiates [p], and that ones of the form of Un-p mean that everything instantiates [p]. More complex cases would be harder to translate in this way, the difficulty growing with every increase in the depth of nesting of quantifiers and thus in the number of different Blanks contained in a single sentence. Eventually we should stop plodding through a series of rules, one for each depth of nesting, and adopt the strong conjecture that Ex and Un obey the absolutely general rules given above, regarding this conjecture as reasonable so long as independent inquiries do not falsify it. In fact, our inquiries will neither falsify *nor support* most of the content of the rules: for instance, we are unlikely to encounter any sentences containing 37 Exes and 422 Uns, in the ordinary linguistic life of the tribe; yet the rules assign meanings to such sentences. This raises the infinity matter which I shall discuss in §81 below.

In the tribe's use of quantifiers, as of Dem, there could be a Gricean practice of using linguistic regularities to express part of one's meaning and relying upon one's hearers to complete it by considering what one is likely to intend. Schematically: a tribesman utters Ex-p where he means that something *of kind K* instantiates [p], his hearers being left to identify K through their knowledge of what his intentions are likely to be. For example, what he utters means that something is burning, and he relies upon his hearers to infer that something which is nearby is burning, because they know he has no reason to communicate information about distant fires. This Gricean mechanism could also aid the use of the universal quantifier.

9

STRUCTURE

This final chapter will treat some issues which are raised by my presentation of Tribal semantics. Some of them are prominent in the current literature: the concept of syntax and how it relates to semantics (§§74–5), the notion of deep structure (§76), Quine's strictures on the notion of meaning (§§77–8), and the relation of meaning to truth (§79). Others concern aspects of my own handling of semantic structure: the presentation of structure on the basis of meaning-regularities (§80), the implication that there are infinitely many Tribal sentences (§81), and the differences between my account and two broadly comparable predecessors of it (§§82–3).

§74. The independence of syntax

I have described the semantic structures of Tribal, by offering generalizations enabling one to infer the meanings of sentences from facts about their structures and about the meanings of their parts. What about the syntax of Tribal? Presumably syntax is a theory about sheer grammaticalness – something which specifies what counts as a Tribal sentence, without giving a clue as to what any sentence means. I now offer such a theory, as a prelude to a discussion of how semantics relates to syntax.

The theory starts with certain lists of Tribal expressions. One is headed 'Names', and contains Tribal names and also Self; another is headed 'Predicates' and contains unstructured predicates, subdivided into monadic, dyadic etc.; a third contains the propositional operators And, If, Imp etc., and a fourth contains the attitude operators Fear, Believe, etc. There is also some way of identifying the Dems, the Blanks, and the Quantifiers (the Exes and the Uns, but syntax does not distinguish between these). Objection: 'In constructing and labelling these lists, you must invoke facts about meanings: how, for example, can you know that something is a Predicate without knowing something about what it means?' I shall answer this later. In the meantime, let me have the lists.

Here are the rules for sentencehood in Tribal (still using '-' to mean 'immediately followed by'):

(1)   Something is a *sentence* of Tribal if and only if it consists of
    (a)   an *n*-adic predicate - *n* designators
    (b)   an *n*-adic propositional operator - *n* sentences
    (c)   an attitude operator - one designator - one sentence
    (d)   a quantifier$_i$ - a clause containing Blank$_i$

Those four rules, aided only by the initial lists, do not let us classify anything as a sentence: (a) and (c) because they use the still unexplained 'designator', (d) because it uses the still unexplained 'clause', and (b) and (c) because they require that we have already identified some sentences. Let us proceed:

(2)   Something is a *designator* in Tribal if and only if it consists of
    (a)   a Name
    (b)   Dem$_i$ - a clause containing Blank$_i$.

The first of these, together with the initial list of Names, lets us classify certain items as designators; then through (1a) we can identify some sentences, and, through (1b) and (1c), further sentences still. But we still cannot use (1d) or (2b), because they use 'clause'. Here is its rule:

(3)   An expression is a clause in Tribal if and only if it contains one or more occurrences of Blank$_i$, for some i, and is such that if each occurrence of Blank$_i$ were replaced by a name the result would be a sentence of Tribal.

This requires that we already have some sentences at our disposal, but so we have. Now that we can apply (1d) and (2b), all our conditions are hard at work.

Parentheses are not needed in Tribal, as they are in some languages, e.g. to show where one clause ends and another begins. This is because I have based Tribal on the Łukasiewicz notation for quantification theory, which is known to be free of syntactic ambiguities although it uses no parentheses.

That theory of sentencehood for Tribal used certain lists labelled 'Name', 'Predicate' and so on. These need not covertly appeal to meanings. Although I originally explained 'name', 'predicate' etc.

in terms of meanings, those labels are of no importance to the syntax of Tribal. All that syntactic theory needs is that the lists be available under some labels – they could be called the Georges, the Henrys and so on.

But must one not appeal to meanings to decide which list a given expression belongs in? No, for the basis for the lists could be purely syntactical. One needs only to discover that certain ways of classifying Tribal are serviceable in an efficient theory of sentencehood: those classifications are then justified by their utility in that theory. One could reach this result by tentatively classifying expressions, while tentatively conjecturing about the syntax of Tribal, with each side influencing the other; until finally one had syntactical generalizations, and classifications underlying them, in which one could be confident. The labels 'Name', 'Predicate' etc. can now be explained syntactically: a newly encountered Tribal expression can be classified as a Name or a Predicate etc. according to how it fits with other expressions to make sentences, and without regard to its meaning. Chomsky may be right, then, when he suggests that 'semantic considerations' do not 'play a role in the choice of the syntactic ... component of a grammar'.[1] It seems clear that one can construct a theory of sentencehood for Tribal, at least, without giving semantic force to any of its theoretical terms.

Furthermore, it can be done for every language. There is some evidence that English syntax needs to distinguish 'abstract nouns' from 'concrete nouns', and it might be thought inevitable that that distinction must rest upon meanings; but really it need not. I shall show this late in §75, in the course of showing also that the independence thesis – that syntax never needs help from semantics for its classifications – is, though true, not interesting.

§75. The dependence of syntax

Even if the syntax of every language can dispense with help from semantics for its classifications, I shall argue that syntax still depends upon facts about meaning. Indeed, it does so in two different ways, of which I shall take the less important first. It concerns the problem of explaining what one means by 'sentence of Tribal'.

If a theory of sentencehood for language L is to have empirical content, it must be refutable. That is, when it implies that a given string of phonemes is a sentence of L, there must sometimes be a way of

[1] Chomsky (1965), p. 226.

independently checking on whether that string really is a sentence of *L*; and so we need an account, other than the one provided by the syntactic theory, of what a sentence of *L* is.

It is often maintained, I think rightly, that the notion of 'sentence of *L*' must be explicated in terms of the notion of 'whole-utterance type which has a meaning in *L*'; which implies that syntax does after all depend in a certain way on the semantic notion of meaning. Chomsky is sceptical about this dependence,[2] but it is not clear that he can manage without it.

Perhaps sentencehood should not be simply equated with that-*P* meaningfulness. Chomsky has plausibly offered 'Colourless green ideas sleep furiously' as a meaningless sentence;[3] and, conversely, there are non-sentences which hearers would in practice accept as meaningful ('Shall we go swimming?' 'Yes! No sooner said the better!'). But these divergences between meaningfulness and sentencehood must rest on a developed theory of sentencehood for English – a theory which is centrally answerable to facts about which whole utterances have meaning in *L*, or so I contend. Since divergences between 'sentence of *L*' and 'meaningful whole utterance of *L*' must be relatively rare, and heavily theory-dependent, their existence does not prevent sentencehood from being explicated primarily in terms of meaningfulness.

Anyway, what other non-theoretic account of sentencehood is there? Chomsky invokes the native *L*-speaker's intuitions about sentencehood: 'The speaker–hearer's linguistic intuition is the ultimate standard that determines the accuracy of any proposed grammar.'[4] But intuitions cannot serve *instead of* facts about meaning. How can we know what 'intuitions about sentencehood' someone has? (a) If we go by how he uses sentences in everyday linguistic life, then our knowledge of his intuitions must rest upon what we can discover about which expressions he endows with meaning. (b) Alternatively, we may ask him 'Is *S* a sentence?' for many values of *S*. But his answers are pertinent only if he means by 'sentence' what we do; which brings us right back to the problem of explaining what a sentence is. If our informant's alleged 'intuitions of sentencehood' do not square with the facts about what *L*-speakers treat as meaningful, his intuitions are bad evidence

[2] Chomsky (1957), pp. 14–15; Chomsky (1965), p. 32.
[3] Chomsky (1957), p. 15. For some illuminating comments on this example, and on the notion of 'intuitions of grammaticality' which has been associated with it, see Barbara Hall Partee, 'Linguistic Metatheory', in W. O. Dingwall (ed.), *A Survey of Linguistic Science* (University of Maryland, 1971), pp. 663–4.
[4] Chomsky (1965), p. 21; see also Chomsky (1957), p. 13.

about sentencehood: either his grasp of L is poor, or he has misunderstood our questions (perhaps through misunderstanding 'sentence'). If, on the other hand, his intuitions do square with the relevant facts about meaningfulness, then we can trust them all right; but now they are not the fundamental data to which the syntactic theory is answerable, but merely quick and convenient pointers to such data. When our informant declares S to be a sentence, or shows somehow that he finds S 'acceptable' or the like, this gives us a short-cut to a conclusion which otherwise we might have had to establish laboriously in the field, namely that P-speakers generally would accord a meaning to S.

There seems to be no escape from the conclusion that 'the main job of a modest syntax is to characterize meaningfulness (or sentencehood)'.[5]

Still, someone could agree, and yet maintain the independence of syntax from semantics. If he took the province of semantics, rather than being as broad as the domain of the concept of meaning, to be restricted to uses of that concept in statements about *what* various expressions mean, he would have room to contend that the concept of meaningfulness or having-a-meaning is a syntactic one. This is the view that syntax is the theory of meaningfulness, and semantics the theory of meanings. If syntax, thus viewed, is to be an autonomous empirical discipline, we must be able to discover what is meaningful in L without discovering what anything means in L. That seems to be theoretically possible, through attention to which linguistic performances are 'uttered without reactions [on the part of the hearers] suggesting bizarreness of idiom'.[6]

However, syntax rests upon semantics in a deeper way which cannot be eliminated by relocating the boundary between them. This relationship does connect syntax with facts about the meanings of expressions – with their meaning this and that, not merely their being meaningful. The connection consists in this: the fundamental structural facts about a language are those which constitute its semantic structure; and syntactic structure is an abstraction, a selection of certain aspects from this larger whole.

Chomsky says: 'The theory of syntax should be designed so that the syntactic structures exhibited for particular languages will support

---

[5] Donald Davidson, 'Truth and Meaning', *Synthese*, vol. 17 (1967), p. 308; see also Quine (1951).
[6] Quine (1951), p. 53.

semantic interpretation.'[7] I warmly concur. But Chomsky sometimes evokes a wrong picture – one in which syntax stands on its own feet and, if all goes well, carries semantics on its shoulders. '[By] the formal study of grammatical structure . . . a syntactic framework is brought to light which can support semantic analysis. Description of meaning can profitably refer to this underlying syntactic framework, although systematic semantic considerations are apparently not helpful in determining it in the first place.'[8] To see that this is misleading, imagine a syntax which supported no semantics. Suppose that for some language *L* we have a syntactic theory *T* which demarcates the sentences of *L*; but what the sentences of *L* mean must be either (a) separately learned for each sentence, or (b) worked out with the aid of a semantic theory which has nothing significant in common with *T*. If (a) obtains, *L* is uninteresting because its repertoire of sentences is so small. If (b) obtains, then we can presumably extract from the semantic theory an alternative syntactic theory *T'*; in which case we should ignore the semantically sterile *T*, attending instead to *T'*. For what is the use of knowing what the sentences of *L* are, if one does not know what they mean?

If I am wrong in supposing that there is a syntactic theory nested within any semantic theory, *T* might not have a semantically fruitful rival syntax *T'*. But that would not strengthen *T*'s claims on our attention. Indeed, whether or not it had a rival its existence would be at once boring and mysterious. Boring, because *T* would describe useless structure; and mysterious, because it would be puzzling that a language should have elaborate, useless structural features. In short, any syntactic theory that is to merit our attention *must* 'support semantic interpretation'. The converse does not hold. It is not essential that any semantic theory should admit of being split into a syntactic foundation and a semantic overlay. Even if that kind of separation can be done for every semantic theory, I can find no general reasons for thinking that it is a necessary or even a desirable way of describing semantic structure.

Chomsky has exhibited a vehement desire to get as much as possible into the realm of syntax and out of that of semantics, although he has also said that 'any attempt to delimit the boundaries of these domains must certainly be quite tentative'.[9] This empire-building without maps is puzzling, but I think I can explain it. One striking example of

---

[7] Chomsky (1965), p. 226.   [8] Chomsky (1957), p. 108.   [9] Chomsky (1965), p. 163.

syntactic imperialism occurs in a discussion of 'subcategorizations' such as the classing of 'sincerity' as an abstract noun. Chomsky says:

It is an interesting question whether or to what extent semantic considerations are relevant in determining such subcategorizations . . . A linguist with a serious interest in semantics will presumably attempt to deepen and extend syntactic analysis to the point where it can provide the information concerning subcategorization, instead of relegating this to unanalyzed semantic intuition, there being, for the moment, no other available proposal as to a semantic basis for making the necessary distinctions.[10]

This remarkable takeover bid deserves comment. Why should 'a serious interest in semantics' make one hope that the answers lie in syntax? Chomsky's answer is, in effect, that syntax contains principles whereas semantics, 'for the moment', can steer only by 'unanalyzed semantic intuition'. What would it be like for semantics to be based on something more principled than 'intuition'? I conjecture that as soon as facts about linguistic structure become expressible in highly general theories, Chomsky will automatically count them as syntactic. There is a reason for this. Semantic structure is the fundamental reality, I have argued, and syntactic structure is abstracted from it. But what syntax abstracts is, really, all the structure – it merely leaves behind the facts about what the structure is for, what it does for the language-user. Now if one takes syntactic structure as basic and self-sufficient, and defines semantics as whatever must be added to syntax to get a complete theory of meanings in the language, one may be puzzled to know what to add. And it will seem clear that whatever is added will not include any very general statements, for those would describe structure and would thus already be in the syntax. Consider, for instance, the classifying of some nouns as 'abstract'. If some syntactic generalization can be found which fits all and only the abstract nouns, that automatically yields a syntactic basis for the classification: an 'abstract noun' can be defined as one which obeys that syntactic principle, just like the syntactic basis for classifying various expressions as Names, Predicates etc. in my syntax for Tribal. There is nothing wrong with this, so long as it is understood. If it is not, one may mistake necessities for contingencies, and thus be led to think that *so far* semantics has lacked general principles. This could lead in turn to describing as a desire for a syntactic treatment of problems what is really just a desire for a principled treatment of them.

[10] Chomsky (1965), p. 75.

§76. Deep structure

The structures in Tribal are child's play: as well as being very simple, they are also all *surface* structures. Chomsky has argued powerfully that natural human languages involve 'deep structures' of a kind that Tribal totally lacks. Many arguments for deep structure come from the needs of syntax, but some concern meanings. Consider:

(1) You are too quick to take offence.
(2) You are too young to take snuff.

These differ in meaning, in ways which are not fully explained by the meaning-difference between 'quick' and 'young', and between 'offence' and 'snuff'. *Those* differences cannot explain why (1) is a criticism whereas (2) may not be, or why (2) gives a reason whereas (1) does not, or why (1) implies 'You sometimes take offence' whereas (2) does not imply 'You sometimes take snuff'.

One gets some purchase on the difference by saying that (1) means (1') 'You take offence too quickly' while (2) means (2') 'People as young as you ought not to take snuff'. That is a correct, *ad hoc* meaning-analysis which any sensitive English-speaker might give. But there are countless similar cases; and it would be good to have a theoretical basis for dealing with them, rather than having merely to bring one's *Sprachgefühl* to bear on each separately. There is a kind of syntactic theory which provides such a basis – a kind in which the concept of *deep structure* plays a vital role.

This kind of theory was invented by Chomsky. It contains rules which generate certain structures which sentences of the given language may have. For instance, $S \rightarrow NP + VP$ means that a sentence may have the form of a noun-phrase followed by a verb-phrase; and $VP \rightarrow VP + NP$ means that a verb-phrase may consist of a verb-phrase followed by a noun-phrase; and the two together yield a further rule $S \rightarrow NP_1 + VP + NP_2$ (think of 'The man hit the dog'). In addition to these 'phrase structure rules' there are 'transformation rules', each of which 'operates on a given string . . . with a given constituent structure and converts it into a new string with a new derived constituent structure'.[11] For example:

If S_1 is a grammatical sentence of the form

$$NP_1 - Aux - V - NP_2$$

[11] Chomsky (1957), p. 44. The example is from *Ibid.*, p. 43.

then the corresponding string of the form

$$NP_2 \text{ - Aux} + \text{be} + \text{en} - V - \text{by} + NP_1$$

is also a grammatical sentence.

It is that rule – plus some other material which I shall omit – which certifies that because 'John admires sincerity' is a sentence, so also is 'Sincerity is admired by John'.

The aim of such a theory is to give rules which generate everything which is, and nothing which is not, a sentence-form of the language in question. If the theory succeeds, then it assigns to each sentence a 'transformational history', which is a rule-governed route from a simple 'S' to that sentence. If the transformational history of our sentence (1) included, somewhere along the way, the form of (1'), and if the history of (2) included the form of (2'), then we could adduce (1') and (2') not merely to describe but partly to explain the difference in meaning between (1) and (2). And the concept of 'deep structure' comes in as follows. Sentences (1) and (2) do not differ in surface structure: the differences between them, as they meet the eye or ear, are merely those between 'quick' and 'young', and between 'offence' and 'snuff'. But the sentences also differ in their transformational histories, and that contributes to the meaning-difference between them. We can think of a sentence as carrying its transformational history with it; so that the facts of that history do not merely concern how the sentence fits into a certain theory of 'generative grammar', but also affect what it is like in itself. So the sentence has features which do not meet the eye or the ear; and they must be structural features, since they are determined by a purely structural theory. We thus arrive at the notion of the sentence's *deep structure*. If we have a sound generative grammar which puts (1') into the transformational history of (1), and (2') into the history of (2), then we have unarbitrary grounds for saying that the meaning-differences between (1) and (2) are partly explained by how their deep structures differ, the latter difference being indicated by that between (1') and (2'). Chomsky goes as far as this:

The meaning of a sentence is based on the meaning of its elementary parts and the manner of their combination . . . The manner of combination provided by the surface . . . structure is in general almost totally irrelevant to semantic interpretation, whereas the grammatical relations expressed in the abstract deep structure are, in many cases, just those that determine the meaning of the sentence.[12]

12 Chomsky (1965), p. 162.

This sounds extravagant if one focuses on 'in general', less so if one attends to 'in many cases'. But I shall not argue about that. The main point is that the concept of deep structure can be very helpful in the study of semantic structures.

But not in Tribal, to which the concept of deep structure is inapplicable. Any Tribal sentence has a 'history'; that is, we can say how the syntax of Tribal generates it. I did not present the syntax in generative form, but it is a routine matter to do so, using rules like

$$S \rightarrow \text{MonPred} + \text{Des}$$

and

$$\text{MonPred} \rightarrow \text{DyPred} + \text{Des}$$

and

$$\text{Des} \rightarrow \text{Dem} + \text{Clause}$$

and so on. But if the syntax of Tribal is expressed in generative rules, they will be phrase-structure and not transformation rules. That implies that the effect of applying them is always additive: as the rules go through the successive stages of generating a given sentence, the procedure is one of steady lengthening, by addition or insertion, with no other changes at all. Tribal sentences therefore lack deep structure simply because all their structure lies on the surface: they show on their faces every fact about their transformational histories. In contrast with this, the transformational rules for English, and probably for any actual, natural language, do not merely add, but also delete, substitute, and re-arrange; which is why many aspects of an English sentence's transformational history do not meet the eye or ear in the final, surface structure.

In depriving Tribal of deep structures, I make it easier to describe but harder to speak. In general, the features of human languages which challenge the grammarian's ingenuity also serve to make them efficient instruments of communication. For example, consider the sentence 'If that grey dog barks, the white one will too'. The Tribal equivalent of this has the form: 'If (it will be the case that) (that item such that) it (is grey) and it (is a dog) barks (it will be the case that) (that item such that) it (is white) and it (is a dog) barks.' Each bracketed portion would be a single word in Tribal, so that the sentence could be described in this form (where B, D, G and W connote barking, canineness, greyness and whiteness respectively):

If-Future-*B*-Dem$_1$-And-*D*-Blank$_1$-*G*-Blank$_1$-Future-*B*-Dem$_1$-And-
D-Blank$_1$-*W*-Blank$_1$,

which shows, as did the bracketed-English version, that Tribal needs
seventeen words to do what normal English can do in ten. Yet a proper
grammatical description of the ten-word English sentence involves
complexities from which the Tribal one is free.

Tribal's lack of deep structure, as well as simplifying its grammar,
smooths out the theory of how it might be learned. But that advantage
is only one of degree, not of kind. It may be true that every English-
learner attributes deep structures to the sentences he hears. That is, it
may be that the only coherent route from (a) his learning-data to (b)
the sentences which define his resultant competence is through a
grammatical theory in which (a) and (b) are all generated by rules which
attribute deep structures to many sentences. But this feat on the English-
learner's part is on a continuum with theorizing or generalizing which
even the Tribal learner must do. I have nothing to add to my discussion
of this matter in §49 above.

The growing school of 'generative semantics' uses the concept of
deep structure, but replaces Chomsky's stress on the autonomy of
syntax by an approach which is semantic right from the outset. The
idea is that any sentence's meaning can be expressed in something like
the language of quantification theory (or Tribal); and then there are
rules which transform that representation of the meaning into the
sentence which actually meets the ear or eye. Again we have the concepts of deep structure and of transformational history; but now the
transformation rules must preserve meaning, not just meaningfulness or
sentencehood, and they take us through a new kind of deep structure
up to the old familiar kind of surface structure. This would also help to
explain meaning-differences on the surface: the suggested explanation
of the 'too quick'/'too young' example would be provided by generative semantics, if the route to (1) from its deep structure contained
(1'), and the route to (2) contained (2') – the deep structures here being
understood to be quantificational representations of the meanings of
(1) and (2).

If one could express in the language of quantification all the meanings
which English sentences could have, then generative semantics could
undertake the Chomskyan task of finding rules to generate all and only

the sentences of English; but if it succeeded it would not only generate the sentences but also assign meanings to them.[13]

If someone tried to find systematic ways to teach my tribe the whole of English, by teaching them permissible transformations of Tribal sentences, his endeavour would be tantamount to the search for a generative semantics for English.

I have no opinion on the comparative merits of this programme and Chomsky's one. I have argued that the divorce of syntax from semantics is an abstraction, an artificiality; but that implies nothing about how theoretically useful the divorce is.

It is presumably clear that Tribal provides no raw material for either kind of theory. Whether deep structures are thought of as syntactic or semantic, Tribal does not have them. I take it that nobody will contend that a system which lacks deep structures cannot be a language.

§77. Quine's inextricability thesis

In this section and the next I shall relate the present work to two famous theses of Quine's, each of them hostile to the concept of meaning. They are sometimes taken to be aspects of a single doctrine, but I shall argue that this is wrong. I start with the view which Dummett has called Quine's 'inextricability thesis'.[14]

Suppose that someone says, in the course of describing a box, 'It is cubic'. If he believes what he says, then he believes that it is cubic; and this belief coincides exactly with the meaning of his sentence. Some of his beliefs are parts of the belief that the box is cubic, and thus parts of the meaning of 'The box is cubic': for instance, that the box is regular and convex, that it has plane sides, and so on. Others, perhaps, are not clearly parts of the meaning of 'The box is cubic' although they are logically entailed by it: for instance, that on any side of the box a pair of diagonals will make four right-angled triangles. I shall not discuss this supposed line between what is meant and what is entailed by what is meant. My concern is with the line which lies further out still, namely that between (a) what is meant and (b) what is contingently implied by what is meant – i.e., between (a) the meaning of 'It is cubic' and (b) propositions which are not parts of the sentence's meaning but which follow, by virtue of well-entrenched contingent beliefs which

[13] See Gilbert Harman, 'Deep Structure as Logical Form', in D. Davidson and G. Harman (eds.), *Semantics of Natural Language* (Dordrecht, 1972).
[14] Dummett (1974), p. 365.

nearly everyone holds, from 'It is cubic'. For example, the proposition that the box would not roll as well as most balls do.

Quine has argued that there is no sharp line between what a sentence means and what it implies through well entrenched contingent generalizations.[15] His thesis is not that we cannot discover exactly where the line falls, but rather that there is no line, only a continuous shading from what clearly falls within the sentence's meaning to what clearly falls outside it. In other words: from the total content which a given sentence would convey to most members of a given linguistic community, we cannot extricate a core of pure meaning. Hence the label 'inextricability thesis'.

The inextricability thesis implies that there is no determinate class of analytic sentences, that is, sentences which are true solely by virtue of what they mean and without appeal to what is contingently implied by what they mean. One upshot of this is that there are, at best, degrees of analyticity; another is that analyticity turns out to be uninteresting.[16]

One of those who came to the defence of analyticity was Grice,[17] and soon after that his 'Meaning' paper appeared. Could it help against Quine? One might think so, for the following reason. Part of Quine's strategy was to examine various attempts to distinguish what is meant by a sentence from what is contingently implied by it, or to distinguish analyticity from truth by virtue of facts. He argued that each attempt fails unless it is qualified in some manner which presupposes that the line has already been sharply drawn. For instance: if S is analytic, then the proposition it expresses could not be false, so if S came to express something false it would have to be *by coming to express some other proposition*. But that means '. . . by changing its meaning', and so this partial explanation of 'analytic' achieves nothing unless we already have 'meaning' at our disposal. So in Quine's hands the problem took the form: how can one draw the *first* line? How, for instance, can one distinguish analytic from synthetic before one has distinguished what is meant from what is contingently implied? It is natural to see Grice's paper as a response to this – an explanation of 'meaning' in

[15] Quine (1950), Quine (1951).

[16] In this sketch, I follow Dummett (1974), and also J. Bennett, 'Analytic–Synthetic', first published in 1959 and reprinted, with disclaimers of the anti-Quinean parts, in L. W. Sumner and J. Woods (eds.), *Necessary Truth* (New York, 1969). A different interpretation is advanced in Gilbert Harman, 'Quine on Meaning and Existence', *Review of Metaphysics*, vol. 21 (1967).

[17] H. P. Grice and P. F. Strawson, 'In Defence of a Dogma', *Philosophical Review*, vol. 64 (1956).

terms which do not use 'analytic' or 'proposition' or any of those others. But really it is not, and nor are the descendants of it which have been presented by Schiffer, Armstrong, myself and others.

Gricean meaning-theory does give us one kind of initial leverage on the concept of meaning, but that does not entail that it meets Quine's challenge. For it might give us leverage only on a *coarse* concept of meaning, that is, one which will let us say '*S* means that *P*' without enabling us to extricate what is meant from what everyone would confidently infer from what is meant. Even if Grice's theory is true, therefore, it may nevertheless fail to meet Quine's challenge by enabling us to extract the pure core of sheer meaning from what is said.

To use Gricean theory to meet Quine's challenge, one would have to argue as follows. Gricean theory bases 'means that *P*' upon 'intends to get someone to believe that *P*'. With a sufficiently refined behavioural theory of belief and intention, we could sharply delimit what a given person intends to communicate on a given occasion. For instance, we could discover that someone meant that *The box has six plane sides*, and not that *The box would not roll as well as a ball*, even though he knew that if the former was true the latter must be also; for we could discover that he had some reason to communicate the former but not the latter. So we could have a refined concept of 'intends to communicate *P*', which would sustain a refined concept of 'means that *P*'; and Quine would be answered.

This argument fails completely, though; and that failure reinforces the case for the inextricability thesis.

Let us grant, though it may not be true, that there is no limit in principle to how finely someone's beliefs can be discriminated on the evidence of his non-linguistic behaviour (see §36 above). That certainly does not imply that we can finely discriminate what he intends to get someone else to believe; and I think that my discussion in §38 above suggests that the latter discrimination is usually impossible. However, in order to get on with my main argument I shall concede that point also: individual communicative intentions can be discriminated as finely as you like, with the aid of a perfect behavioural theory of belief and intention.

Suppose, then, that we have a finely drawn concept of what a speaker means on one occasion by a particular utterance. To meet Quine's challenge, we must get from that to finely drawn meanings for sentences, which are re-usable utterance-*types* belonging to a public language. But that move may be impossible, for it might be that every attempt to classify utterances into types yielded only coarse meanings for the types. I contend that that is what would happen if the users of the language were sensible. If S means roughly what 'It is cubic' means in English, the communicational intention with which S is uttered might sometimes focus on how the thing would look in a certain position, sometimes on how it would roll, sometimes on what the upshot would be of a proper count of its sides, sometimes on what would result if it were cut in half, and so on. If all of these matters are firmly interlinked through generalizations which the tribe confidently accept, then the tribe has good reason to associate them all with a single utterance-type which could be efficiently used for any of them. Thus, even if on each individual occasion there is some more constricted propositional content which the speaker is interested in communicating, the meaning of S should be taken to spread over all those contents; and around the edges the meaning of S will shade off, as one comes to propositional contents which are less firmly linked – through tribe-wide belief – with the having of six plane sides etc.

Objection: 'Even if S-utterers may want to communicate one or other of the propositions you have mentioned, they are only upshots of S's meaning, not parts of it. Indeed, your account is not coherent unless S does have a central meaning which holds those other propositions together.' I see no reason to believe that. Presumably S's 'central meaning' is supposed to be a propositional minimum which is common to all the normal communicational intentions with which S is uttered. But why should there be any such common element? Because without it those propositions could not be suitably linked to a single utterance-type? That is false. The set of propositions which are associated with S and which constitute its 'coarse' meaning may form a *cluster* – this being not merely a metaphor but something truly explanatory which Putnam has enabled us to understand.[18]

The foregoing argument uses Gricean meaning-theory to support the inextricability thesis as applied to utterance-types, while apparently conceding that it may be false for utterance-tokens. The appearance is misleading, however. In granting, for purposes of argument, that we might have a finely drawn concept of communicational intention, I was giving maximal weight to the notion of what someone cares about communicating on a particular occasion; but we cannot move directly from 'this is all he was anxious to communicate when he uttered that

[18] Hilary Putnam, 'The Analytic and the Synthetic', reprinted in *Mind, Language and Reality* (Cambridge, 1975).

S-token' to 'this is all he meant by (uttering) that S-token'. If the question of what he meant by (uttering) the token is to connect seriously with the inextricability thesis, then it must be a question about *what expressive powers the token had* on that occasion. What the inextricability thesis says about utterance-types is that they have no power to convey some of their import (meaning) in one way and the rest of it (obvious contingent consequences of meaning) in a sharply different way. There is, says the thesis, nothing about utterance-types or their use which gives them such a power. But utterance-tokens do not have it either, even if they are backed by very finely drawn communicational intentions. If a speaker says 'It is cubic', and cares about communicating that the thing has six sides but not about communicating that it would not roll well, the limitations on his concerns do not imply corresponding limitations on what the utterance-token will convey to hearers or on what he expects it to convey to them. The limitation on what he cares about is discoverable, but it is not embodied in the utterance-token and is indeed not typically available to the hearers. Our only way of learning about it is by independent inquiry into the speaker's motives: that is needed for learning language, but it actually subverts the chief purpose of language, which is to communicate *through* utterances (see §48 above).

If *U* says 'I have just shot a rabbit', caring only to communicate to *A* that he has shot something edible, no one would say that *U* means by that utterance-token only that he has shot something edible. The utterance is explained by an intention which is restricted to edibility; but nothing stops the expressive powers of the token from stretching as far as rabbithood.

I conclude that Gricean meaning-theory does not refute the inextricability thesis, and indeed tends to support it, for utterance-tokens as well as -types. If Quine were, as some have thought, contending that the concept of meaning is so shoddy that no coherent explanation of it can be given – not even one which makes it a coarse concept – then of course Grice answers him. But that would be a misreading of Quine.

§78. Quine's indeterminacy thesis

More recently, Quine has argued that there is an unavoidable slack or indeterminacy in one's understanding of those parts of any language which do not relate very immediately to the speakers' experience.[19]

[19] Quine (1960).

This thesis, which is quite distinct from the inextricability thesis,[20] poses a challenge to my offerings in chapter 8 above.

To facilitate discussion, I shall pretend that my results in chapter 8 were expressed in the form

S means the same as '. . . . .'
S' means the same as '- - - - - -'

with English sentences on the right-hand side. In fact, I did not *mention* any English sentences, but merely *used* them in statements of the form

S means that . . . .
S' means that - - - - -.

or in higher-level principles which entailed such statements. However, Quine addresses himself explicitly to 'translation', which he construes as a mapping of sentences onto sentences; so I retroactively adopt that form, in order to link this part of Quine's work directly with what I have been doing.

I have claimed, then, that with the support of a good behavioural theory of belief, intention and meaning, and aided by hard work and some luck, we could map all the sentences of Tribal onto sentences of English in such a way that each Tribal sentence means the same as its English counterpart. Even if we are using a somewhat coarse concept of meaning, our sentence-pairs could still be fairly exactly synonymous. Quine, however, says that any evidence which supports one mapping will also support a rival to it: any language can be translated in either of two equally good ways, one of which translates some sentence by one English sentence while the other translates it by another – the two English sentences being ones 'which stand to each other in no plausible sort of equivalence however loose'.[21]

Quine later repented of that formulation, saying that he 'disliked having to appeal thus to equivalence . . . in the very formulation of a thesis that casts doubt on notions of translation or synonymy or equivalence'.[22] This scruple was ill-founded; for the formulation really says just that one sentence might be translated by two English sentences which would not be deemed synonymous even by those who think that

---

[20] Here I agree with Dummett (1974), and Hilary Putnam, 'The Refutation of Conventionalism', reprinted in *op. cit.*

[21] Quine (1960), p. 27.

[22] W. V. Quine, 'Reply to Harman', in D. Davidson and J. Hintikka (eds.), *Words and Objections* (Dordrecht, 1969), at pp. 297–8.

some sentence-pairs are synonymous; and that, rather than 'appealing to' synonymy, merely says something about people who have 'synonymy' in their vocabularies. Quine's misplaced scruple has seduced him into some bad formulations of the thesis. The basic claim is that two translation-systems Tr_1 and Tr_2 map a single Tribal sentence S onto two English sentences E_1 and E_2, respectively; and something must be said about how E_1 differs from E_2; for it is not enough merely that they are *different*, as 'There is gorse on the hills' is different from 'There is furze on the hills'. Quine has been led to say that they may differ in truth-value. But we must not know which of the two is true, for then we could prefer one translation to the other, on Quine's principle that a good translation will as far as possible translate sentences which the tribe accept into sentences which we deem true. Accordingly, he has taken refuge in the idea that we may know that E_1 is the contradictory of E_2 but not know the truth-value of either of them.[23] This is surely unacceptable. If our agreement 'in withholding verdicts on both sentences' arises from curable ignorance, let us cure it and then adjudicate between Tr_1 and Tr_2. The indeterminacy thesis is supposed to concern something which threatens any translation of any language into any other; and so it cannot rest on such temporary contingencies as factual ignorance on the part of the translators.[24] The alternative is to say that E_1 and E_2 permanently lack truth-values. That would be a curious thing for Quine to say, since in other contexts he has fought hard against truth-value gaps, describing our tolerance of them as an 'idiosyncrasy of ordinary language'.[25]

Cutting a long and tangled story very short, I conclude for those reasons that Quine should have retained the formulation in which E_1 and E_2 differ because they would not be deemed 'synonymous' even by those who think that some pairs of sentences are synonymous. That is clear enough, and poses a definite challenge to my claims in chapter 8 above.

When Quine first presented the indeterminacy thesis, he did not

[23] This possibility was offered to Quine by Gilbert Harman, 'An Introduction to "Translation and Meaning"', in *Ibid.*, pp. 14–16; and Quine seems to have accepted it, in 'Comment on Michael Dummett', *Synthese*, vol. 27 (1974), p. 399.

[24] Thus Dummett (1974), pp. 382–4, 414.

[25] W. V. Quine, *Methods of Logic* (London, 1952), §37; see also *The Ways of Paradox* (New York, 1966), p. 143. Harman (*loc. cit.*) handles the topic through an illustrative model, which is an axiomatic system; that supports the notion of *independence from the axioms*, which is Harman's analogue for *permanent lack of truth-value*. But that just shows that a frozen axiomatic system is a misleading model for a natural language which has a flexible, growing, all-in epistemic basis.

argue for it. He has subsequently offered one argument in its favour, and I shall now try to show that it fails.[26] It goes as follows.

If we are to discover the meanings of Tribal sentences, we must note how the tribe's utterings relate to their experience of the world. In particular, if we are to translate the sub-set of sentences which constitute their science, we must discover what science *would* be accepted by a tribe with their perceptual and intellectual level and their experience. That is, we must attribute to them that science which best fits the world as they know it, and then so translate Tribal that a sub-set of its sentences, which the tribe deem true, come out as expressing that science. This assumes that we can know what their epistemic strengths and weaknesses are, but so we can; and for simplicity's sake I shall assume that they are perceptually and intellectually on a par with us. Even if they are good scientists, they may be unlucky ones – that is, they may have been seduced into false theories and happened to escape experiences which refute them. But we can set that possibility aside, too, for Quine is supposing that we have access to the facts about 'all possible observations' which the tribe might make of their world.[27] Even then, he argues, we cannot determinately translate Tribal, because no one scientific theory is *the* one which best fits the world as the tribe know it. Quine is here relying on the widely held doctrine that 'Theory is under-determined by data', i.e. that any range of empirical facts, even an infinite one, is covered by at least two perfectly adequate theories. For instance, there are facts which could be explained by the theory that space is non-Euclidean and that measuring-rods have certain properties, or by the theory that space is Euclidean and that measuring-rods have different properties.[28] From this Quine infers that our knowledge of the tribe's experience of the world could never conclusively entitle us to attribute to them any given scientific theory; for there would always be a rival theory which would fit their facts just as well. The argument concludes: since we cannot decisively attribute to them one science, we cannot decisively apply to their language one system of translation. If, for all we can tell, they might hold either of two scientific theories Th_1 and Th_2, we cannot choose between the corresponding translation-systems Tr_1 and Tr_2 – where Tr_1

[26] W. V. Quine, 'On the Reasons for Indeterminacy of Translation', *Journal of Philosophy*, vol. 67 (1970).

[27] *Ibid.*, pp. 179, 183.

[28] This example is used to illustrate the indeterminacy thesis in Edwin Levy, 'Competing Radical Translations: Examples, Limitations and Implications', in R. C. Buck and R. S. Cohen (eds.), *Boston Studies in the Philosophy of Science*, vol. VIII (Dordrecht, 1972).

maps some of their accepted sentences onto the English sentences which express Th_1, while Tr_2 maps those sentences onto the ones which express Th_2. There is therefore an inevitable indeterminacy in our translation of their language. Q.E.D.

This argument reflects Quine's empiricist and behaviourist approach to language, but it is none the worse for that. In his particular way of tying language to experience there are details which I disagree with, but they are not relevant to whatever is wrong with the indeterminacy thesis. What is wrong, I submit, is as follows. Quine writes as though one's only guide in constructing a translation consists in all the facts about the tribe's sensory contact with the world, together with all the facts about which sentences they accept. If that were our only evidence, and if data always under-determine theory, then we should indeed have a choice about which science to attribute to the tribe and thus about how to translate their language. But that is not our only evidence. We can also have copious evidence about how the tribe link parts of their total sensory intake with parts of their total linguistic output – which experiences they count as creating difficulties for which bits of their science, which pairs of sentences they take to be intimately linked and which pairs they connect only through many intermediate sentences, and so on. There is no reason to think that any range of data can be brought under two sciences which are so related that any inference in either is paralleled by an inference in the other, any problem for either is a problem for the other, any experiment which bears on one bears in an exactly analogous way upon the other, and so on. Certainly, in any of the cases we actually know about, the two theories differ in *how* they are fitted to the facts, so that there could be abundant behavioural evidence about which of them the tribe accepted.

'But even if we cannot point to known instances, a given range of data might be covered by two rival theories which are so interrelated that we couldn't tell which of them a tribe accepted. And this bare, abstract, logical possibility is enough to refute some mentalistic theories of meaning.' It is not clear to me how mentalism can be refuted by an argument which has behaviourism as a premiss; and I can imagine a mentalist accepting Quine's argument and using it contrapositively, as a *reductio ad absurdum* of the behaviourist approach to meaning. Anyway, there is no point in discussing the implications of this abstract logical possibility unless it is indeed a possibility. I shall argue that it is not.

Consider a case of the sort which, according to the indeterminacy thesis, is always on the cards: two optimal translation-systems translate S by, respectively, E_1 and E_2, which nobody would regard as synonymous with one another. Quine thinks that the two translations may both be safe from refutation because E_1 and E_2 will be 'highly theoretical statements', so that: '[Their] connection with extralinguistic stimulation consists pretty exclusively in the reverberations across the fabric ... Commonly such statements are scarcely to be judged otherwise than by coherence, or by considerations of overall simplicity of a theory whose ultimate contacts with experience are remote as can be from the statements in question.'[29] But the 'reverberations across the fabric' have their own detectable pattern; and the two translations of S cannot both be secure unless E_1 and E_2 both reverberate in precisely similar ways. For example, if any experiences would render problematic the acceptance of E_1 but not that of E_2, then there could be behavioural evidence favouring the translation of S by one of them rather than by the other. Or if E_1 were relevant to some theoretical issue, while E_2 did not have an exactly analogous relevance to an exactly analogous theoretical issue, then again there could be a basis for preferring one translation. In short, every single fact about E_1 must be mirrored by a fact about E_2. By any reasonable standard, therefore, the two sentences are synonymous, and so the indeterminacy of translation thesis is false.

The thesis has another strand which should be mentioned. Quine says that even if Tr_1 and Tr_2 assign the same overall meaning to S, they might give different accounts of what contributions its various parts make to the total meaning. He infers from this that 'reference' is 'behaviourally inscrutable', meaning that on the behavioural evidence we cannot determinately settle what a given Tribal expression refers to.[30] He illustrates this with 'the problem of deciding between "rabbit" and "undetached rabbit part" as translation of "gavagai"', the point being that 'whenever we point to different parts of the rabbit, even sometimes screening the rest of the rabbit, we are pointing also each time to the rabbit [and when] we indicate the whole rabbit with a sweeping gesture, we are still pointing to a multitude of rabbit parts'. One might think that increasing knowledge of the semantic structures

[29] W. V. Quine, 'Speaking of Objects', reprinted in *Ontological Relativity and Other Essays* (New York and London, 1969), pp. 16–17.

[30] W. V. Quine, 'Ontological Relativity', reprinted in *op. cit.* This and all remaining quotations in the present section are from pp. 29–34 of this work.

of Tribal would enable us to choose between 'rabbit' and 'undetached rabbit part' as translations for 'gavagai'; for we might observe that the tribesmen accept a sentence which we translate as 'This "gavagai" is the very same as the one we saw an hour ago', where they had viewed its head on the first occasion and its hind-quarters on the second. But Quine points out that that depends upon our translating a certain Tribal expression as 'is the very same as', rather than as 'belongs with'. If it means 'belongs with', then the sentence doesn't mean 'This rabbit is the very same as the one we saw an hour ago' but rather 'This rabbit part belongs with the one we saw an hour ago'. That is as far as Quine takes the example; but he 'suggests' that any further attempts to rule out 'rabbit part' as a translation of 'gavagai' might be foiled by further 'compensatory adjustments in the translation of accompanying native locutions'. Because of 'the broadly structural and contextual character of any considerations that could guide us' in theorizing about the semantic structures in Tribal, Quine says, 'There seem bound to be systematically very different choices, all of which do justice to all dispositions to verbal behaviour on the part of all concerned.'

I do not think that this example will work. As we learn more about the semantic structure of Tribal, it will become ever harder to devise the required 'compensatory adjustments': the 'systematically very different choices' which are supposed to confront us will become ones which we cannot make, or even formulate and consider. Quine might agree about that. In one place he says, of a 'workable' alternative translation of some Tribal expression, not that it 'seems bound' to be available but only that 'perhaps' it is. So his basic point may be merely that the envisaged alternative – e.g. 'gavagai' translated as 'undetached rabbit part', and compensating adjustments made – is abstractly logically possible. This apparently more modest claim might still be valued as an antidote to the view that 'the meanings of the words are . . . determinate in the native's mind, his mental museum, even in cases where behavioural criteria are powerless to discover them for us'. The 'mental museum' metaphor tends to evoke not merely a kind of mentalism that might be objectionable, but also a wrong view about how the meanings of utterance-parts relate to the meanings of whole utterances. It suggests a view according to which the meanings of the separate words in a sentence somehow exist independently of any facts about how they might be assembled to yield a meaningful sentence; to which Quine opposes the correct picture in which one starts with a sentence's meaning and finds reasons for distributing it amongst the constituent words. Quine often writes as though this were the main point of his doctrine of the inscrutability of reference, as when he emphasizes 'the broadly structural and contextual character' of the facts which let us assign meanings to words and short phrases, and when he says that 'the secret' of the whole matter is that we run into difficulties by 'cutting language into segments too short to carry [determinate] meanings'. The point is indeed extremely important; but the doctrine of the inscrutability of reference is at best a shaky illustration of the point, and has no tendency to support or confirm it. Confronted by the inscrutability doctrine, a proponent of the 'mental museum' might well say: 'If putting sentence-meaning first leads to a fundamental, unremovable uncertainty about whether "gavagai" means "rabbit" or "undetached rabbit part", that shows how wrong it is to put sentence-meaning first.' He is more likely to be converted by being shown what evidence we have for things we do all confidently say about word-meanings. To try correcting his error by deploying the doctrine of the inscrutability of reference is just to offer him an antidote which he will not swallow.

§79. Meaning and truth

Little enough has been said about truth in my account of meaning and language, and yet for some philosophers – notably Davidson – truth is the key to meaning. Any major thread in Davidson's work leads to most of the remainder; but I do not think that I shall be doing Davidson any injustice by picking out and partly isolating certain aspects of his total doctrine about meaning and truth.

I approach the first of them by picking up a thread which in itself seems not to interest Davidson much; but it interests me, and it leads to him. It concerns the nature of conceptual analysis.

For some decades before Quine's papers of the 1950s, conceptual analysis was taken to be the pursuit of illuminating analytic biconditionals. The tie-up between 'analysis' and 'analytic' was seductively tempting, and it reflected the view that conceptual analysis was one kind of exploration of meaning. When Quine attacked the concepts of meaning and analyticity in the 1950s, his views were resisted partly from a fear that his attack threatened to leave philosophers with no coherent way of defining their discipline.

However, this work of Quine's looks less destructive if one sees him not as attacking the concept of meaning but rather as arguing that it is a *coarse* concept (see §77 above); and as saying not that there is no such thing as analyticity but rather that there is no sharply demarcatable class of analytic sentences. There could still be an unsharply delimited class of analytic sentences, namely those whose truth is warranted by considerations which lie fairly near to the centre of the meanings of the terms which are involved. According to the inextricability thesis, on my construal of it, something's pertaining to the meaning of an expression is a matter of degree: that the box will not roll is *less* a matter of the meaning of 'It is cubic' than is its having six plane sides; and so a sentence's being analytic is also a matter of degree. This approach is clearly extractable from Quine's writings, as I have demonstrated elsewhere.[31] Quine himself has shown no interest in salvaging 'analytic', even as used coarsely, but his work does support such a salvage.

Still, 'analytic' may not be worth saving. It tends to mislead, unless accompanied by a loud avowal that it is being used coarsely; perhaps it would be better to replace the use of 'analytic' and the accompanying cautions by something which more directly and openly says what ought to be said. Since the primary use of 'analytic' is just in a single statement characterizing the aim of analysis, we could just drop the word and say that conceptual analysis seeks to establish biconditionals (or, as in my inquiry into the concept of meaning, conditionals) which are rather deeply embedded in our totality of accepted sentences. The metaphor of 'embeddedness' can be unpacked: it is largely a matter of how much intervening material there is sheltering a given sentence from revision in the face of recalcitrant experience. Another angle on the metaphor will be presented shortly.

As well as a post-Quinean way of describing the aims, we need a post-Quinean way of expressing the results, of conceptual analyses. One might retain the old forms:

S means that . . . . . .
S means, in part, that . . . .

and

S expresses part of the meaning of the statement that . . . .

and accompany these with warnings that 'mean' is here used coarsely. It would be intolerable, though, to have to give the warning every time; and yet without it one may be misunderstood by philosophers

[31] See note 16 above.

who still think one can distinguish nicely between what S means and what could be inferred from S by moves which, though obviously truth-preserving, are not licensed by S's meaning alone.

One solution is to eschew the use of 'mean' in these contexts, and express one's results instead in statements about S's truth-conditions:

S is true if and only if . . . .
S is true only if . . . .

and

S is true if . . . .

A shining example of this kind of formulation is in Goodman's famous paper about counterfactual conditionals:[32] it first appeared in 1947, but its use of the 'if and only if' formulation is presumably a response to the inextricability thesis, which Goodman suggested to Quine in the first place.[33]

(In expressing one's results in the language of truth-conditions, one avoids, *a fortiori*, the worst form of the refined-concept-of-meaning view, namely the assumption that claims about meanings are directly answerable to what speakers have in mind when they use the expressions in question. This assumption can lead to the rejection of one analysis of counterfactuals because when someone says 'If it hadn't rained we would have gone swimming' he is not thinking about the law-derivability of some propositions from others, and to the rejection of another analysis because the speaker is not thinking about classes of possible worlds. By this standard, it seems, any correct analysis would have to be rather trivial; but even when that consequence was noticed, many philosophers, instead of dropping the standard, announced the discovery of something called 'the paradox of analysis'. That whole way of thinking vanishes, happily, when we move to the language of truth-conditions; though it could also be destroyed by a more careful handling of pre-Quinean lines of thought.)

---

[32] Nelson Goodman, 'The Problem of Counterfactual Conditionals', reprinted in *Fact, Fiction, and Forecast* (London, 1954).

[33] 'Dr. Nelson Goodman has suggested (in conversation) the dismal possibility that what we think of as synonymy may be wholly a matter of degree, ranging from out-and-out orthographical sameness of expressions on the one hand to mere factual sameness of designatum . . . on the other. In this case analyticity in turn would become a matter of degree – a measure merely of our relative reluctance to give up one statement rather than another from among a set of statements whose conjunction has proved false.' W. V. Quine, 'The Problem of Interpreting Modal Logic', *The Journal of Symbolic Logic*, vol. 12 (1947), p. 45 n.

There is a difficulty. Suppose that I am discussing counterfactuals, right now, and I say this:

'If it had rained this morning I would not have used the hose' is true if and only if $2+2 = 4$.

That biconditional is true, because the quoted sentence is true and $2+2 = 4$. The following is also true:

'If I had not been alone in the house this morning I would have thrown a party' is true if and only if $2+2 = 5$;

for in this case the statements which flank the 'if and only if' are both false. Obviously, neither of these two biconditionals, true though they are, helps to explicate the meanings of the quoted counterfactuals. There is no tolerable concept of meaning – no residuary legatee, however coarse, of pre-Quinean meaning – for which 'if and only if' is a reasonable substitute in either of the above biconditionals.

Davidson has addressed himself to this difficulty.[34] He envisages a situation where we have a strong, complete, interlocking theory which implies a set of T-sentences – ones of the form 'S is true if and only if P' – which assign truth-conditions to every sentence in the language. Such a theory will not imply T-sentences like the two above, true though they are, because there is no theoretical connection between any arithmetical facts and the truth of 'If it had rained . . . etc.' or the falsity of 'If I had not been alone . . . etc.' Davidson conjectures that the T-sentences which were implied by such a theory would strike us as elucidating the meanings of the sentences mentioned in them, or, in terms he prefers, would strike us as 'interpretations' of those sentences.

To this persuasive line of thought, something should be added. Even if we have a theory which implies truth-conditions for every sentence in the language, and assuming that it has no rivals like those postulated in Quine's indeterminacy thesis, we still have the option of strengthening or perhaps weakening it to a certain degree. Given a theory which embodies only information which strikes us as pertaining to meaning (or 'interpretation'), we might enrich it, feeding in further highly general biconditionals which add to the content of many of the T-sentences. One could then consider whether this enrichment had gone beyond sheer 'interpretation', taking us out of the province of meaning into that of physics, say. The answer would be a matter of degree.

If that possibility did not exist, Davidson would have laid the basis

[34] Davidson (1973), §3; Davidson (1974), pp. 319–20.

for a sharp-edged concept of meaning or 'interpretation'. For then we could have a unique theory, not admitting of enrichment or impoverishment, which would be determinately related to each T-sentence: either it does imply the T-sentence or it does not, and so the T-sentence either does or does not *interpret* the sentence which is mentioned in it. But when my point in the preceding paragraph is made, Quine's matter-of-degree concept of meaning or interpretation is reinstated.

I have credited Davidson with views about conceptual analysis, mainly on the strength of his clear preference for a truth-conditions manner of recording *all* facts about meanings. But he has not said much about conceptual analysis as such, if that is taken to be a matter of T-sentences in which puzzling sentences of our language are interpreted through less puzzling ones. Davidson is more interested in two other sorts of T-sentence: each of them yields 'interpretations' also, but not of the kinds ordinarily associated with 'conceptual analysis'.

Firstly, there are those which exhibit what he calls the 'logical forms' of sentences, that is, which state their truth-conditions in the language of quantification-theory in a manner which explains their logical powers. For instance, he has argued that the best explanation of the fact that

John walks slowly entails *John walks*

is that the logical form of one of these is

$(\exists x)(x$ is a walking & x is by John & x is slow$)$

while the form of the other is

$(\exists x)(x$ is a walking & x is by John$)$;

so that the one-way entailment between them is a matter of simple formal logic. And these claims about 'logical form' are expressible in T-sentences: 'John walks slowly' is true if and only if $(\exists x)(x$ is a walking ... etc.). This is not the place to discuss quantification over events, or to evaluate the programme of exhibiting logical forms (which Davidson also calls 'deep structures' – see §76 above). If the programme is a good one, it presumably belongs to the larger programme of conceptual explanation and puzzle-removal which could all be called 'conceptual analysis'. Davidson uses that phrase more narrowly, and repeatedly *contrasts* 'giving the logical form of S' with 'giving a conceptual analysis of S'; but it would not be sensible to quarrel with that choice of words.

Davidson's other chief interest in this area is in the question of how one might establish the set of *T*-sentences which interpret all the sentences of a radically foreign language. This programme of 'radical interpretation', which resembles what I have tried to do for Tribal, is what brings Davidson closest to my present concerns and is the real motivation for the present section. Davidson links it with the previous topic, for he thinks that a 'radical interpretation' should include assignments of logical forms to all the foreign sentences; but I am concerned with a different aspect of 'radical interpretation' which lets me now drop logical form. I want to discuss Davidson's views about what our basic data are for understanding a radically foreign language, and what concepts those data should be brought under.

Despite the great merits of the use of *T*-sentences to state the meanings of sentences, I believe that any attempt to understand a radically foreign language must use the concept of meaning in ways which are not derived from statements about truth-conditions. Specifically, I believe that the whole inquiry must rest upon discoveries of the form: When *U* uttered *S* at *T*, he *meant* by it that *P*. (We could steer around 'mean' by using 'he was saying that *P*'; the basic point remains the same.) I have shown how I think that 'he meant that *P*' enters the picture. I cannot prove that it must do so; but I can object to Davidson's attempt to keep it out.

For he does try to keep it out. He wishes to use *T*-sentences as a basis for everything of a meaning-stating or interpreting kind: truth-conditions are the foundation of his whole semantic theory, and so his data for 'radical interpretation' must not include anything like 'When he uttered *S* he meant that *P*'. In Davidson's account, the theory of truth-conditions for the language under study – call it Tribal – is based upon observations of which sentences, perhaps in specified circumstances, the tribe *hold to be true*.[35] Given enough data of this sort, pertaining to a good variety of sentences, we can begin to establish some general theory about when they hold various kinds of sentences to be true. Then we can ascend to generalizations about when various kinds of Tribal sentences *are* true – i.e. to our theory of truth-conditions for Tribal – by discovering when the tribe are in error. This requires a theory of tribal belief. Davidson is cramped here by his refusal to get belief under way independently of language, but he has a suggestion about how a theory of belief might be developed *pari passu* with the theory of truth-conditions.[36]

[35] Davidson (1973), §2; Davidson (1974), p. 320.   [36] Davidson (1974), pp. 320–1.

I have no complaint with all this, as far as it goes. Nor would I deny that it treats certain problems profoundly. Yet it is also shallow, in not digging below the level where one knows that the tribe have a language, and which are its sentences, and when a tribesman is asserting a sentence or otherwise showing that he holds it to be true. I applaud Davidson's claim that 'the evidence for the adequacy of a theory of interpretation . . . must be describable in non-semantic, non-linguistic terms';[37] but the 'non-linguistic' requirement is discarded, for a page later he says that the evidence consists in facts about 'when a speaker holds a sentence to be true'. Davidson may envisage cashing out 'holds true' in some non-semantic, non-linguistic terms; perhaps in terms of uttering in a certain tone of voice. But whatever plausibility that might have depends on the assumption that what is being uttered is *a sentence*. Presumably Davidson does not aim to give a 'non-linguistic' account of what a sentence is.

Below the level which is Davidson's ground floor, there are further problems about evidence and theory-construction; they concern the marshalling of evidence which really is 'non-semantic, non-linguistic', and the Gricean approach can make some headway with them. Although Davidson apparently does not notice that the 'non-linguistic evidence' he seeks cannot be found at his chosen level, he does acknowledge the existence of the lower levels: 'An attempt to build on even more elementary evidence, say behavioristic evidence, could only make the task of theory construction harder, though it might make it more satisfying. In any case, we can without embarrassment undertake the lesser enterprise.'[38] That is not very disarming, though, for Davidson is not humbly agnostic about the 'greater enterprise'. On the contrary, he has strong views about the lower levels – especially about what they do not contain. He envisages basing 'true' on 'holds true', and basing the latter only on notions which are in no way semantic: he speaks guardedly of 'even more elementary evidence, say behaviouristic evidence'; but if he has any candidates other than sheerly behavioristic evidence for the 'more elementary' role, he gives no hint of what they are. He certainly does not envisage grounding 'x holds S to be true' in behavioural evidence through a chain which leads from (1) behaviour to (2) beliefs and intentions, thence to (3) occasion-meanings, thence to (4) regular meanings, and thence to (5) Davidson's ground-floor where there is a language some of whose sentences are held to be true. He will

37 Davidson (1974), pp. 311–12.
38 *Ibid.*, p. 310. For a superb treatment of the shallowness issue, see Strawson (1969).

not put (3) or (4) below (5) because he proposes to found meaning entirely upon truth. He will not put (3) below (4) because he flatly rejects meaning-nominalism: 'To interpret a particular utterance it is necessary to construct a comprehensive theory for the interpretation of a potential infinity of utterances.'[39]

Furthermore, Davidson clearly sees no chance of giving (2) a role anywhere below (5), because: 'Making detailed sense of a person's intentions and beliefs cannot be independent of making sense of his utterances.'[40] I have tried to refute that; and one wonders why Davidson is so sure of its truth that he is willing to assert it without argument. (He has much to say about the attempt to distill out separate belief and meaning components from the total import of a linguistic utterance; but that is a world away from the attempt to attribute beliefs where there is no language. General slogans such as 'Meaning and belief are interlocked' tend to blur that vital distinction.) Perhaps the word 'detailed' is carrying a lot of weight. On the same page, Davidson speaks of the impossibility of verifying without appeal to language 'the existence of detailed, general and abstract non-linguistic beliefs and intentions', and cites the example of 'trying to learn without asking him whether someone believes there is a largest prime'. Is it assumed that the concept of language can be based on pre-linguistic concepts of intention and belief only if one could pre-linguistically attribute every belief which is expressible in language? I hope not (see §30 above), but then what is the point of the example?

Anyway, despite this unclarity in Davidson's position, there is no uncertainty about his attitude to, specifically, the Gricean treatment of the lower levels. Still on the same page, he dismisses Grice with a breath-taking snub:

> There is a principled, and not merely a practical, obstacle to verifying the existence of detailed, general and abstract non-linguistic beliefs and intentions, while being unable to tell what a speaker's words mean. We sense well enough the absurdity in trying to learn without asking him whether someone . . . intends, by making certain noises, to get someone to stop smoking by that person's recognition that the noises were made with that intention. The absurdity lies not in the fact that it would be very hard to find out these things without language, but in the fact that we have no good idea how to set about authenticating the existence of such attitudes when communication is not possible.

I have tried, through a series of presentations culminating in §43 above, to give a 'good idea' of what might 'authenticate the existence' of that

---

[39] Davidson (1974), pp. 316–17.   [40] *Ibid.*, p. 312.

intention. Of course, somebody might reasonably predict that it could not be done; perhaps someone might, after the event, reasonably judge my attempt a failure. But I do not know what to make of someone who can sheerly 'sense well enough the absurdity' of the attempt, and who deems this to be a 'principled obstacle' to success.

§80. Structure before regularities

I said in §5 above that I would move from the meanings of whole utterances to the meanings of utterance-parts; and so I did. My way of doing this involved assigning meanings to *types* of utterance-part on the basis of what they contribute to the meanings of *types* of whole utterance containing them. Could I instead have introduced the notion of the meaning of an utterance-part before endowing the tribe with any re-usable, regularly or conventionally meaningful, utterance-types? I used to think not. I accepted what I call 'the recurrence thesis', namely that an utterance-part cannot be meaningful unless it instantiates a type which recurs in several different whole-utterance types. That implies that the meaning-nominalist programme must be restricted to whole utterances. It would be important if it were true, but it is false. I learned this from Michael Beebe, and the present section derives mainly from a paper by him and other help he has given me.

Suppose that a tribesman U does something thereby meaning that *the fish are biting*, this being an isolated, iconic case, and not an instance of any meaning-regularity. Specifically, he sketches a fish in the air with his hands, and then jumps as high as he can, snapping his mouth open and shut at the top of the jump. If this two-part action means that *the fish are biting*, one naturally suspects that the first part means something about fish while the second means something about biting. I shall rest nothing on suspicions and impressions, however: the aim is to show what could soberly entitle us to attribute those separate meanings to the two parts of the utterance.

Here, as always before regularities are at work, meaning is determined directly by intention. U's overall intention is to get his audience A to believe that the fish are biting. If we could resolve that into two sub-intentions, and establish that U sketched a fish with one sub-intention, and jumped up and bit with the other, we should have a basis for assigning the desired separate meanings to those two parts of his total utterance. That would be neat, if it were not impossible: the whole intention cannot be resolved into two such sub-intentions. Consider what the latter would have to be like. Each must be an intention to affect A – how? If neither intended effect is a belief, then they will not jointly constitute a belief, which is contrary to hypothesis. If one is a belief and the other not, they will not automatically add up to the intended overall belief: for instance, if U intends to get A (1) to think about fish and (2) to believe that something is biting, those intentions would be fulfilled by A's believing that something is biting the fish. And if we strengthen (2) to 'believe that the fish are biting', that makes it equivalent to the whole intention, thus rendering (1) otiose. (This point is handsomely illustrated by an asymmetry in Searle's very careful handling of reference and predication. His 'rules of reference', which govern 'successfully and non-defectively perform[ing] the speech act of singular identifying reference', require that the reference be part of some larger speech act, but no details of the latter are specified.[41] In contrast, the 'rules of predication', which state the conditions for 'successfully and non-defectively predicat[ing] P of an object X', explicitly require that the predication be associated with 'a successful reference to X'.[42])

If we try to direct each sub-intention towards the production of a belief, things get no better. What can the intended beliefs be? That *the fish are doing something* and that *something is biting*? Someone who had those two beliefs *might* be led to guess that the fish are biting; but intending to communicate those two beliefs is not the same as intending to communicate that the fish are biting. It has been suggested that *the fish are biting* might be resolved into *there are fish* and *they are biting*; but the words 'they are biting' do not express any proposition except in a context which fixes the referent of 'they'; and in our present context the words express the proposition that *the fish are biting* – which again renders the first belief, and thus the first sub-intention, otiose.

I conclude that we cannot associate each of the two utterance-parts with a distinct intention. But we can associate each with a different feature of the single intention with which the whole thing is uttered. In general, when someone acts with one indivisible intention, the latter may have features which severally explain features of his action. For instance, he threw the rock high into the air, intending to produce a loud splashing sound when it hit the water: the *height* of the throw is explained by the *loudness* of the intended sound. Sometimes a feature of the intention explains the action's having a certain part. For example, I surreptitiously dump garbage on your study floor, and also drop

41 Searle, pp. 94–5.   42 Searle, pp. 126–7.

there Smith's wallet, my overall intention being to make you angry with Smith. The action has parts, which are explained by aspects of the intention: I leave garbage because I intend to make you angry, and I leave Smith's wallet because I intend the anger to be directed at Smith. This cannot be put in terms of distinct sub-intentions, each aimed at a distinct upshot. For if the 'upshots' made sense at all, either they would fall short (to make you angry with someone, to give you some attitude to Smith), or else one would engulf the other (to make you angry with someone, to direct your anger towards Smith).

Now I can explain why the first part of U's utterance seemed to mean something about fish and the second something about biting. His sketching a fish in the air is explained by a fish-involving feature of his intention: had he intended to communicate something about birds rather than fish, that part of his utterance would have been different. Similarly, his jumping-and-biting is explained by the biting-involving aspect of his intention: that second part of his utterance would have been different if he had wanted to communicate that the fish were swimming, or dying.

That, I submit, *justifies* the impression that one part meant something about fish and the other something about biting. I conclude that an utterance-part has a meaning which contributes to the meaning of the whole utterance if that part is explained by a feature of the whole meaning, so that if the whole meaning had differed in respect of just that feature, the whole utterance would have differed in respect of just that part. To know this, one must have relevant general knowledge, but not necessarily knowledge about regularly meaningful utterance-types. Beebe is thus right in contending that the recurrence thesis is false.

This result would lose interest if we needed two accounts of utterance-part-meaning – one based on intention-features, for isolated cases, and one based on regularities. But that split can be avoided, for both kinds of utterance-part-meaning can be brought under a single honestly unified account; and the latter does not conflict with anything in chapter 8, but on the contrary provides the underlying rationale for that chapter.

Suppose that an utterance-type x-y regularly means that the fish are biting, and has no iconic relationship with its meaning. Now consider the hypothesis that x means something about fish and y means something about biting. I treat this exactly as I treated the previous case where there were iconic relationships and no regularity. That is, I take the hypothesis that x is about fish and y is about biting to imply that when U utters x-y his uttering x (but not his uttering y) is explained by his intending to communicate something about fish, and that his uttering y (but not his uttering x) is explained by his intending to communicate something about biting. How could these claims be true if there is no iconic relationship between x and fish or y and biting? They could be true because of facts about the meanings of other utterance-types. If several different utterance-types all contain x and all mean different things about fish, that is evidence that the x-including aspect of x-y is explained by the fish-involving aspect of the meaning. (Furthermore, it seems to be the only kind of evidence we could have. In the absence of icons and of recurrences of x and/or of y in other utterance-types, we could have no sound reason to associate x with fish and y with biting, To see that such an association would be groundless, pit it against rival associations – e.g. of x with biting and of y with fish, or of x with fish-biting and of y with affirmative-present-tense. It would be like saying that in the word 'brother', 'bro' means 'male' and 'ther' means 'sibling'.)

Michael Beebe has helped me to realize that I took a short-cut in assigning structure to Tribal in chapter 8 above. If x occurs in various utterance-types which all mean something about fish, that does not directly imply that x means something about fish. But it provides good evidence that the occurrence of any x-token is explained by the speaker's intending to communicate something about fish; and *that*, by the theory I am now adopting, immediately implies that that x-token means something about fish. It is then a routine further step to say that the type x means something about fish.

This presupposes something which I did not mention in chapter 8, namely that when I based claims about the semantic structure of Tribal on various generalizations about meanings in Tribal, I was assuming that those generalizations reflect the tribesmen's minds in some way. For example, I was assuming that if B-D-C regularly means that the chief is bitten by his dog, someone's uttering this sentence (rather than B-X-C, say) is in part *explained* by what he *knows* about the meanings of various sentences in which D occurs. Perhaps he cannot say what he knows; he certainly need not consciously theorize about the semantic structures in Tribal; but he must somehow be guided by those structures in his use of Tribal. This is a safe assumption, for all it amounts to is that our generalizations do not report mere coincidences, and will sustain predictions and counterfactuals about the use of Tribal. But it should be stated explicitly, because it is essential to the unified treatment of utterance-part-meaning.

The meaning-regularities are not merely evidence about intentions: they are also what make the intentions possible. If U's mind had not been affected in a certain way by the regular use of D in sentences which mean things about the chief's dog, it could not be the case that U included D in his utterance because he wanted to communicate something about the chief's dog. But I think Beebe is right that the fundamental reality lies not in the regularity but in the fact about intentions.

This section, incidentally, is neutral with respect to whether speakers rely on the Gricean mechanism or something simpler for the realization of their intentions.

§81. An infinity of sentences

The rules for Tribal assign meanings to infinitely many sentences. This is due partly to the rules for operators, which enable the tribe to say things with meanings like that of: 'If either John comes to the party or Mary stays away, then it will be the case both that Henry hopes that James wins the prize and also that Jane fears that unless Helen goes swimming Charles will expect that the party will be raided by the police.' That is the merest beginning: there is no end to the length and complexity of the Tribal sentences which are assigned meanings by the rules for operators. Furthermore, that generates an infinity of clauses, and thus an infinity of designators; and so the stock of sentences is stretched still further. In Katz's words: 'These rules are finitely statable, yet they specify an infinite output because they are capable of being endlessly reapplied to their own output to yield an unbounded set of formal objects.'[43]

Why should our theory of this system of behaviour which we call Tribal make room for the idea of a sentence which it would take 10^{10} years to utter? If the tribe are anything like humans, we shall never encounter a Tribal sentence with more than 3,000 significant expressions in it, say. We could bring the Tribal operators under rules which generate every Tribal sentence we shall ever encounter, while sparing us that oppressive infinity. For example, the rule for each operator could specify that its sentential variables range only over sentences which contain at most seventeen operators. If seventeen seems too low, make it seventeen hundred; the infinity is still avoided.

[43] J. J. Katz, *The Philosophy of Language* (New York and London, 1966), pp. 122–3.

So there is a case for finitism about the number of sentences in a language. Still, finitism is wrong.

It would be all right to bring operators under non-recursive rules – i.e. ones which could not be 'endlessly reapplied to their own output' – if the rules corresponded to determinate cut-off point(s) in the tribe's linguistic behaviour. If we found that every tribesman could manage many sentences to which my rules assigned meanings of the form '*x* believes *P*', but none could make sense of ones with meanings of the form '*x* believes that *y* believes *P*', we could reasonably trim the rule for 'Believe' so that it did not generate sentences of the latter kind. Again, if they could all manage conditionals, but none could produce or comprehend conditionals with conjunctive antecedents or consequents, the rule for 'If' might be restricted so as to reflect that fact. Similarly with the various other operators.

If the tribe are much like us, though, there will be no clean cut-off points. Rather, each tribesman will move smoothly from sentences he can easily understand to ones he cannot understand at all, through a middle region of sentences he can understand when he is fresh but not when he is tired, or which he can understand when he has thought about them but not immediately upon hearing them. Furthermore, the line between intelligible and unintelligible, smudged as it is, will be differently placed for different tribesmen, depending upon intelligence, memory, attention-span, and so on.

There is therefore no clear work to be done by any particular finitist rule for any operator. Any rule which allows everything the brightest tribesman can understand will be far too generous for the linguistic performances of the duller members of the tribe. We could adopt different rules for different tribesmen, but it is better to explain the behavioural facts by differences in general intellectual abilities, rather than to postulate different dialects of Tribal. 'Still, if we equip the rules for operators with restrictions which are liberal enough to allow for the best that the brightest tribesmen can manage, the restrictions can be useful as reminders that there are limits to what any tribesman can produce and comprehend.' True; but that reminder can be given much more economically – for instance by simply saying *There are limits to what any tribesman can produce and comprehend.*[44]

As for positive grounds for not restricting the rules for operators:

---

[44] For more on this, see Katz's long helpful footnote, *Ibid.*, pp. 121–2; though I am more sceptical than he is about the supposed distinction between 'theory of performance' and 'theory of competence'.

the only one I know is the general principle favouring simplicity and smoothness in theories. This is in the spirit of a remark of Quine's. Taking it that the sentences of a language are those which are or could be uttered in the relevant community, Quine says: 'Our basis for saying what "could" be generally consists . . . in what *is* plus *simplicity* of the laws whereby we describe and extrapolate what is.'[45] The situation might change if facts about Tribal could be linked with facts about the tribe's brains. A science of cerebro-linguistics might isolate some cerebral function which is uniquely associated with recursive rules; and that would give grounds, deeper than mere theoretic elegance, for using recursive statements in describing the structure of Tribal. In the absence of anything like that, however, we have the simplicity desideratum.

Since I wrote this section, up to here, as a dutiful exposition of an uncontroversial point, Ziff has broken the calm by arguing that 'There is no important sense in which it is true that there are infinitely many English sentences'.[46] He allows that the syntax of English probably has to allow an infinity of sentences: 'It seems to be almost impossible . . . to give any precise cut-off point from a syntactic point of view.'[47] But although syntax may have to generate an infinity of sentences, 'there's no reason to believe that the semantics of English . . . is of a consonant or even comparable character'. His arguments for this are of two kinds.

He first attacks one alleged source of infinity, namely the forming of sentences by taking ones of the form '[Noun] is . . . [adjective]' and putting many occurrences of 'very' in the blank. Ziff says that 'He is very very very very very very very very old' is semantically defective – for instance because it could never be right to say 'No he isn't very very very very very very very very very old; though he is admittedly very very very very very very very very old'. That seems right. A semantic theory for English should deal firmly with such repetitions of 'very', not by banning them but by giving them the same meanings as sentences in which 'very' occurs twice. (Ziff prefers to speak of a sentence's 'significance' rather than of its 'meaning'; but his reasons for that, to be discussed in my next section, are irrelevant to the present issue.) Let us say, then, that sentences with three or more occurrences of 'very', all in

[45] Quine (1951), p. 54.
[46] Paul Ziff, 'The Number of English Sentences', *Foundations of Language*, vol. 11 (1974).
[47] *Ibid.*, p. 526. The remaining quotations in this section are from *Ibid.*, pp. 528–30.

a row, are *senselessly extended* sentences. I presume that a semantic theory for English could define a category of senselessly extended sentences, whose members would include 'I sat there while he talked and talked and talked and talked and talked and talked', and 'Don't hit me again – please, please, please, please, please, please!' It seems likely that a generative semantics for English (see §76 above) could locate and properly handle senselessly extended sentences.

Then this round goes to Ziff. We want the question 'How many English sentences are there?' to be anchored in semantics, not syntax; so we may take it as asking 'How many English sentences are there with distinct meanings?'; and then senselessly extended sentences must not be allowed to inflate the answer.

Still, Ziff has not yet won, as he acknowledges. For there are also ways of forming ever-longer sentences which are not senselessly extended, using methods of extension in which each addition changes the meaning. For instance, 'My father's maternal grandmother's youngest aunt's mother's father's paternal grandmother's first husband was a crusader'. Eliminating anything from this would alter the meaning of the whole, as Ziff points out. But he does not count this sort of thing among the sentences of English either, not because of 'what one says' because of 'how one says it'. This part of his argument apparently rests on the claim that as sentence-length increases one starts producing 'sentences that are utterly incomprehensible to speakers of the language'. So indeed one does. But the question 'How many English sentences are there?' does not mean 'How many sentences are there which would be understood by speakers of English?', and no one would give the answer 'Infinitely many' to the latter question. Ziff's point may be that we *ought* to limit the class of 'English sentences' to the class which some speakers would understand. But he does not defend that, and it seems indefensible. Certainly it does not follow from Ziff's basic premiss that 'How many?' questions should be answered on the basis of 'the semantics of English'. A semantics-based answer to the question might be one which specified how many English sentences there are with distinct meanings; I cannot extract from the phrase 'the semantics of English' any stronger constraint than that. But then Ziff's conclusion would have to be that there are only finitely many English sentences which have distinct meanings (or significances). That seems false, and Ziff does not try to show that it is true. On the contrary, he says that 'My father's grandmother's . . . etc.' is defective not because of what is said but because of how it is said; which concedes that something *is* said. Something which syntax declares to be an English sentence, and to which semantics assigns a determinate meaning or significance, is surely entitled to be included in the count of 'English sentences'.

The notion of what has meaning is admittedly founded upon the notion of what is understood, but the two are not co-extensive. There are good reasons, sketched earlier in this section, for saying that there are sentences – infinitely many of them – which have meanings yet would not be understood.

§82. Ziff's strategy

In some of its broad aspects, my approach to the meanings of utterance-parts resembles that of Ziff's *Semantic Analysis* more than anything else in the literature. This work has helped my thinking, though its author might wonder how, and I shall now sketch some similarities and differences. None of them pertains to sentence-infinities: it is coincidence that my two sections concerning Ziff are adjacent.

The large overall similarity is that Ziff theorizes at length about (1) the behavioural facts which show what sentences mean, and (2) the facts about the meanings of sentences which show what words mean. I do not know of any other book, before my present one, which extensively treats both these topics.

Not that Ziff would describe his strategy in that way. He says: 'Words are generally said to have meaning . . .; not utterances and not sentences.'[48] That seems to be true; we tend to speak of the 'meanings' only of items which are often used; so that words clearly have meanings, short phrases and sentences less clearly so, and long sentences less clearly still. This seems to be an unimportant fact about our use of the word 'meaning', as Ziff implies: 'That words primarily, but not utterances or sentences, are generally said to have meaning is not an inevitable fact about language. If we were not the sort of creatures we are, we might talk of the meaning of an utterance.'[49] I am puzzled by Ziff's explanation of why we do not assign 'meanings' to large linguistic units, and I prefer my own in terms of frequency of recurrence; but the point is in any case a superficiality. It reflects Ziff's concern with the *mot juste*, which I do not share. From now on, I shall attach no weight to the difference between 'significance' and 'meaning': it clearly does

[48] Ziff, p. 149.
[49] Ziff, p. 151, quoted with several deletions.

not produce any of the substantive differences between Ziff's approach and mine.

One substantive difference was noted in §48 above: where I interpret sentences through generalizations of the form 'Whenever anyone utters S he intends to communicate P', Ziff prefers the form 'Whenever anyone utters S, it is the case that P'. In general, Ziff gives little prominence to speakers' intentions, and that is also relevant to the two levels immediately adjacent to the one where sentences get their significances.

The level below, which does not occur in Ziff's book, is where one asks what makes something a sentence or an utterance. For example, why does not the truth of 'Whenever anyone screams, he is in pain' confer a linguistic kind of significance upon a scream? If Ziff were to answer this, he might distinguish screams from utterances on the grounds that the scream–pain link is not systematically related in suitable ways with other comparable behavioural regularities. I prefer a meaning–nominalist answer, which makes the distinction without appealing to language or to anything systematic or regular (see §3 above). My answer does involve speaker's intentions, for it says that screams do not have the required kind of meaning or significance because they give intention-free evidence for pain.

The level above the sentence-significance one is occupied by the question of how to base claims about word-meaning on facts about the significances of sentences. Ziff's handling of this matter gave me my start in chapter 8 above: he ties the meaning of a word to the effects it has on the significance of sentences containing it:

> The problem of finding regularities pertaining to m_i then has two distinct parts ... First, there is the problem of finding tentative semantic regularities pertaining to the syntactically nondeviant whole utterances ... in which m_i occurs. [Secondly] there is then the problem of tentatively attributing something about the regularities to the occurrence of m_i in the utterances; e.g. suppose one finds that if the utterance 'Look at that swine!' is uttered then generally there is a swine present ...: one could not attribute the regularity to the occurrence of 'at' in the utterance.[50]

That is all of a piece with my treatment of unstructured predicates in §66 above. But I have sought in §80 to relate these facts about regularities to deeper-lying facts about speakers' intentions; and that is a further move which Ziff could not easily make, and perhaps would not want to.

In its details, Ziff's move from sentence-significance to word-

[50] Ziff, pp. 44–5.

meaning differs tremendously from mine. He puts no large emphasis upon semantic *structure*, apparently because he assumes that syntactic structure comes first and that semantics is built upon that. In advance of assigning meanings to any words, Ziff says, 'I shall assume [a syntactic] analysis of the corpus that yields imperative utterances, interrogative utterances, declarative utterances, and so on as elements as well as syntactic subjects, predicates, noun phrases, and so on'.[51] This leads him into a treatment of meanings in which structure plays no evident part, apparently being relegated to the province of syntax; and this makes it hard to be sure what facts about word-meanings *can* be established by Ziff's methods.[52]

The difficulty is increased by his thinking that before assigning meanings to words he can cut sentences into 'morphemic segments' (out of which 'morphemes' are logical constructs). A morphemic segment is a stretch of a sentence which could be replaced by any one of a range of alternatives, without harming the sentence's status as a sentence.[53] Ziff says that in 'I want to go', 'to' is a morphemic segment only by remainder, because 'I' and 'want' and 'go' are morphemic segments: he thinks that one cannot grammatically fill the blank in 'I want . . . go' with anything which does not include 'to'. That is false, for the blank could be filled by 'half an hour alone with someone who hopes that I shall', or 'a ticket for everyone who can', and countless others. Perhaps Ziff would object that those change the sentence's syntax; but that just highlights the difficulty created by his reliance upon a syntax, not actually presented, whose scope within the total account is left unclear.

In his account of word-meaning, Ziff tries for precision. Where I am interested in word-meaning only as a by-product of an account of a language's semantic structures, that is of a theory which centrally aims at saying what sentences mean, Ziff really does want to determine precisely the meanings of individual words. His book opens thus: 'What does the word "good" mean?', and closes thus: 'This is what "good" means: answering to certain interests.' This leads him to consider some evidence about word-meaning which I have neglected, especially facts

---

[51] Ziff, p. 13.

[52] See J. J. Katz's review of *Semantic Analysis* in *Language*, vol. 38 (1962), especially pp. 64–5. For other difficulties in Ziff's thoughts about syntax and semantics, see Paul Ziff, 'About what an Adequate Grammar Couldn't Do', *Foundations of Language*, vol. 1 (1965); Gilbert Harman, 'About What an Adequate Grammar Could Do', *Ibid.*, vol. 2 (1966); Paul Ziff, 'Some Comments on Mr. Harman's Confabulations', *Ibid.*, vol. 3 (1967).

[53] Ziff, p. 14.

about which uses of a word count as 'deviant' or 'somewhat odd' or the like.[54] So Ziff's ambitions aim higher than mine in two ways: he seeks a theoretical basis for the attribution of *precise* meanings to words in an *actual* language. By contrast with this, my endeavour to display the main semantic structures of Tribal, a mythical language which is devised so that its structure would be simple and manageable, looks simplistic. But I have been trying to make certain points clear – to say things which would illuminate some aspects of the concept of meaning. The extreme difficulty of *Semantic Analysis* is no doubt partly explained by Ziff's refusal, apparently on principle, to go out of his way to be helpful: 'What I have to say is of interest to me. I suppose it will be of some interest to some others. But I have never given serious thought to such matters.'

My purpose has been to describe and compare, rather than to criticize. However, there is one aspect of *Semantic Analysis* against which I need to defend myself. Ziff and I both think that a word's meaning is determined by what it can contribute to the significance of sentences containing it, and this view has sometimes been expressed in the slogan that 'the meaning of a word is its use in the language'. Ziff says that this 'is not even a good slogan' because 'the use of a word depends on many factors many of which have nothing to do with questions of meaning'.[55] That is indeed fatal to the claim that the meaning of a word *is* its use in the language, but perhaps we can still say that the meaning of a word is determined by its use in the language, or even that it is a sub-set of the facts about its use in the language. Ziff would reject that too, and not just because it is vague. He writes: 'Contemporary enjoiners to examine the use of a term to find out what it means are open to [an] objection. Misuses of words occur. [One] cannot find out what a word means by examining its actual usage unless one can recognize misuses and deviant uses. But how is one to recognize a misuse? or a deviant use?'[56] My answer is that one recognizes misuses by their special relationship to one's semantic theory for the language; and this is consistent with one's basing that theory upon one's observation of uses – including misuses. It would help if the theory were well established before we encountered any misuses, as in my idealized account of the translating of Tribal. But so long as misuses were a small minority of uses, we should be able to cope with them *ambulando*. And even if they were not a minority, they might still be identified as

[54] Ziff, p. 195.   [55] Ziff, p. 158.   [56] Ziff, p. 70; see also p. 189.

misuses just so long as the proper uses of each term were not out-numbered by any one, patterned class of misuses. Even if these remarks are a glibly optimistic treatment of a difficult matter, they at least point in the right direction. Ziff, by contrast, refuses to point. He says that any interesting 'regularities' about English will be true of only 'a proper part' of the totality of English utterances; but he will say nothing about what proper part, except that it is not to be marked off as involving use rather than misuse, or by any fact about relative frequency.[57]

§83. Grice's strategy

Of Grice's three papers to date on the analysis of the concept of mean-ing, only the 1968 one says anything about the meanings of parts of utterances. It is a mere preliminary sketch – an attempt to introduce 'some such notion as [that of] a predication of β (adjectival) on α (nominal)'[58] – but a highly suggestive one. I want to explain why I have not followed its lead.

Given an utterance x-y which means that Jones's dog is shaggy, how can we justify saying that x refers to Jones's dog and that y means *shaggy*? Abstractly stated, Grice says, what we need are two correlations of different sorts – one linking x with Jones's dog, and one linking y with the class of shaggy things. If we can get those right, we shall be well on the way to being entitled to say that x-y means what it does because it means that the x-correlated particular belongs to the y-correlated class. Everything depends on the two sorts of correlation.

Grice distinguishes 'explicit' from 'non-explicit' correlations. Although he discusses the former only in connection with y and shagginess, and the latter only in connection with x and the dog, his view seems to be that either sort of correlation may be used with either sort of utterance-part.

One may explicitly correlate y with the class of shaggy things either by offering a verbal definition of y as meaning 'shaggy' or 'hairy-coated' or the like, or by ostensive definition; and something similar presumably holds for explicitly correlating x with a particular dog. (Grice does not use the term 'definition': he describes the procedures wholly in terms of physical, including linguistic, behaviour engaged in with certain intentions.) Grice points out that we cannot tie word-

[57] The three parts of this sentence relate to Ziff, pp. 22–4, 21–2, and 26–7 respectively.
[58] Grice (1968), p. 236. All further quotations are from *Ibid.*, pp. 240–1.

meaning just to such deliberate procedures as these, because 'many correlations', for names as well as predicates, 'seem to grow rather than to be created'. He accordingly introduces 'non-explicit correlation' between x and the dog. A speaker non-explicitly correlates x with Jones's dog if: he *would* explicitly correlate x with the dog if he were asked to give an explicit correlation for x.

Such a request must be made in a highly structured language, and that is worrying. Grice might reply that we need not share a structured language with our speaker in order to know what he *would* do *if* we could get a certain request across to him. I shall show later that if we could get evidence to support that risky counterfactual, we could find better uses for it; but in the meantime I shall drop the point.

There is another cause for worry. Grice notes that there is an un-clarity about the request for an explicit correlation for x: 'He might quite well take it that he is being asked to make a stipulation in making which he would have an entirely free hand. If he is not being asked for a stipulation, then it must be imparted to him that his explicit correlation is to satisfy some non-arbitrary condition.' This is troubling, because 'asked for a stipulation' here must mean 'asked for a stipulation as to what x is to mean', in contrast with 'asked to do something which shows what x does mean'. The contrast between these assumes that the speaker does at least realize that he is being asked for something bearing on the meaning of x. This seriously compromises the whole endeavour, considered as an entering wedge for semantic structure, that is, as a launching of the notion of word-meaning comparable with the launching of utterance-meaning in Grice's 1957 paper. But I shall drop that too, for the bit about 'stipulation' could be a slip. Grice is in any case right that we must tighten up the notion of 'being asked to make an explicit correlation with x', for otherwise the request is so unspecific that mere compliance with it would be uninformative.

He lays a 'non-arbitrary condition' on the explicit correlation which the speaker is to be thought of as being asked to give, namely that the correlation be one 'which would generate relevant existent procedures'. Grice describes a 'relevant procedure' for the name x, namely:

to predicate β on x when one wants to communicate that Jones's dog belongs to the class of things correlated with β.

In that formulation, 'β' is a variable ranging over predicates. The 'procedure' can be implemented only by someone who has at his disposal a range of predicates, that is, of utterance-parts each of which is correlated with a class of objects. And the 'relevant procedure' for the predicate y would presumably have the form:

> to predicate y on α when one wants to communicate that the object correlated with α belongs to the class of shaggy things.

Here 'α' is a variable ranging over names. So this procedure could be implemented only by someone who had at his disposal a range of names, that is, of utterance-parts each of which is correlated with an object.

This might look circular, but really it is not. The basic picture is as follows. The speaker in question has at his command a range of names $x_1, \ldots, x_n$ which are associated with particular objects $X_1, \ldots, X_n$ respectively; and he has a range of predicates $y_1, \ldots, y_k$ which are associated with classes $Y_1, \ldots, Y_k$ respectively; these associations being established by his uses of these expressions in utterances. The crucial fact about his uses of the expressions is something like this: for any i and j, he utters x_i–y_j only if he intends to communicate that the object X_i belongs to the class Y_j.

That is like my own treatment of names and predicates (§§66–7 above); though I have exaggerated the similarity by smoothing out a wrinkle through which Grice allows for ambiguous utterances. Yet on this sound foundation Grice erects a shaky superstructure. He explains what a speaker means by a name or a predicate on

> facts about *how the speaker would behave if he were successfully asked to do something which related in a certain way to* his uses of those utterance-parts.

The italicized portion of that causes tremendous difficulties for Grice's position. (1) As noted earlier, it requires either that we share a powerful language with the speaker, or that we discover how he *would* behave *if* we shared such a language with him and used it to make a certain request. (2) How should the correlation relate to the relevant procedures? Grice says that it should be such as 'would generate' the procedures, but it is not clear how a correlation can generate a procedure, or, to use another of his formulations, how a procedure can 'result' from a correlation. (3) Grice notes that in an explicit correlation for a predicate, the ostensive samples, being finite in number, will belong to classes other than the intended one. This compels him to say that the meaning of a predicate is determined by which class the speaker *intends* to correlate with the predicate when he displays his ostensive samples. So our knowledge of what 'explicit correlation' he has performed involves knowledge of a rather recherché fact about his intentions. The appealingly down-to-earth, physicalistic appearance of the correlations is lost.

Those are serious problems, and my account of names and predicates avoids all of them by simply omitting the italicized phrase. In my account, what a speaker means by a name or a predicate is explained by his uses of them, not by how he would behave if he were asked to do something relating in a certain way to his uses of them. This loses nothing which Grice has, except problems.

SELECT BIBLIOGRAPHY

Armstrong (1971)   D. M. Armstrong, 'Meaning and Communication', *Philosophical Review*, vol. 80, pp. 427–47.

Armstrong (1973)   D. M. Armstrong, *Belief, Truth and Knowledge* (Cambridge), Part I.

Beebe   Michael Beebe, 'The Basis of Semantic Structure', *Dialogue*, forthcoming.

Bennett (1964)   Jonathan Bennett, *Rationality* (London).

Bennett (1973)   Jonathan Bennett, 'The Meaning-Nominalist Strategy', *Foundations of Language*, vol. 10, pp. 141–68.

Bennett (1975)   Jonathan Bennett, 'Stimulus, Response, Meaning', in N. Rescher (ed.) *Studies in Epistemology (American Philosophical Quarterly* Monograph no. 9), pp. 55–88.

Chomsky (1957)   Noam Chomsky, *Syntactic Structures* (The Hague).

Chomsky (1965)   Noam Chomsky, *Aspects of the Theory of Syntax* (Cambridge, Mass.).

Chomsky (1967)   Noam Chomsky, 'The General Properties of Language', in F. L. Darley (ed.), *Brain Mechanisms Underlying Speech and Language* (New York and London), pp. 73–81.

Chomsky (1968)   Noam Chomsky, *Language and Mind* (New York).

Davidson (1970)   Donald Davidson, 'Mental Events', in L. Foster and J. W. Swanson (eds.), *Experience and Theory* (Amherst, Mass.), pp. 79–101.

Davidson (1973)   Donald Davidson, 'Radical Interpretation', *Dialectica*, vol. 27, pp. 313–28.

Davidson (1974)   Donald Davidson, 'Belief and the Basis of Meaning', *Synthese*, vol. 27, pp. 309–23.

Dummett (1973)   Michael Dummett, *Frege: Philosophy of Language* (New York).

Dummett (1974)   Michael Dummett, 'The Significance of Quine's Indeterminacy Thesis', *Synthese*, vol. 27, pp. 351–97; and 'Reply to W. V. Quine', *Ibid.*, pp. 413–16.

Grice (1957)   H. P. Grice, 'Meaning', *Philosophical Review*, vol. 66, pp. 377–88.

Grice (1968)   H. P. Grice, 'Utterer's Meaning, Sentence-Meaning, and Word-Meaning', *Foundations of Language*, vol. 4, pp. 225–42.

Grice (1969)   H. P. Grice, 'Utterer's Meaning and Intentions', *Philosophical Review*, vol. 78, pp. 147–77.

Lewis   David K. Lewis, *Convention* (Cambridge, Mass., 1969).

Nagel   Ernest Nagel, *The Structure of Science* (New York, 1961), ch. 12.

Quine (1950)   W. V. Quine, 'Two Dogmas of Empiricism', in *From a Logical Point of View* (Cambridge, Mass., 1953), pp. 20–46.

Quine (1951)   W. V. Quine, 'The Problem of Meaning in Linguistics', reprinted in *Ibid.*, pp. 47–64.

Quine (1960)   W. V. Quine, *Word and Object*, (New York and London), chs. 2, 6.

Schiffer   Stephen R. Schiffer, *Meaning* (Oxford, 1972).

Searle   John R. Searle, *Speech Acts* (Cambridge, 1969), chs. 2, 4, 5.

Strawson (1964)   P. F. Strawson, 'Intention and Convention in Speech Acts', reprinted in *Logico-Linguistic Papers* (London, 1971), pp. 149–69.

Strawson (1969)   P. F. Strawson, 'Meaning and Truth', reprinted in *Ibid.*, pp. 170–89.

Taylor   Charles Taylor, *The Explanation of Behaviour* (London, 1964), chs. 1, 2.

Williams   Bernard Williams, 'Deciding to Believe', in *Problems of the Self* (Cambridge, 1973), pp. 136–51.

Ziff   Paul Ziff, *Semantic Analysis* (Ithaca, N.Y., 1960).

INDEX

SUBJECTS

NAMES